An Administrator's Guide
for Evaluating Programs and Personnel

Second Edition

An Administrator's Guide for Evaluating Programs and Personnel

An Effective Schools Approach

Edward F. DeRoche
University of San Diego

Allyn and Bacon, Inc.
Boston London Sydney Toronto

Library of Congress Cataloging-in-Publication Data

DeRoche, Edward F.
  An administrator's guide for evaluating
programs and personnel.

  Bibliography: p.
  Includes index.
  1. Educational evaluation—United States—
Handbooks, manuals, etc. I. Title.
LB2822.75.D47 1987   371.2   87-1400
ISBN 0-205-10512-2

Printed in the United States of America

10 9 8 7 6 5 4 3 2 1 92 91 90 89 88 87

Contents

Chapter 6
Evaluating the Effectiveness of the Student
Activities Program 165

Chapter 7
Evaluating the Effectiveness of Pupil Personnel
Services and Personnel 193

Chapter 8
Evaluating the Effectiveness
of School-Community Relations 213

Chapter 9
Evaluating the Effectiveness of Office, Food, and Transportation Services 249

Chapter 10
Evaluating the Effectiveness of Managing School Plant and Facilities 281

Preface

When the first edition of this book was published in 1981, the author stated that it was based on three assumptions. These assumptions are now facts—facts supported by research on the effective school. These three facts are: (1) school administrators are educational leaders, or at least want to be; (2) determining the effectiveness of a school begins with a self-examination by principals, teachers, and staff; and (3) progress toward quality education begins at the building level; that is, education is only as good as an individual school's principal, faculty, and staff. The challenge for today's educational leaders is to set an example that clearly demonstrates that schools can be the one institution where human relationships are enhanced while meeting the demands of society in general, and communities, in particular; and that a school can be a human and humane enterprise as it deals with internal and external evaluation processes and accountability requirements.

Determining the effectiveness of the school's programs and personnel is one of the major tasks faced by principals. They, more than other educators, must respond to the public's pleas for quality education, for finding ways to enhance teaching and learning, and for helping parents and the community cope with the problems of raising children in a dynamic, rapid-paced society.

One of the first questions a reader should ask about a second edition is, "What are the differences in content between the first and second editions?" After all, books are expensive. Is the cost of the second edition worth it? You will have to be the judge, but the author has made a comprehensive revision for this second edition, retaining what administrators told him were important and helpful, while incorporating many of the new insights and new developments produced by effective schools research and practices. All chapters have been revised, combined, or replaced by new content as illustrated in the following.

In Chapter 1 the premises for effective schools are examined, and the factors that make for quality education are highlighted. The case is made for the important role of the school principal as a leader and an evaluator.

In Chapter 2 the broader picture of school life and its culture is evaluated. The material about classroom climate that appeared in the first edition is retained. An audit procedure for examining the principal's vision of his/her school, the school's mission and goals, its environment and culture, and other factors that make for effective schools is featured in this chapter.

Chapter 3 deals with the issue clearly delineated by the research: namely, that the principal must be an instructional leader in the school. An evaluation scheme, using an instructional improvement framework and staff development recommendations highlight this chapter.

In Chapter 4 the ever-present problem of teacher evaluation is discussed. Among the new content are evaluating the induction program for new teachers and new ideas for evaluating tenured, experienced teachers.

Effective schools have an articulated, coordinated K–12 curriculum. In Chapter 5, evaluating effective curriculum designs and practices help the administrator make decisions.

Chapter 6, evaluating the effectiveness of the student activities program, has little new content not only because of the value of the content in the first edition but also because there has been little new research on the topic since 1981.

Evaluating the effectiveness of pupil personnel services and personnel, the title of Chapter 7, presents new material including a discrepancy evaluation plan, new suggestions for evaluating school counselors and the services they provide, and an update on the content that appeared in the first edition.

Chapter 8 focuses on ways to evaluate and improve school-community relations. Much of the original content is updated, but also included are ways to evaluate the adopt-a-school or partnership programs.

Evaluating the effectiveness of office, food, and transportation services is the theme of Chapter 9 and basically includes a rewriting of two chapters into one chapter with new ideas for evaluating these services.

The final chapter, Chapter 10, updates the content and provides some new ways for evaluating the effectiveness of how well principals manage the school plant and its facilities.

It should be noted that the ideas in each chapter of this book insist that determining the effectiveness of the school's programs and its personnel is a team effort. The point is made again and again that evaluation requires the understanding and cooperation of all school personnel. The school principal and other administrators have to establish procedures that create a positive climate for evaluation and insist that the quest for quality education is worth the effort.

While this book provides many examples, ideas, illustrations, and suggestions, most suggestions are not all-inclusive, but intended to generate further ideas. For example, as a school principal shares the ideas in the chapter on curriculum with teachers, other suggestions, maybe better ones, will result. If this happens, then the purpose of this book has been accomplished because the underlying intent is to encourage individual school personnel, guided by the leadership of the school principal, to take an active role in evaluating and determining the effectiveness of what is done in the day-to-day operation of the school.

This book is filled with useful ideas in conducting assessments and self-evaluations. But self-evaluation and the use of survey instruments, opinionnaires, and questionnaires, by themselves, are insufficient for decision making. The use of additional data to supplement what you find out from using the instruments in this book is also necessary. For this reason, each chapter provides you with descriptions of evaluation instruments that have been found valid, reliable, and helpful in gathering additional data for making decisions. The detailed, step-by-step assessment methods and procedures, coupled with the numerous evaluation instruments in the text and references, will help you to better determine what works and what doesn't work in your school.

Another feature of this book is that each chapter is designed to promote a team effort utilizing a problem-solving approach. A plan of action is carefully described that includes problem identification, data collection, data reporting, drawing conclusions, and making recommendations. Over the past twenty years, I have witnessed the frustration of teachers and others serving on innumerable committees trying to decide the best way to get the job done. Much time is wasted. Enthusiasm is drained. Frustration results. The suggestions in this book, properly used, should alleviate this problem.

Throughout this book, I have attempted to be positive, practical, and realistic while at the same time using research and theory to support the major themes described in each chapter. Each chapter examines the major evaluation responsibilities of administrators and teachers at the building level. Some of the material will have to be adapted by those implementing these ideas because of the school climate, the level of education (elementary, middle, high school), and other unique situational factors. To provide a well-balanced and useful guide that may be used with confidence by those that value evaluation, and in an attempt to meld theory with practicality, numerous charts, scales, inventories, forms, and checklists have been included for the purpose of duplication and testing in each school.

Thus, this administrator's handbook on evaluation, this ready-to-use reference, is designed to help today's school principals and other administrators carry out their evaluative responsibilities. It is a book for administrators who believe it is important to know where one is before one can determine where to go and in what direction; in other words, it provides evaluation for decision making.

Although the focus is on principals and teachers at the building level, superintendents, assistant principals, supervisors, curriculum specialists, board members, and others who wish to assess programs and personnel will find the material indispensable. The book is also recommended for those studying to be administrators. Experienced administrators and teachers as well as graduate students will find ideas, suggestions, and strategies which will help them solve many problems found in today's schools.

Recognition and appreciation go to three major sources of support during the writing of this second edition. First, to the University of San Diego for promoting and supporting excellence in teaching and scholarship. Second, to all who help type, critique, and retype the manuscript. And thirdly, to my family who, once again, were understanding, cooperative, and patient.

CHAPTER 1

Effective Schools
and Evaluation

We can, whenever and wherever we choose, successfully teach
all children whose schooling is of importance to us. We already
know more than we need to to do that. Whether or not we do
it must finally depend on how we feel about the fact that we
haven't done it so far.

Ronald Edmonds

The purpose of this chapter is to set the framework for the other
chapters in this book. To do so, five topics will be discussed. The first deals
with the characteristics of effective schools; the second with evaluation itself, and the need to define certain words and terms. The third subject
focuses on the principal as evaluator. Organizing for evaluation outlines
steps for involving others in the evaluation process. The final topic ad-
dresses the issue of individual school autonomy.

EFFECTIVE SCHOOL INDICATORS

"Effective" is the word of the decade in the education business, emanating
from research on the topic. Every school administrator should know about
this research and the suggestions for implementing its findings. While the
research doesn't provide a specific strategy for all schools, it does provide
models that are systematic, comprehensive, and implementable, and that
will, in all likelihood, contribute to school improvement.

What are the characteristics, the indicators, the factors that make for
effective schools? In providing the answers to this question, you might
look at the information as an evaluative checklist against which you can
rate your own leadership and your school. The early studies on determining the characteristics of effective schools reported five specific correlates:

1

1. A school climate that has a safe, orderly environment conducive to teaching and learning.
2. An instructional leader-principal who is active in solving instructional problems and in observing classrooms.
3. A principal and faculty who have high expectations for all the children in the school.
4. A sense of purpose with common goals and a standard curriculum.
5. An educational program that is designed to insure student achievement on standardized tests.[1]

Purkey and Smith[2] in two definitive articles provide a model for school improvement, a portrait of an effective school summarized in these thirteen indicators:

1. School-site management and democratic decision making.
2. Instructional leadership.
3. Staff stability.
4. Curriculum articulation and organization.
5. Schoolwide staff development.
6. Parental involvement and support.
7. Schoolwide recognition of academic success.
8. Maximized learning time.
9. District support.
10. Collaborative planning and collegial relationships.
11. Sense of community.
12. Clear goals and high expectations commonly shared.
13. Order and discipline.

Murphy and Hollinger[3] report the following characteristics of some of the most instructionally effective high schools in California as having:

- A clear sense of purpose.
- A core set of standards within a rich curriculum.
- High expectations.
- A commitment to evaluate each student as completely as possible.
- A special reason for each student to go to school.
- A sense of community.
- A resiliency and problem-solving attitude.

Larkin[4] reports that principals of effective schools are:

- Assertive leaders, achievement oriented.
- Evaluators of the school and its program.
- Willing to hold the staff accountable; active supervision.

- Able to balance strong leadership with autonomy for the faculty.
- Willing to involve staff participation in school policies and plans.

He also reports that the organizational characteristics of effective schools includes:

- Clear goals and consensus about the goals.
- Maximized learning time.
- Aligned and articulated curriculum.
- High academic standards.
- A sense of community.
- Staff autonomy.[5]

The school climate of effective schools, according to Larkin,[6] includes these factors:

- High expectations of success.
- Schoolwide recognition of academic achievement and programs.
- Order, discipline, businesslike atmosphere.
- Cooperative and friendly atmosphere.
- Safe, clean, and adequate physical facilities.
- A faculty responsible for educational outcomes.

There you have it. A little repetitious but intentionally so because of the importance of these characteristics for improving schools, for increasing student achievement, and for setting the basis for the discussion in each chapter of this book.

EVALUATION: CONTEXT AND DEFINITION

It is recommended that each principal have an evaluation plan for school programs and personnel. This recommendation should be viewed within the context of the accountability-assessment schemes required by state and local school districts. In most cases, state and district requirements focus on assessing student achievement, determining the extent to which students have mastered the basic skills, and comparing results with other schools in the district and sometimes among school districts.

It is obvious that the principal must include state and district requirements in the school's evaluation plans. It would be foolhardy not to do so. But it must be recognized that many evaluation schemes are quite narrow, focusing on student academic achievement only. So the principal must design an effective evaluation plan that meets the assessment requirements from outside the school and insures that the school is a good place to get an education and a good place to work. The ideas in this book provide a broad-brush attempt to help you do just that.

Uses and Types of Evaluation

What is evaluation? It is the process used for determining the value, amount, or worth of something—a program, a product, a procedure, or other factor. Whatever, in the judgment of the principal and teachers, is worth the time and effort for data collection, analysis, and decision making, can be evaluated.

There are three uses of evaluation posed by Stufflebeam and Shinkfield: evaluation for improvement, evaluation for accountability, and evaluation for enlightenment. Evaluation for improvement provides "information for assessing the quality of a service or for improving it." Evaluation for accountability provides clientele with summative reports on the results of "completed projects, established programs, or finished products." Evaluation for enlightenment might be used in the context of research to promote increased understanding of the phenomena that are involved in the evaluation.[7]

The two types of evaluation are formative and summative evaluation. The former refers to evaluation that gathers and uses information during the process of doing something. It is on-going, requiring continual feedback for decision making and change along the way. This book favors the use of formative evaluation because I believe that principals and teachers benefit from feedback during on-going evaluation processes, when they can change or redirect something, rather than waiting for the completion of a program or project.

Summative evaluation is the typical end-of-the-year assessment used to determine the effects of a program, project, or procedure. It leads to one of three decisions at the completion of something—to continue it, change it, or cancel it.

Quantitative-Qualitative Measures

There are three kinds of tests used in schools: objective-referenced tests, criterion-referenced tests, and norm-referenced tests. Objective-referenced tests (sometimes labeled "diagnostic tests") are designed to find out what students know about a particular subject. Criterion-referenced tests examine how much students know in relation to criteria set by teachers. ("If you want an A on this test, you'll need to answer 90 percent of the questions correctly.") Your driver's license test was a criterion-referenced test. Norm-referenced tests are standardized achievement tests. Achievement test results usually are published by the local newspaper with the implication that these results are a measure of the school's success—the quality of education one can expect while attending a particular school.

Each of these tests will be recommended for use as you go about collecting quantifiable information to help you make judgments about the quality of instruction and learning. But *quality* is an elusive word, and educating children and young people may be more an art than a science. To this end, attention should be given to other kinds of measures (for all subjects and activities, but particularly for the arts).

Educational connoisseurship and educational criticism are two evaluation processes recommended by Elliot Eisner. Eisner believes that "the major contribution of evaluation is contributing to a heightened awareness of the qualities of (classroom) life so teachers and students can become more intelligent within it."[8] Many of the qualitative methods are those that anthropologists use as their research methods. Such methods may be helpful when the focus is on quality, when there is a need to be unobtrusive (less disruptive), when the focus is on program improvement, when performing implementation evaluation, when evaluating to determine the extent to which the program services meet the individual needs of students, and when conducting process evaluation (the internal workings of a program).[9]

Responsive evaluation is characterized by three criteria. First, those teachers and administrators engaged in responsive evaluation should be responsive to actual program activities. (Who is doing what? Concerned about what? Values what?) Second, evaluation that is responsive meets the information needs of a variety of audiences. There are many publics your school serves, each with varying information needs and ideas. Third, evaluation is responsive to participants and audiences' value perspectives.[10] Stake and Hoke write, "we who take the 'responsive evaluation' approach complete our studies without strong proof that the program was a success or failure and even without hard data for making good comparisons—but we often end up with people understanding their program better."[11]

Graham Maxwell describes a rating scale for assessing the quality of responsive evaluations.[12]

Curriculum

The curriculum includes those programs, subjects, and experiences designed specifically for children, youth, and adults who participate in the school. The curriculum finds its content in the needs of society, the needs of individuals in attendance, and contemporary influences (legislative, technological, societal).

Faculty and Staff

Faculty refers to full-time or part-time teachers, assistant principals, librarians, teacher aides, para-professionals, etc. *Staff* refers to all other school personnel—secretary, custodian, cafeteria director, and the like.

Effectiveness and Efficiency

These words are used throughout the book to describe how well something is being done and at what cost in time, energy, money (effectiveness), and how it is being accomplished while preserving personnel worth (efficiency).[13]

Sampling

Many of the instruments in this book are designed for specific audiences. Time, energy, and cost may prohibit you from polling, studying, and testing everyone in your school or in the community. For this and other reasons, it is important to know about sampling techniques.

In certain chapters in this book, the term *random sampling* is used; that is, each individual in your population has an equal chance of being selected for your study. In addition, it is important that you know about two methods of random sampling: stratified random sampling and proportional sampling.

For example, you wish to find out how the public feels about your school. A questionnaire has been designed and you wish to send it to a random sample of the population. An analysis of your population suggests that there are several subpopulations (parents, graduates, citizens who live in the school's attendance area but have no children attending the school, etc.). Using the *stratified random sampling* technique you would take a random sample from each of the subpopulations.

Proportional sampling is a technique whereby you select samples that are in proportion to the population. For example, you wish to sample your graduates concerning the value they place on the education received at your school. In studying the population you note that 75 percent of the graduates were female, 25 percent male. The proportional sampling technique would require that you randomly select 75 percent female graduates for your study and 25 percent male graduates. These and other techniques are worthy of further study.[14]

THE PRINCIPAL AS EVALUATOR

Informal evaluation is taking place in and out of school everyday. The building principal has the major responsibility for formalizing the evaluation process. Legally the building principal is the chief administrative officer, the supervisor, and the decision maker. A principal's attitudes and procedures can make the evaluation program an enlightening, interesting, exciting venture or one that is frustrating, based on fear, and viewed negatively by those involved. What the principal does and how it is done determines, to a large extent, the effectiveness of the school district's and an individual school's evaluation program. Therefore, the following guidelines are suggested as you carry out your role in the evaluation process:

1. A principal must be knowledgeable about the school district's goals and objectives.
2. A principal has to assist the superintendent in effectively carrying out the policies and procedures resulting from the school district's goals and objectives.
3. A principal should demonstrate leadership in formulating plans and procedures for the evaluation of these goals and objectives.
4. A principal must provide the students, parents, and teachers with the necessary information about the district's and school's evaluation program.
5. A principal must capitalize on the talents of the faculty, parents, students, and community personnel in helping formulate plans and procedures for carrying out the evaluation program at the individual level.
6. A principal has to provide a plan and secure resources for helping personnel get the job done.

In order to help you in your role as evaluator you might try the following suggestions:

1. Assess your current knowledge about evaluation.
2. Improve your knowledge and attitude about evaluation.
3. Find out how other principals plan for evaluation.
4. Determine what skills you have and what you will need for evaluating your school's programs and personnel.
5. Determine how your faculty and staff feel about evaluation.
6. Find out what knowledge and skill your faculty and staff have about evaluation.
7. Compare your current evaluation procedures with those suggested in this chapter and other chapters.
8. Promote a positive view of evaluation in the school and community.
9. Encourage self-evaluation techniques among school personnel, including students.

There are, of course, areas that should be avoided, as in the following:

1. Evaluation should not be used as a threat to faculty and staff.
2. Do not assume that you are the only evaluator in the school.
3. Too much evaluation should not occur at any one time.
4. Evaluation should not be done without specific objectives and plans of action.

5. Do not use evaluation plans that do not involve the entire faculty and staff.
6. Do not allow someone outside the school to prepare evaluation plans that do not include you and your faculty and staff in the process.
7. People who want to evaluate for the purpose of finding scapegoats or cutting the budget should not gain your support.
8. Do not become discouraged if, as a result of your self-evaluation, you judge yourself too critically. You're only human.

These guidelines, suggestions, and cautions are based upon some basic principles of evaluation.

PRINCIPLES OF EVALUATION

The eighteen principles of evaluation are guidelines for the discussion of topics in this book. These principles should be discussed by you, the faculty, and any evaluation committee created to assess programs and/or personnel.

1. Evaluation should help clarify the school's goals and objectives and the extent to which these are being accomplished.
2. Evaluation is a cooperative, team function and should be seen in a positive, optimistic way.
3. Evaluation should be an ongoing, continuous process.
4. Performance evaluation should be required of all school personnel.
5. Performance evaluation should be honest, open, and free from threats.
6. Evaluation should contribute to the improvement of attitudes, relationships, and morale.
7. Program and performance improvement should be the major purpose of a school's plans for evaluation.
8. Time, assistance, training, and an appropriate budget should be provided to each school for evaluation purposes.
9. Evaluation should help school personnel develop short- and long-range plans.
10. Evaluation should contribute to program and behavior changes.
11. Self-evaluation strategies should be an integral part of any school evaluation plan.
12. External evaluation plans (accrediting agencies) should contribute to and help with internal evaluation plans.
13. Evaluation should be a humane process designed to determine the strengths and weaknesses of programs and personnel.
14. Through the evaluation process teachers, parents, students, and

citizens should be able to clarify and understand the objectives and programs of the school.

15. The evaluation process should promote a positive attitude toward self-appraisal and self-improvement.
16. The evaluation program should provide opportunities for school personnel to diagnose difficulties, strengthen existing programs, and establish pilot programs or projects to test new approaches.
17. Evaluation should be a process that will help teachers and learners determine the extent to which each has been successful in the teaching-learning process.
18. Evaluation should encourage a team effort, a cooperative spirit, and a feeling by the community that we are all accountable for the education of our young people.

The effective schools movement has produced numerous evaluation strategies, instruments, and plans that offer useful alternatives to the above. Information regarding these resources will be found in the reference sections to each chapter in this book.

ORGANIZING A SCHOOL EVALUATION COMMITTEE

Evaluation at the school district level should be an ongoing process that can be a part of or incorporated into an individual school's evaluation plans. The aim here is to provide principals and teachers with ideas for evaluating their programs, in their school, involving their own personnel. To do this, the principal should consider establishing a school evaluation committee initially by appointment or by requesting volunteers and eventually by election or some combination of election and appointment methods.

Membership on the evaluation committee will depend on the size of the school. For example, if a school has a faculty of thirty or more members, then the committee probably should consist of nine to twelve members. About one-third of these should be department heads (if a high school) or other administrative personnel, one-third teachers, and one-third representatives from other areas (such as custodian, nurse, secretary, parents, students, and selected community leaders). In small schools, the committee should have a membership of about six to nine people with about one-third of that number representing teachers, support personnel (custodian, nurse, secretary, etc.), and parents and selected community leaders.

Once you and your faculty select a method of organizing for evaluation, be it a single evaluation committee, several subcommittees, or *ad hoc* committees, the work to be done should be organized in some way. There are many ways to plan. Other chapters will include plans for evaluating specific things, i.e., teacher effectiveness. A more general plan follows:

Step I—Purpose of Evaluation.   Early in the process, evaluation committees should take the opportunity to decide the purpose for which they have organized. Answering the following questions will help:

- Why has our committee organized?
- What are our immediate objectives?
- What might be our long-range objectives?

Step II—Evaluation Needs.   After answering the questions about the purposes of evaluation, the committee should decide what needs to be evaluated and when. To do this, the committee should solicit information from school personnel and others in the community (if you wish) regarding what and when something should be evaluated. Figure 1-1 shows an evaluation inventory that has been used successfully to identify evaluation needs.

Part II of Figure 1-1 enables the committee to determine priorities as viewed by those surveyed. It also assists the committee in planning for the current school year as well as at least three years ahead. Long-range planning is tentative, however. You may find that what is listed for evaluation two years from now will not carry a high priority at that time. It is best to go back to those surveyed people and tell them what the priorities were two years ago and ask if these items continue to carry a high priority and should be evaluated. In any case, the idea does generate results useful in establishing immediate evaluation priorities. However, it would be foolhardy for the committee to attempt to evaluate all facets of education taking place in their school at one time. Some items that receive a high priority can be evaluated in less time than other items. For example, it takes less of the principal's or evaluation committee's time to evaluate field trips, attendance policies, study halls, meetings, etc., than it does to evaluate school goals and objectives, policies and procedures, or school-community relations. Time is a factor that is worthy of consideration. It is important at this stage to determine the evaluation design. It will also be helpful to consider the answers to these questions:

- What kinds of in-service programs will be needed to help personnel acquire some skills, competencies, and ideas in the evaluation process?
- What kinds of professional assistance will be needed? (For example, it would be wise for the committee to seek professional assistance from a computer programmer, who could advise the committee on ways to use a computer and its programs for recording, summarizing, and analyzing the data.)
- What kinds of facilities, equipment, and materials will be required?

Directions: The school evaluation committee requests your help in deciding what areas of schooling should be evaluated and when it is best to evaluate that area. Please complete each item by checking the appropriate blank.

Part I

Items to Be Evaluated	*Definitely Evaluate*	*Could Be Evaluated*	*No Need to Evaluate*
1. School goals and objectives	——	——	——
2. School rules, regulations, and policies	——	——	——
3. School-community relations	——	——	——
4. Parent-teacher conferences	——	——	——
5. Grading and reporting practices	——	——	——
6. Report cards	——	——	——
7. Student needs and interests	——	——	——
8. Instructional objectives	——	——	——
9. Extracurricular activities	——	——	——
10. Faculty meetings and other school meetings	——	——	——
11. In-service programs	——	——	——
12. PTA meetings	——	——	——
13. School assemblies	——	——	——
14. Field trips	——	——	——
15. School fairs	——	——	——
16. Student council	——	——	——
17. School clubs and organizations	——	——	——
18. Secretaries, custodians, etc.	——	——	——
19. Paraprofessionals and teacher aides	——	——	——
20. Reading program	——	——	——
21. Substitute teachers	——	——	——
22. Math program	——	——	——
23. Science program	——	——	——
24. Social studies program	——	——	——
25. English-Language Arts program	——	——	——
26. Physical education program	——	——	——
27. Vocational program	——	——	——
28. Guidance program	——	——	——
29. Foreign language program	——	——	——
30. Instructional materials and equipment	——	——	——
31. Teacher effectiveness	——	——	——
32. Teacher evaluation techniques	——	——	——
33. Student learning	——	——	——
34. Student values and attitudes	——	——	——
35. School administration	——	——	——

(cont.)

FIGURE 1-1
Evaluation Needs Inventory

Items to Be Evaluated	Definitely Evaluate	Could Be Evaluated	No Need to Evaluate
36. Attendance policies	____	____	____
37. Teaching strategies	____	____	____
38. Student-teacher relationships	____	____	____
39. Discipline	____	____	____
40. Instructional materials center, library, etc.	____	____	____
41. Study halls	____	____	____
42. School plant and facilities	____	____	____
43. Audio-visual materials	____	____	____
44. School organization (grouping, graded, nongraded, etc.)	____	____	____
45. Others_____	____	____	____

Part II

Please list five items that you identified in Part I as *Definitely Evaluate* and check the appropriate space in the column at the right.

	Sometime During the Next Three School Years	Sometime During the Next School Year	Sometime During This School Year
1. _____	_____	_____	_____
2. _____	_____	_____	_____
3. _____	_____	_____	_____
4. _____	_____	_____	_____
5. _____	_____	_____	_____

FIGURE 1-1 (*cont.*)

Step III—Data Gathering. By using the results of the evaluation schedule, the committee determines what needs to be evaluated. To prepare the implementation phases of this evaluation plan, the committee should:

- Specify objectives.
- Decide what information to collect.
- Decide how to gather the information.
- Decide when to collect the information.
- Decide who will collect the information.

Step IV—Organizing and Analyzing Data. The people responsible for the previous steps should also be active in organizing and analyzing data. The subcommittee, if this is the procedure selected, would review what data have been collected and be responsible for categorizing and summarizing it. The method of analysis will depend upon the objective and the evaluation design.

Step V—Reporting the Data. The committee needs to plan a method for reporting the data. The contents should include the *objectives* (why this item/program/procedure was evaluated), the *procedure* (how was it evaluated), the *results* (what was found as a result of the evaluation), and the *implications* (what one does with the results). The implication section of the report should include strengths and weaknesses found as a result of the study, as well as how to improve weaknesses while maintaining strengths. Questions such as the following will be helpful:

- What does the study reveal about strengths and weaknesses?
- What are the suggestions for further study?
- What program alternatives might be necessary?
- What appears to be the best solution (the best way to proceed)?
- What personnel resources are required?
- What additional information is needed?
- What financial commitments should be made?

The evaluation committee should involve others in deciding what should be done about the evaluation report. In other words, now that you have all of this information, what are you and your faculty going to do about it? All factors—programs, alternatives, suggestions, cost, time, effort—should be considered. This is a crucial step for the school principal because it is here that leadership and cooperative decision making can be demonstrated.

DEVELOPING AN EVALUATION PLAN

Be prepared! Plan carefully! These two warnings imply that you not launch into a self-evaluation or the evaluation of programs or personnel without some preparation and a plan of action. The idea presented here is one of many that a principal could use. This plan is merely illustrative. It does require you to think about what is to be evaluated and why.

Purpose. You should have an objective or two in mind about something or someone you wish to evaluate, including self-evaluation. Objectives should be carefully written and as specific as possible. Questions that are of value at this beginning stage include:

- What is the purpose of this evaluation?
- What are my objectives?
- Why do I want to evaluate this?

Orientation.   You should prepare yourself as well as those who will be involved in the evaluation plan. Anyone who will be evaluated or asks to contribute to the plan should have an understanding of the purposes and objectives. In addition, participants should know what will be expected of them. There should be no surprises nor any hidden agendas.

Instruments.   You will have to determine what methods and instruments will be used to assess those factors you wish to evaluate. The instruments must be selected on the basis of which ones will do the best job of assessment based on the statement of objectives. This should be done cooperatively with your faculty and staff. It could be of value to get some feedback from selected faculty and staff about some of the self-evaluation instruments you may wish to use.

Schedule.   An evaluation schedule is important and useful, but it must be flexible. You should estimate the amount of time it will take you and others to carry out the evaluation program or self-evaluation ideas. The schedule should include target dates for orienting participants; for designing, preparing, or purchasing instruments; for collecting data; for collating, summarizing, and analyzing the data; and for preparing the final report.

Results.   When you reach this stage, you should ask yourself the following questions:

- What am I going to do with the results?
- What do the results confirm, reveal, or suggest?
- Do these results help me determine the extent to which the objectives have been accomplished?
- With whom will I share the results of this evaluation?

Follow-up.   Data collection and analysis are futile exercises unless something is done with the results. You might ask yourself the following questions:

- What procedures are suggested as a result of my analysis of the results?
- Should I change some or all of our procedures or practices?
- Have I shared the results with those concerned and given them an opportunity to suggest ways to improve?
- Should I plan additional evaluative procedures to determine progress in correcting weaknesses and maintaining strengths?
- Do these results suggest other areas that should be evaluated?

To summarize this evaluating plan in question form, and to serve as a guide to principals, you must decide:

1. What is to be evaluated?
2. Why is it to be evaluated?
3. How is it to be evaluated?
4. When is it to be evaluated?
5. By whom is it to be evaluated?
6. How are the data to be collected?
7. How are the data to be analyzed?
8. How are the data to be reported?
9. To whom will the reports be presented?
10. What will be done with the results in the report?

These questions apply to self-evaluation techniques the principal uses as well as to the evaluation of any phase of the school operation and the evaluation of personnel. They are questions that you should refer to every time you wish to conduct an evaluation.

The effective schools movement has produced numerous education strategies, instruments, and plans that offer useful information to school administrators interested in improving schools. Information regarding these resources will be found in the reference sections of each chapter in this book.

INDIVIDUAL SCHOOL AUTONOMY

I am convinced of the need for more evaluation and decision-making autonomy for principals at the school-site level. The basic, most fundamental element of education is the interaction between a group of students and their teacher. All other school services, be they legislative, judicial, or administrative, are supportive and should be rendered in the context of enhancing the quality of teaching and learning.

The truth of the matter is that most parents want to know whether their child or teenager is getting a good education. The focus is on the school their sons and daughters attend. So effectiveness for them is determined by what the principal and teachers "deliver." Teacher problems, student problems, parent problems are all local in nature, to be solved, for the most part, at the school-site level.

In discussing the nine commandments for enhancing school effectiveness, Chester Finn makes the point that the school as the "key organizational unit" should implement the broad goals and standards set by the state or school district in their own way, with "more budgetary authority" and with its effectiveness determined by what the people inside the school do.[15]

Experience and common sense suggest that if education is to do the things we say it should do, it must be accomplished at the building level. Studies reported in *Looking Behind the Classroom Door*[16] clearly subscribe to the view that educational change will be most effective when it resides with the principal, teachers, students, and parents in the individual school. Francis Roberts states it best:

> Nearly a quarter century of regular contact with the schools, including six years as a public school principal and nearly seven years as a school superintendent, leaves me thoroughly convinced there will be no early reform of American elementary and secondary education until the individual school is freed from system-wide entanglement of curriculum sequences, staffing patterns, and bureaucratic routines. Until the school, each school, is acknowledged as a separate and significant social institution, real, meaningful, no deep reform can take place. . . . Whereas the "school district" is an abstraction existing only on paper (maps, policy manuals, tax bills and the like), the school has significant reality. In short, it forms a community, for better or worse, and its catalyst, also for better or worse, is the principal.[17]

Finally, research studies suggest that large, centralized organizations tend to place reliance on codification of tasks and observation of rules (formalizing the organization). As a result, its members find little autonomy over tasks they are to perform and little participation in decision making, all of which tends to lead to alienation from work and from relationships with colleagues. Such a malady seems to appear in some of our large school districts.[18]

Therefore, the ideas for organizing and administering a plan for evaluation at the school building level and the viewpoints expressed about accountability have at their core the interest of classroom teachers with their twenty-five to thirty youngsters. However, before implementing evaluation plans, before you try some of the ideas, tools, and strategies presented in this book, you must understand and appreciate the nature, purpose, and procedures for evaluation at the individual school level.

A FINAL COMMENT

At the risk of being repetitious, let's review once again those factors that have been found in schools where quality education is evident. Current research has helped us to delineate and describe these factors, each of which has been selected for discussion throughout this book. The nine quality indicators are:

1. There is a commonly held sense of mission/vision for the school with goals and objectives that have an academic focus.

2. There is strong administrative and instructional leadership both at the district and the school-site level coupled with collaborative planning and collegial relationships.
3. There is a school culture that promotes a sense of community; that is supportive, orderly and safe; and that is conducive to a positive teaching-learning climate where achievements and success are recognized and rewarded.
4. There is well-coordinated, articulated curriculum.
5. There are high expectations and standards for all students because equity and excellence are seen as synonymous.
6. There is an instructional program that has high performance standards for teachers; that emphasizes teacher-directed instruction, maximum use of instructional time, regular homework, a variety of teaching strategies; and that maintains reasonable staff stability.
7. There is frequent monitoring of student progress both in the cognitive and affective domains of learning and living during the school year.
8. There are continued efforts to involve parents and the community in the programs and services offered by the school.
9. There are school and district-wide professional development opportunities for teachers and administrators.[19]

It is clear, or at least it should be, that you, in collaboration with the faculty, staff, and district office personnel, should utilize evaluative procedures to determine the extent to which these nine quality indicators are present in your school. The ten chapters in this edition will help you do just that.

NOTES

1. Lawrence W. Lezotte, "The Five Correlates of an Effective School," *The Effective School Report* 1 (November 1983): 3–4.
2. Stewart C. Purkey and Marshall S. Smith, "Effective Schools: A Review," *The Elementary School Journal* 83 (March 1983): 427–452; and "School Reform: The District Policy Implications of the Effective School Literature," *The Elementary School Journal* 85 (January 1985): 353–389.
3. Joseph Murphy and Phillip Hollinger, "Effective High Schools—What Are the Common Characteristics?" *Bulletin of the National Association of Secondary School Principals* 69 (January 1985): 18–22.
4. Ronald F. Larkin, "Achievement Directed Leadership," *The Effective School Report* 2 (September 1984): 3.
5. *Ibid.*, p. 3.
6. *Ibid.*, p. 3.
7. Daniel L. Stufflebeam and Anthony J. Shinkfield, *Systematic Evaluation* (Boston: Kluwer-Nijhoff Publishing, 1985), p. 7.

8. Elliot W. Eisner, *The Art of Educational Evaluation: A Personal View* (Philadelphia: The Falmer Press, 1985), p. 92.

9. Arline Fink and Jacqueline Kosecoff, "How to Use Qualitative Evaluation Methods," *How to Evaluate Education Programs: A Monthly Guide to Methods and Ideas that Work* (Capital Publications, Inc., January 1985).

10. Robert E. Stake and Gordon A. Hoke, "Evaluating An Arts Program: Movement and Dance in a Downtown District," *National Elementary School Principal* 55 (January/February 1976): 52–59.

11. *Ibid.*, p. 54.

12. Graham S. Maxwell, "A Rating Scale for Assessing the Quality of Responsive/Illuminative Evaluations," *Educational Evaluation and Policy Analysis* 6 (Summer 1984): 131–138.

13. Howard J. Demeke, "Theory in Educational Administration: A Systems Approach" in *A Systems Approach to Educational Administration*, eds. Robert C. Maxson and Walter E. Sistrunk (Dubuque, IA: W. C. Brown Co., 1973), p. 33.

14. See Clifford J. Drew, *Introduction to Designing Research and Evaluation* (St. Louis: C. V. Mosby, 1976), Chapter 5.

15. Chester E. Finn, Jr., "Nine Commandments for School Effectiveness," *Phi Delta Kappan* 65 (April 1984): 518–524.

16. John I. Goodlad and M. Frances Klein, *Looking Behind the Classroom Door* (Worthington, OH: Charles A. Jones Publishing Co., 1974).

17. Francis Roberts, "School Principal: Minor Bureaucrat or Educational Leader?" *Urban Review* 8 (October 1975): 243.

18. Michael Aiken and Jerald Hage, "Organizational Alienation: A Comparative Analysis," *American Sociological Review* 31 (August 1966): 497–507.

19. See, for example, *Raising Expectations: Model Graduation Requirements* (Sacramento: California State Department of Education, 1983); Stewart C. Purkey and Susan Degan, "*Beyond Effective Schools to Good Schools*," *R and D Perspectives* (Eugene: University of Oregon, Spring 1985); Wilbur Brookover et al., *Creating Effective Schools* (Holmes Beach, Florida: Learning Publications, Inc., 1982); and *The Effective School Reports* (New York: Kelwynn Inc., 1983–85).

REFERENCES

Brookover, Wilbur; Beamer, Lawrence; Efthin, Helen; Hathaway, Douglas; Lezotte, Lawrence; Miller, Stephen; and Passa/Acqua, Joseph. *Creating Effective Schools.* Holmes Beach, Florida: Learning Publications, Inc., 1982.

Chrispeels, Janet, and Meaney, David. *Building Effective Schools: Assessing, Planning, Implementing.* San Diego: San Diego County Office of Education, 1985.

Cronbach, Joseph L. *Designing Evaluation of Educational and Social Programs.* San Francisco: Jossey Bass, 1982.

Cuban, Larry, "Effective Schools: A Friendly But Cautionary Note." *Phi Delta Kappa* 64 (June 1983): 695–696.

Datta, Lois-Ellin, and Perloff, C., eds. *Improving Evaluation.* Beverly Hills: Sage Publications, 1979.

Guba, Egon G. *Effective Evaluation.* San Francisco: Jossey Bass, 1981.

Madaus, George F.; Airasian, Peter W.; and Kellaghan, Thomas. *School Effectiveness: A Reassessment of the Evidence.* New York: McGraw-Hill Book Company, 1980.

Manlove, Donald C., ed. *K–12 School Evaluation Criteria: A Guide for School Improvement.* Falls Church, VA: National Study of School Evaluation, 1983.

Mann, Dale, and Inman, Deborah. "Improving Education Within Existing Resources: The Instructionally Effective Schools' Approach.'' *Journal of Education Finance* 10 (Fall 1984): 256–269.

Wilson, Bruce L. ''The School Assessment Survey.'' *Educational Leadership* 42 (March 1985): 50–53.

Young, Rufus. ''Development of a Process for an Effective School Model.'' *The Effective School Report*. New York: Kelwynn, Inc., Part 1, June 1984; Part 2, May 1985.

CHAPTER 2

Evaluating the School Culture
and Classroom Climate

> While it seems a bit mystical to say it, when school climates are
> well established, they take on a life of their own. . . . They gain
> their stability and influence from the beliefs people have about
> them, the stress and myths that make up their traditions and in-
> structional mechanisms that are developed to reinforce them.
>
> *Willis D. Hawley and Susan J. Rosenholtz*

In the first edition of this book, this chapter was titled "Evaluating
School and Classroom Climate." Since the writing of the first edition, research studies suggest that school climate is one of the five correlates of
effective schools. Additional research in the business world suggests that
"climate" may be too narrow a concept, that one has to examine an organization's culture. This being the case, four questions are worth discussing in this chapter. First, what is the school culture? Second, how are
culture and climate similar and different? Third, how does one conduct a
"culture audit"? Fourth, how can classroom climate be evaluated?

SCHOOL CULTURE

Deal and Kennedy point out in their book, *Corporate Culture*, that corpo-
rations spend a lot of personnel time and energy enhancing the culture of
the organization—the environment, the values, the heroes, the rites and
rituals, and the networking (formal and informal communication).[1] School
leaders should do no less.

Michael Rutter and his colleagues highlight this concern in their book,
Fifteen Thousand Hours: Secondary Schools and Their Effects on Children, when
they conclude that the school's culture, what they call the "ethos" of a

21

school, is central to its success.[2] Firestone and Wilson[3] suggest that the culture of the school is a key factor for effective instruction and that four factors are related to school culture—its content (commitments, tasks, services, trust, encouragement, individual autonomy); its symbols (stories, myths, legends, trophies, report cards, lesson plans); its rituals (ceremonies, activities); and the communication patterns. These school culture factors will be further defined in the audit process.

CULTURE AND CLIMATE

My colleague, Dr. William Foster, argues that culture is not climate. He makes his case this way:

> "The relationship of climate to culture is like the relationship of a battery to a nuclear plant; they both might give energy, but the one is so much more powerful and complex than the other. Climate implies that we, as organizational leaders, can forecast the climate, and then, through some meteorological trick, produce sunshine when all omens say rain. . . . Culture depends on a long-term commitment, a commitment to creating in the organization a system of meanings which penetrate the core of the individuals involved. It involves heroes, of who has made a difference and why. It involves symbols, of what is important. It involves struggles, of who our enemies are and why we must conquer. It involves sagas, of those times when we were at our best, when we overcame awesome odds. It involves priests, those who can forgive errors and show the way. And it involves leaders, those whom we can turn to for direction, inspiration, and knowledge."[4]

Another viewpoint, my view of the culture-climate relationship, is this. Culture is to meteorology (the study of weather) as climate is to climatology (the study of weather in a specific area or location). The school has a culture, the classroom a climate. Both influence and affect one another. What we have been calling school climate may be better described as the school culture—its organizational health, its safety and orderliness, its rites, rituals and regulations, and so on. While the commitment to improve the culture of a school may take some time, it seems that principals, teachers, and others can begin to improve some of the climate factors immediately. But since the school culture and the classroom climate are interrelated it is best not to focus on the dichotomy but rather to suggest that both can be enhanced to improve the quality of the education taking place in the school. For the purposes of assessment the remainder of this chapter will use the term "culture" for school factors and "climate" for classroom factors.

CULTURE AUDIT

Culture is the glue that holds the elements of an organization together. It is the presence of shared meaning, a sense of mission that binds individuals in the organization to each other. It is composed of elements that broadly define its productivity, its effectiveness, its worth. Willis J. Furtwengler reports that the culture of effective schools reflects: "(1) structure and order, (2) support for social interactions and acceptance of people as individuals, (3) support for intellectual or learning activities, and (4) strong commitment to a clearly articulated school mission and to a shared vision for the school."[5]

Some of these elements are discussed in this proposal for a school culture audit. The recommended approach to gather data for the audit will be questionnaires and interviews with the emphasis on question asking. "Successful leaders, we have found, are great question-askers, and they do pay attention."[6]

This audit strategy suggests that the school principal select a team of teachers, students, parents, and community leaders. The team, as suggested in chapter one, should plan to carry out a specific set of tasks for gathering, collating, and reporting the information.

Vision

As it says in the Old Testament: "Where there is no vision the people perish." The reality of this dictum is that the school leader, the school principal, must have a vision for the school, must be able to gather followers to support that vision, and must be able to use persuasion and other methods for implementing that vision.

Bennis and Nanus say: "A vision is a target that beckons. It may be as vague as a dream or as precise as a goal or mission statement. A shared vision of the future also suggests measures of effectiveness for the organization and all its parts."[7]

Bill Honig, California's Superintendent of Public Instruction, believes "that the proper state role is to work to achieve a common vision of excellence, to develop strong constituencies in the educational and general communities for the vision and to help organize support to assist those who are committed to improve."[8]

A. Lorri Manasse wrote in *Principal* magazine: "The importance of this personal vision or image of the school as a whole is a recurring theme in studies of effective principals."[9]

Team Audit Questions:

1. Does the school principal have a vision for the school?
2. Has he/she talked to you about this vision?

3. Is this vision in writing?
4. Has this vision been shared with others in the school?
5. Does the principal actively seek followers to support the vision?

Mission/Goals.   An effective school is one that has a clear and concise statement of the district's and school's mission, goals, and objectives, with the objectives being defined by course and by grade level for each of three categories—knowledge, skills, and attitudes. It is obvious, but worth repeating, that teaching methods, learning activities, instructional materials, and assessment strategies must be directly related to the school's goals and objectives.

Team Audit Strategies:
1. Find and review the *district's* statement of its mission, goals, objectives.
2. Find and review the *school's* statement of its mission, goals, objectives.
3. Determine the relationship of one with the other. Do the school's goals and objectives flow from the statements made by the district?
4. Are both sets of statements clear, concise, precise, understandable, implementable?
5. Use the recommendations for curriculum evaluation in chapter five to determine ways to indicate whether the courses, the materials, and the assessment strategies follow naturally from the statement of goals and objectives.

Environment/Climate.   An effective school is one where everyone in the school is free from bodily harm and where there is a safe and orderly atmosphere. This means that there is a discipline code, that there are rules and regulations regarding behavior, that student rights and responsibilities are clearly delineated, that enforcement is fair and consistent, and that everyone has been well informed. It also means that the school is a pleasant place with an attractive, bright, clean physical appearance. The culture is such that it promotes a sense of pride, a sense of responsibility, and a series of activities (assemblies, rallies, slogans) that involve everyone in enhancing the quality of school life and its organizational health.

Team Audit Strategies
The team should use the instruments in this chapter to gather data, discuss findings, and develop action plans.

Students.   An effective school is one where students are expected to master the basic skills, the core curriculum, and engage in higher order thinking skills. In effective schools, students recognize and appreciate the need for high standards and high expectations for performance. They understand the need for frequent monitoring of their academic progress and use the feedback from such monitoring to help themselves improve or enhance their performance. In effective schools, students recognize the necessity to use their time effectively and efficiently and not to allow instructional time to be disrupted by student misbehavior. In such schools, students learn to appreciate the need for good work, for achievement, and for success. They appreciate the opportunities that the school provides for acknowledging their efforts through rewards, displays of material, informing parents and the like.

Team Audit Strategies

There are several chapters in this book that assess the factors listed above. The audit team should use specific strategies to help determine the extent to which students in the school:

A. Master the basic skills.
B. Engage in high order thinking skills.
C. Have high expectations for performance.
D. Are awarded for their performance.
E. Receive feedback about their progress.
F. Use their time adequately.
G. Do their homework.
H. Limit disruptions.
I. Demonstrate positive behavior.
J. Show a sense of pride and accomplishment in the work they do.

Home-School-Community Relations. An effective school is one where parents have an understanding of the mission, goals, and objectives of the school; where parents are given information about their children's progress; where school personnel look to parents as educators of their children and thus provide help in developing parenting skills; where parents are given information to help their children with school work and homework; and where parents are encouraged to participate in school affairs and to use community resources to enrich home and school life. An effective school also makes use of community resources and engages in cooperative programs with local businesses, agencies, and groups.

Team Audit Strategies

Use the recommendations in chapter eight for assessing school-home-community relationships and developing action plans.

Teachers. An effective school is one in which teachers provide direct instruction in the basic skills, higher order thinking skills, and the core curriculum, with the expectation that all children in their classrooms can master the content and skills. Effective school teachers are flexible in their grouping patterns, use a variety of teaching methods and materials, and monitor student progress frequently, informing both students and parents of this progress. Effective school teachers protect student learning time, using management techniques that minimize loss of instructional time. These teachers use multiple assessment methods to check for student understanding of skills, content, and attitudes and, when necessary, they alter instruction to meet the needs and talents of the students in their classes.

Team Audit Strategies
1. Use the recommendations in chapters four and five.
2. Study how other districts evaluate teachers and reward teachers for excellence in teaching.
3. Consult with the school principal and district supervisors to determine the extent to which teachers in the school are performing according to the criteria stated in effective school literature and research regarding good teaching practices.
4. Design methods that support the teachers in their efforts to improve instruction, to maintain standards, to maintain high expectations for student performance, and to reduce classroom interruptions.
5. Monitor the curriculum to be sure that there is articulation among program objectives, course content, instructional materials, and testing materials.

These suggestions are but one way to monitor the school's culture. As mentioned earlier, culture includes the school's organizational health. We now examine one way of assessing your school's organizational health.

ASSESSING YOUR SCHOOL'S
ORGANIZATIONAL HEALTH

A healthy school climate is a prelude to change. Organizational health has long been considered an important factor for change, innovation, and individual and group productivity. As part of this discussion about school climate, it is imperative that you, the principal, recognize the conditions that promote organizational health because organizational health influences the school's culture and the potential for change and innovation. Suggestions have been provided for evaluating the culture of the school. What can a principal do to determine the *health* of a school?

Kimpston and Sonnabend[10] completed a study designed to determine whether there is a relationship between a school's organizational health and innovation in schools. Specifically, they ask whether faculty members view their school's organizational health more positively when the school is engaged in some innovative practices. Twenty junior or senior high schools were identified as least innovative, and twenty were identified as most innovative. Using an instrument that they developed (see Figure 2-1) and administered to the faculty (1134 people) in these forty schools, these researchers found that faculty members in innovative schools viewed the school's organizational health more positively, particularly on factors of decision making (the extent to which a building administration involves staff in the decision-making process for solving problems), innovativeness (how the staff members feel about trying new methods, new designs, and

---

Directions: The purpose of this questionnaire is to secure a description of (1) the organizational behaviors of public school faculty, and (2) the organizational conditions under which faculty members work. The items in the questionnaire describe typical behaviors or conditions that exist within a secondary school. Please indicate to what extent each of these descriptions characterizes *your school*. Do not evaluate the items in terms of "good" or "bad" behaviors or conditions. Respond in terms of how well the statement describes the conditions in your school. Read each item carefully and mark your answers by placing a check mark on the appropriate line. Your response will remain anonymous. Be as candid as possible.

	Strongly Agree (A)	Mildly Agree (B)	Mildly Disagree (C)	Strongly Disagree (D)
1. Teachers willingly spend time after school with students who seek their help.	___	___	___	___
2. There is a feeling of togetherness within the faculty.	___	___	___	___
3. Teachers are willing to try innovations in this school.	___	___	___	___
4. The school administration provides needed information to the staff.	___	___	___	___
5. Decision making in this school could best be described as democratic.	___	___	___	___
6. Students are involved in decision making in this school.	___	___	___	___
7. Efforts are made by the faculty to discuss this school's goals.	___	___	___	___
8. Problems are solved in this school and not just ignored.	___	___	___	___

(cont.)

FIGURE 2-1
Organizational Health Description Questionnaire*
*Richard D. Kimpston and Leslie C. Sonnabend, Mimeograph. Reprinted by permission from the authors.

	Strongly Agree (A)	Mildly Agree (B)	Mildly Disagree (C)	Strongly Disagree (D)
9. A deterrent to change in this school is the stress which accompanies that change.	____	____	____	____
10. Feedback information is secured and utilized in conducting and sustaining change in our school.	____	____	____	____
11. Teachers value their professional association with this faculty.	____	____	____	____
12. In our school there is willingness to respond to community requests but the action taken is based upon professional knowledge.	____	____	____	____
13. Teachers feel threatened by community pressures.	____	____	____	____
14. Faculty members are aware of instructional resources available to them within their community.	____	____	____	____
15. Many school problems are solved by individual faculty members because the organization is generally unresponsive.	____	____	____	____
16. There is generally a pessimistic atmosphere in this school.	____	____	____	____
17. Teachers in this school present new ideas for improvement.	____	____	____	____
18. The goals of this school are seen as achievable by faculty members.	____	____	____	____
19. Teachers feel that communication lines are open with the school administration.	____	____	____	____
20. In general, teachers' opinions are valued in decision making.	____	____	____	____
21. Faculty opinions are solicited but seldom used in our school.	____	____	____	____
22. Educational changes are generally made in our school without sufficient study and preparation.	____	____	____	____
23. Our school has procedures for identifying school problems.	____	____	____	____
24. Many school problems are solved by group action.	____	____	____	____
25. The right person is doing the right job in this school.	____	____	____	____

(cont.)

	Strongly Agree (A)	Mildly Agree (B)	Mildly Disagree (C)	Strongly Disagree (D)
26. Innovativeness is uncharacteristic of this school.	___	___	___	___
27. Community requests receive scant attention in this school.	___	___	___	___
28. Resource personnel available within this school district are utilized in this school.	___	___	___	___
29. Faculty members view school goals as appropriate.	___	___	___	___
30. The public is made aware of our school's activities.	___	___	___	___
31. Any faculty member in this school may assume leadership responsibilities.	___	___	___	___
32. Solutions to problems are actively sought from the staff.	___	___	___	___
33. This school has an ongoing plan for facilitating change.	___	___	___	___
34. The strengths of faculty members are utilized in this school.	___	___	___	___
35. Teachers enjoy getting together informally with other faculty members.	___	___	___	___
36. Ideas for improvement generally receive support in this school.	___	___	___	___
37. Teachers in this school are given considerable latitude in carrying out instruction.	___	___	___	___
38. Faculty members are generally unaware that goals exist for this school.	___	___	___	___
39. Procedures for communication with the community have been established.	___	___	___	___
40. Decision making in this school could best be described as undemocratic.	___	___	___	___
41. It is difficult to change anything in this school.	___	___	___	___
42. In our school, procedures have been established to evaluate our effectiveness in resolving school problems.	___	___	___	___

(cont.)

	Strongly Agree (A)	Mildly Agree (B)	Mildly Disagree (C)	Strongly Disagree (D)
43. There is general agreement by faculty members as to the appropriateness of the school goals.	——	——	——	——
44. Most teachers make an effort to communicate with the administration.	——	——	——	——
45. There is no opportunity for faculty to grow and develop professionally in this school.	——	——	——	——
46. Many teachers attend school social functions.	——	——	——	——
47. Most teachers would rather teach in this school than someplace else.	——	——	——	——
48. A climate of experimentation pervades this school.	——	——	——	——
49. Teachers are protected from unreasonable community and parental demands.	——	——	——	——
50. The teachers in this building enjoy their work.	——	——	——	——

FIGURE 2-1 (*cont.*)

new programs), and community relations (how well the school staff act and react with the surrounding environment).

You might find the results of the questionnaire interesting and informative. Rather than obtaining a total score it may be best that you examine the teachers' rating for each characteristic so that you can plan for change—improvement if it is needed. It is easiest to give each teacher a score sheet, as shown in Figure 2-2, for this purpose.

An item analysis is also possible and informative. For example, have the teachers rate each of the five statements regarding "innovativeness." How many of your teachers willingly innovate by trying new ideas for improvement? Is there an atmosphere and support for change and for trying new ideas? How many of your teachers feel that change, innovativeness, and trying new ideas is not a priority?

Is it possible for a principal to administer a school with an unhealthy climate? Probably so—at least for a short period of time. I have seen situations where school principals, because of their own insecurities and distrust of people, contributed to a school climate that warped faculty attitudes. These principals encouraged only responses that they wanted to hear, promoted superficial change, were master manipulators of individ-

Directions: Your name is not necessary. Please take the Organizational Health Description Questionnaire that you just completed and *circle* the number that corresponds to the letter you circled for each item. Add your circled numbers for each characteristic and place it on the line.

Characteristic	Items	A	B	C	D	
Goal	7	4	3	2	1	
Focus	18	4	3	2	1	
	29	4	3	2	1	
	38	1	2	3	4	
	43	4	3	2	1	___
Communication	4	4	3	2	1	
Adequacy	19	4	3	2	1	
	30	4	3	2	1	
	39	4	3	2	1	
	44	4	3	2	1	___
Optimal Power	5	4	3	2	1	
Equalization	20	4	3	2	1	
	6	4	3	2	1	
	31	4	3	2	1	
	40	1	2	3	4	___
Resource	14	4	3	2	1	
Utilization	25	4	3	2	1	
	28	4	3	2	1	
	34	4	3	2	1	
	45	1	2	3	4	___
Cohesiveness	2	4	3	2	1	
	11	4	3	2	1	
	15	1	2	3	4	
	24	4	3	2	1	
	47	4	3	2	1	___
Morale	1	4	3	2	1	
	16	1	2	3	4	
	35	4	3	2	1	
	46	4	3	2	1	
	50	4	3	2	1	___

(cont.)

FIGURE 2-2
Organizational Health Description Questionnaire Score Sheet

Characteristic	Items	Score			
		A	*B*	*C*	*D*
Innovativeness	3	4	3	2	1
	17	4	3	2	1
	26	1	2	3	4
	36	4	3	2	1
	48	4	3	2	1
Autonomy	12	4	3	2	1
	13	1	2	3	4
	27	1	2	3	4
	37	4	3	2	1
	49	4	3	2	1
Adaptation	9	1	2	3	4
	10	4	3	2	1
	22	1	2	3	4
	33	4	3	2	1
	41	1	2	3	4
Problem-Solving	8	4	3	2	1
Adequacy	21	1	2	3	4
	23	4	3	2	1
	32	4	3	2	1
	42	4	3	2	1

FIGURE 2-2 (*cont.*)

uals and groups, and controlled communication flowing in and out of school. They are among those who resist change and look for excuses such as, "You guys at the college level don't know what it's like to be a principal in the real world!" One can easily lose count of the number of excuses some teachers and principals provide for not solving their problems, for not wanting to change, innovate, or try new things. The most frequent excuse is to blame it on the "system." In city school districts the "system" is usually identified as the central office. "We can't change; we can't do that because it won't sell with the people at central office." In smaller school districts, the "system" is usually the superintendent or sometimes the board of education. For the board of education, the "system" is the public or the community. And so it goes. The "system," that barrier to change, varies according to the people you talk to and their position in the school's organizational structure.

But there are many principals who are leaders, who want their schools to be the best possible, and who encourage and get faculty, parent, and student loyalty, input, and work. There are principals who take educational risks because they believe it will benefit students. There are principals who want to know how they and their faculty and their school are doing. There are principals, armed with information, who plan carefully to change those things that need to be changed.

One recommendation for using this questionnaire is to prepare a graph similar to the example (Figure 2-3) that follows. The example shows the graph prepared for several schools that were pooled in an effective school study project.[11] A school's organizational health could be scored every two or three years and changes plotted on a bar or line graph.

Clark and Fairman[12] report that effectiveness of a planned change may depend more on the organizational health of the school than on the appropriateness of the plan. They use the same categories shown on the questionnaire in Figure 2-2 but rather than using an "agree-disagree" checklist, they use the following format:

"Goal focus is the ability of persons, groups, or organizations to have clarity and acceptance of goals and objectives."

Low level	Average	High

The authors provide definitions for each of the ten dimensions, call for careful reflection of each before checking the level, and suggest that if checks can be provided along the right side of the scale then the school's organizational health is appropriate for change and innovation.

Another option for assessing the school's culture and climate is offered

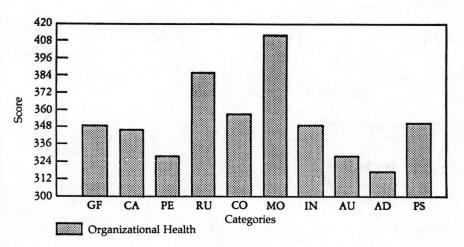

FIGURE 2-3
School Effectiveness Study

by Research for Better Schools, Inc.[13] This group has designed a school assessment instrument that measures a variety of school and organizational factors related to school effectiveness and improvement. The instrument, called the "School Assessment Survey," analyzes nine school climate dimensions: goal consensus, facilitative leadership, classroom instruction, curriculum and resources, vertical communication, horizontal communication, staff conflict, student discipline, and teaching behavior. The survey results provide a school profile, an item analysis, and a written summary.

PRINCIPAL'S COMPETENCY RATING SCALE

The principal, as you might imagine, has the major responsibility for setting the tone for the school's culture and climate.

Klopf et al. have developed a taxonomy of leadership competencies, one of which is the development of a humanistic climate.[14] The authors believe that certain tasks are required if a principal hopes to attain this leadership competency. Each question in the following rating scale contains a competency that implies something you should be doing in your school. For example, the question, "Is the team concept one that you should try to develop among school personnel?" suggests that you, as the principal, should try to create a team effort among school personnel since this may be a factor contributing to a more humanistic climate.

The questions for competency enable you to compare your self-evaluation response (P) with those of the faculty (T) and others (O) you select to complete the scale. Following the scale is a suggestion for scoring and comparing the results.*

Question	Definitely/ Always		Occasionally/ Sometimes		Seldom/ Never
(1) P: Is the team concept one that you try to develop among school personnel?	5	4	3	2	1
T: Has your principal developed or tried to implement a team concept in your school?	5	4	3	2	1

*Permission to reprint the specific tasks has been granted. Copyright 1975, National Association of Elementary School Principals. All rights reserved.

Question	*Definitely / Always*		*Occasionally / Sometimes*		*Seldom / Never*
O: Do you feel that teachers and administrator(s) work together as a team?	5	4	3	2	1
(2) P: Do you delegate leadership responsibility among members of your staff when appropriate?	5	4	3	2	1
T: Has your principal delegated leadership responsibility to teachers and others when appropriate?	5	4	3	2	1
(3) P: Do you make yourself accessible to teachers?	5	4	3	2	1
T: Is your principal accessible to the teachers in this school?	5	4	3	2	1
O: Do you feel that the principal is accessible to the teachers of this school?	5	4	3	2	1
(4) P: Do you encourage teachers to share their problems, needs, feelings, and frustrations with you?	5	4	3	2	1

(cont.)

Question	Definitely/ Always		Occasionally/ Sometimes		Seldom/ Never
T: Can teachers share their problems, needs, feelings, and frustrations with the principal?	5	4	3	2	1
O: Do you feel that teachers are encouraged to share their problems, needs, feelings, and frustrations with the principal?	5	4	3	2	1
(5) P: Have you worked cooperatively with school personnel and its clientele to develop goals and objectives for this school?	5	4	3	2	1
T: Have teachers worked with the principal and others to develop goals and objectives for this school?	5	4	3	2	1
O: Do you feel that the principal, teachers, parents, and others have worked cooperatively to develop goals and objectives for this school?	5	4	3	2	1

(*cont.*)

Question	Definitely/ Always		Occasionally/ Sometimes		Seldom/ Never
(6) P: Do you encourage teachers and other school personnel to implement strategies for carrying out school objectives?	5	4	3	2	1
T: Have teachers been encouraged to implement strategies that will carry out school objectives?	5	4	3	2	1
O: Do you feel that the principal encourages teachers and others to implement strategies that carry out school objectives?	5	4	3	2	1
(7) P: Have you developed with others in the school an assessment program that will determine the school's effectiveness?	5	4	3	2	1
T: Have teachers and others been involved in developing an assessment program to determine the school's effectiveness?	5	4	3	2	1

(cont.)

Question	Definitely/ Always		Occasionally/ Sometimes		Seldom/ Never
O: Do you feel that the teachers, principal, and others have an assessment program that determines the effectiveness of this school?	5	4	3	2	1
(8) P: Do you include classroom teachers, personnel staff, special teachers (art, music, p.e., etc.), and others to share their ideas and perceptions about each child in the school?	5	4	3	2	1
T: Are you involved in sharing your ideas and perceptions about each child in your classroom with pupil personnel staff, special teachers, and others?	5	4	3	2	1
O: Does the school staff (special teachers, guidance counselors, psychologist, aides, and others) share their ideas about each child with the classroom teacher and vice versa?	5	4	3	2	1

(cont.)

Question	Definitely/ Always		Occasionally/ Sometimes		Seldom/ Never
(9) P: Do you help teachers and parents share their ideas and perceptions of a child's strengths, weaknesses, and potential and plan accordingly?	5	4	3	2	1
T: Are you encouraged by the administration to discuss with parents their child's strengths, weaknesses, and potential and cooperatively develop plans to help the child?	5	4	3	2	1
O: Do you feel that teachers are encouraged by the administration to share information with parents and to cooperatively plan ideas that will meet the child's learning needs?	5	4	3	2	1
(10) P: Do you involve school staff to personally recruit parent volunteers?	5	4	3	2	1
T: Are you personally involved in recruiting parent volunteers?	5	4	3	2	1

(cont.)

Question	Definitely/ Always		Occasionally/ Sometimes		Seldom/ Never
O: Do you feel that the school staff is encouraged to personally recruit parent volunteers?	5	4	3	2	1
(11) P: Do you plan and implement parent workshops that will help them work with children in school or at home?	5	4	3	2	1
T: Are workshops for parents planned and implemented by teachers and the principal?	5	4	3	2	1
O: Does this school offer parent workshops that will help them help their child at home and at school?	5	4	3	2	1
(12) P: Do you solicit and use ideas and suggestions from teachers and others when planning the school program?	5	4	3	2	1
T: Are teachers encouraged to share ideas and suggestions with the principal when planning the school program?	5	4	3	2	1

(cont.)

Question	Definitely/ Always		Occasionally/ Sometimes		Seldom/ Never
O: Do you feel that the ideas and suggestions of teachers and others are considered when the school's programs are being planned?	5	4	3	2	1
(13) P: Do you encourage (by some action) a stronger relationship between teachers and instructional aides?	5	4	3	2	1
T: Does your principal implement plans that encourage you and other teachers to develop a positive relationship with instructional aides?	5	4	3	2	1
O: Does the principal encourage a positive relationship between teachers and instructional aides?	5	4	3	2	1
(14) P: Do you meet formally and/or informally with students and encourage them to share ideas, problems, needs, and feelings with you?	5	4	3	2	1

(cont.)

Question	Definitely/ Always		Occasionally/ Sometimes		Seldom/ Never
T: Are the students in the school encouraged to share their ideas, problems, needs, and feelings with the principal?	5	4	3	2	1
O: Do you feel that the students are encouraged to share their ideas, problems, needs, and feelings with the principal?	5	4	3	2	1

Humanistic Climate Summary:

1. Add your score and place it on the line:____
2. Find the mean of the teachers' scores (add their scores and divide by the number of teachers). Place the mean score on the line:____
3. Find the mean score of the "others" (add their scores and divide by the number who completed the scale). Place the mean score on the line:____

Do teachers and others perceive you differently on this competency than you see yourself? What items showed the greater discrepancy between your self-perception and those of teachers and others? What can you do about this? What specific plans can you make that might change their perceptions? Were there items on which you were rated high (5–4) by teachers and yet you rated yourself lower (3–2–1)? What do you feel caused this discrepancy?

The role of a philanthropic foundation in assessing and improving the climate of schools is exemplary. The CFK Ltd., a philanthropic foundation founded by the late Charles F. Kettering II in 1967, exists to be of service to public education by assisting school systems in "developing individualized continuing education programs for their school administrators, developing learning programs for principals and other administrators so that they might serve as climate leaders within their schools and/or school systems and using the results of the above endeavors on non-grant basis."[15]

CFK Ltd. has published two booklets related to school climate. The first is titled *The Principal as the School's Climate Leader: A New Role for the Principalship.* The second, and the one reviewed in this section, is titled *School Climate Improvement: A Challenge to the School Administrator.*

The authors identify two major goals of a humane school climate. One is *productivity;* that is, a wholesome, stimulating, and productive learning environment conducive to academic achievement and personal growth of youth at different levels of development. The other is *satisfaction;* that is, a pleasant and satisfying school situation within which many people can live and work.

The authors list eight factors that affect the climate of a school, all of which are essential to establishing a humane school climate. The authors encourage readers to delete or add items; each factor has broad descriptions summarized as follows:

1. Respect—for students, teachers, administrators, others; a place for self-respecting individuals; no put-downs.
2. Trust—confidence that behavior will be honest, straightforward; belief that others will not let you down.
3. High Morale—school personnel feel good about what is happening.
4. Opportunities for Input—opportunities to share ideas, know that they are considered; self-esteem; part of the decision-making process; use of personnel resources.
5. Continuous Academic and Social Growth—opportunities for students and school personnel to improve their skills, knowledge, attitudes academically and socially.
6. Cohesiveness—a person's feeling toward the school; have a chance to exert their influence in collaboration with others.
7. School Renewal—develop improvement projects; self-renewing; value pluralism, diversity; "new" not seen as threatening; school is organized to approve improvement projects rapidly, effectively without stress, conflict, frustration.
8. Caring—school personnel feel that others care for them; each knows it will make a difference to someone else if he is happy or sad, healthy, or ill.[16]

These qualities, coupled with the basic human needs of school personnel, are essential to a productive and satisfying environment. The basic human needs include physiological needs, safety needs, acceptance and friendship needs, achievement and recognition needs, and needs that maximize one's potential.[17]

SCHOOL CLIMATE PROFILE

The school climate is based on the qualities described above. This profile should be used in conjunction with the comprehensive treatment of school climate provided in Robert S. Fox et al., *School Climate Improvement: A Chal-*

lenge to the School Administrator. The profile is presented in four parts—general climate factors, program determinants, process determinants, and material determinants. The entire instrument takes twenty to twenty-five minutes to complete, but school administrators may administer it in several short sessions. Principals should complete the instrument as well as teachers, students, parents, and other school personnel. The compilation of perceptions from a wide range of people will give the principal a much better "picture" of the climate of the school he or she administrates.

A school's culture and the classroom climate are the direct result of attitudes, behavior, and interactions among teachers, administrators, parents, students, and staff. If a study of a school's culture and classroom climate reveals that there is a lack of trust, a lack of openness, a feeling that the school is not moving toward its goals, that members are not satisfied, and that it is less than a humane place to be, then it would seem that school personnel and parents should be confronted with evidence. Maybe an objective analysis of the evidence will help some people change their behavior and create plans for trying to improve. The evidence of a positive, open, trustful, supportive culture and climate should also be shared with others.

An important part of the school's culture and climate are its rules, regulations and disciplinary practices. We now look at ways to evaluate these three factors.

ASSESSING RULES AND REGULATIONS

There is little need to repeat the litany of statistics documenting the increase in school vandalism, assaults, behavior problems, truancy, and other acts that are adversely affecting the culture and climate of schools and classrooms. The major purpose here is to help you determine whether or not these problems exist in your school to the degree that they interfere with instruction and detract from the positive school culture and climate you and your teachers are working to maintain (note the assumption). In addition, it would be instructive to assess the perceptions of teachers, students, and parents regarding school discipline, safety, and control. Limitations should be noted. There is no attempt here to diagnose and prescribe approaches to behavior problems that teachers encounter in their classrooms.

Rules and Regulations Evaluation

There are several questions that you and the faculty should consider regarding school rules, regulations, policies, and procedures. Each question can be rewritten as a criterion for guiding actions.

1. Are the school rules and regulations based upon board of education policies?
   a. How do you know?
   b. When was the last time you checked?
   c. Might you have one or more rules, etc., that deviate from board of education policies?
2. Are the school rules and regulations available to school personnel?
   a. Does each teacher have a written copy?
   b. Does each student have a copy in a student handbook?
   c. Does each parent have a copy?
3. Is there general agreement on the rules and regulations established for the school?
   a. How do you know?
   b. Have you checked on this lately?
4. Are the rules and regulations stated in a positive manner?
5. Do the rules emphasize responsibility rather than restrictions?

These and other questions can serve as the basis for discussions with faculty and students regarding school rules and regulations. It may be of value to have a committee composed of teachers, students, parents, and an administrator (yourself or an assistant) evaluate existing school rules and regulations. If you decide to do this, this committee should initially obtain copies of all school rules, regulations, policies, and procedures. These materials can be judged on the basis of the five previous questions. In addition, the committee may find it valuable to evaluate these materials by asking teachers, students, and parents to judge them. Figures 2-4, 2-5, and 2-6 are examples of such questionnaires.

In Figure 2-4, a sample teacher questionnaire is provided. One of the basic questions that may come out of a discussion of the items on this questionnaire is whether or not there are rules and regulations in your school that may violate a student's civil rights. Rules governing dress codes, search and seizure, student discipline, and the like, are particularly sensitive to laws and legal rulings about the violation of a student's civil rights.

Figure 2-5 is an example of a student questionnaire regarding rules and regulations. It should be obvious that students should have an opportunity, either in classes or through their student council, to discuss the rationale and necessity for school rules and regulations. Periodic review of rules and regulations is helpful to all parties. It may be best to begin each school year with a review of the school rules in each classroom (homeroom) to clear up misunderstandings and to generate discussion about the need for rules, the need to respect each other's rights, and the need to exercise responsibilities that will insure that these rights are applicable to all.

Figure 2-6 is an example of a parent questionnaire designed to obtain parent opinion. There is an interesting paradox now occurring. Many par-

Grade or Subject Taught_____

1. Do you have a copy of all school rules and regulations?
   ____Yes   ____No
2. Are there any rules and regulations that you feel should be changed?
   ____Yes   ____No
   (If yes, please identify.)

3. Do you feel that parents and students have an understanding of the rules and regulations of this school?
   ____Yes   ____No
   (If no, please explain.)

4. In your opinion, do teachers carry out the rules and regulations as stated?
   ____Yes   ____No
   (If no, please explain.)

5. In your opinion, does the administration carry out the rules and regulations as stated?
   ____Yes   ____No
   (If no, please explain.)

6. Does this school have a good reputation concerning student behavior?
   ____Definitely   ____Not sure   ____I think so
   ____It depends who you talk to   ____Not at all
7. Do teachers seem satisfied with the present school rules and regulations?
   ____Definitely   ____Not sure   ____I think so
   ____Some are, some aren't   ____Many are not
8. Do teachers feel that rules and regulations promote student self-dignity, self-worth, and responsibility?
   ____All or most do   ____Some or a few do   ____Many do not
9. Do teachers feel that most parents support the rules and regulations?
   ____Yes, they do   ____Some do, some don't   ____Many do not
10. Please list the rules and regulations that you feel should be revised or discussed at faculty meetings.

FIGURE 2-4
Teacher Questionnaire Concerning School Rules

Directions: This questionnaire is designed to find out how you feel about school rules and regulations. Please circle the number that represents how you feel.

School_____Grade_____Room_____

	No Opinion	Definitely	Sometimes	Not at All
1. This school has rules and regulations everyone must follow.	1	2	3	4
2. This school has rules and regulations most students should follow.	1	2	3	4
3. Students have very little to say about the rules and regulations established for this school.	1	2	3	4
4. Rules and regulations are well understood by the students.	1	2	3	4
5. Parents generally support the rules and regulations of this school.	1	2	3	4
6. Teachers are understanding in carrying out the rules and regulations of this school.	1	2	3	4
7. Students should be punished or disciplined for breaking the school's rules and regulations.	1	2	3	4
8. The rules and regulations are applied to all students fairly and consistently.	1	2	3	4
9. There should be class discussions on the rationale for rules and regulations.	1	2	3	4

10. Please indicate below which rules and regulations you feel should be revised or discussed.

FIGURE 2-5
Student Questionnaire Concerning School Rules

Directions: The subcommittee is studying school rules and regulations. Reactions and feelings of parents are most important. Please share your opinion by circling the number that best describes your feeling. Thank you for your time and cooperation.

	No Opinion	Definitely	Sometimes	Not at All
1. Most parents support the rules and regulations at this school.	1	2	3	4
2. Parents generally agree with the school's methods of maintaining order and discipline.	1	2	3	4
3. This school has a good reputation concerning student behavior.	1	2	3	4
4. Parents understand the rationale for specific school rules and regulations.	1	2	3	4
5. Most parents feel that students comply with existing school rules and regulations.	1	2	3	4
6. Many parents feel that the administration and teachers are too lenient in carrying out school rules and regulations.	1	2	3	4
7. Many parents feel that the administration and teachers are too harsh in carrying out school rules and regulations.	1	2	3	4
8. It would be beneficial if more parents were involved in developing policies concerning school rules and regulations.	1	2	3	4
9. Most parents agree that the student who disobeys a school rule or regulation should be punished or disciplined.	1	2	3	4

10. Please state below your comments or questions concerning existing school rules and regulations.

FIGURE 2-6
Parent Questionnaire Concerning School Rules

ents and citizens want the schools to "crack down" on students. They are pressuring for law and order almost to the point where they are willing to deny the students their civil rights. Yet many of these same parents will threaten the school with a lawsuit the moment disciplinary action is taken against their son or daughter. In any event, it is important to involve parents in a review of school rules and regulations.

Regardless of the extent of agreement or disagreement about school rules and regulations, and regardless of the amount of involvement teachers, students, and parents have in creating and deciding about school rules and regulations, student misbehavior will not disappear.

Evaluating Discipline Practices

You cannot have learning without discipline. Teachers cannot teach, and learners cannot learn in an environment that is disruptive, distractive, and bound with fear for personal safety. Learning, by its very nature, requires self-discipline. Only individuals can learn, and to do so those individuals must have an environment that encourages and instructs them how to learn and gives them the opportunity to do so. Disruptive and distractive student behavior reduces teaching-learning opportunities. It violates the rights of teachers and students who come to school for this purpose. Yet the school and its personnel have to exhaust every possibility and all existing services to help disruptive and nondisruptive students find success in school.

In relation to the general school climate it may be helpful for you and your teachers to discuss the answers to the following questions:

1. Do teachers enforce school rules and regulations consistently?
2. Do the same groups of teachers complain about student behavior?
3. Do teachers ask for assistance to deal with student behavior problems?
4. Do teachers send behavior problems to the office rather than handle the problem themselves?
5. Does this school need a security officer?
6. Does this school need monitors to keep order?
7. Are teachers and students fearful about coming to school each day?
8. Do students complain that they didn't know they were breaking a school rule when they are caught?
9. Do the penalties students receive fit the misbehavior or rule that was broken?
10. Do parents criticize the school for its lack of discipline?
11. Do students fear using school facilities (halls, toilets, etc.)?
12. Do students criticize the school for its lack of discipline?
13. Do discipline problems have ethnic or racial overtones or implications?

14. Does the administration spend an excessive amount of time handling discipline problems?

ASSESSING CLASSROOM CLIMATE

These questions, particularly the last two questions, deal with the problems and concerns about discipline. Much has been written about this topic. There is a plethora of recommendations for principals and teachers about correcting student behavior, maintaining discipline, providing punishments, emphasizing rewards. Before we examine ways to evaluate the classroom climate, a report on the study of discipline may help both the school culture and the classroom climate.

Discipline

In a study of 500 well-disciplined schools, Wayson and his associates[18] identified several characteristics that seem to make these schools orderly, safe, and productive. These characteristics are reported here in checklist form so that you, the faculty, and others can rate your efforts toward attaining good disciplinary practices.

In this school, my faculty and I:

____ Do things good educators have been recommending for years.
____ Create a school culture focusing on good discipline.
____ View the school as a valuable, successful, productive workplace.
____ Make most decisions for the benefit of students.
____ Focus on behavior causes rather than symptoms.
____ Emphasize positive and preventive practices.
____ Adopt disciplinary practices to meet our own needs and styles.
____ Believe in our students.
____ Believe in ourselves; have confidence we can do the job.
____ Expend a lot of energy in putting our beliefs into action.
____ Spend time being cooperative and supportive.
____ Allow individual teachers to handle routine disciplinary problems.
____ Maintain close ties with parents and the community.
____ Critically and periodically review our school and classroom practices.

It is obvious that school rules, regulations, and discipline practices are directly related to the day-to-day activities and behaviors taking place in each of the school's classrooms. To separate the two is impossible. The factors relating to well-disciplined schools clearly show this relationship. Nevertheless, for evaluative purposes it is important to examine the climate of the classroom. Student misbehavior, student perceptions, and student assessment of their classroom climate will be discussed next.

Directions: This inventory attempts to find out how you feel about the frequency of student misbehaviors/offenses in school (class) and the probable causes. Place a check mark on one of the lines under *Frequency* and circle those numbers that reflect your view of the causes for the misbehavior/offense using the following guide:

1—home environment   5—school or teacher caused
2—parent attitude   6—students have personal problems
3—lack of parent control   7—students have learning problems
4—peer group influence   8—all of the causes

Offenses	Frequency			Causes
	Excessive	Moderate	Rare	
1. Habitual tardiness	____	____	____	1 2 3 4 5 6 7 8
2. Regularly skipping class	____	____	____	1 2 3 4 5 6 7 8
3. Truancy, poor attendance	____	____	____	1 2 3 4 5 6 7 8
4. Cheating	____	____	____	1 2 3 4 5 6 7 8
5. Disruptive behavior	____	____	____	1 2 3 4 5 6 7 8
6. Continual inattention in class	____	____	____	1 2 3 4 5 6 7 8
7. Rowdiness	____	____	____	1 2 3 4 5 6 7 8
8. Persistent silent contempt	____	____	____	1 2 3 4 5 6 7 8
9. Snearing, muttering	____	____	____	1 2 3 4 5 6 7 8
10. Swearing	____	____	____	1 2 3 4 5 6 7 8
11. Carries weapons	____	____	____	1 2 3 4 5 6 7 8
12. Unacceptable sexual behavior	____	____	____	1 2 3 4 5 6 7 8
13. Physical assaults on students	____	____	____	1 2 3 4 5 6 7 8
14. Physical assaults on teachers, other adults	____	____	____	1 2 3 4 5 6 7 8
15. Excessive talking	____	____	____	1 2 3 4 5 6 7 8
16. Lack of interest	____	____	____	1 2 3 4 5 6 7 8
17. Not listening	____	____	____	1 2 3 4 5 6 7 8
18. Destructive of school property	____	____	____	1 2 3 4 5 6 7 8
19. Destructive of student property	____	____	____	1 2 3 4 5 6 7 8
20. Drug/alcohol use	____	____	____	1 2 3 4 5 6 7 8
21. Disrespect, not courteous	____	____	____	1 2 3 4 5 6 7 8
22. Failure to complete school work	____	____	____	1 2 3 4 5 6 7 8
23. Smoking	____	____	____	1 2 3 4 5 6 7 8
24. Other (list)				

FIGURE 2-7
Students' Misbehaviors/Offenses Inventory

Classroom Inventory

It might be of interest to teachers to study the student misbehaviors/ offenses they encounter in the classroom and elsewhere in the school so that when they come together to discuss policies and procedures for implementing good, positive practices, their comments will be based upon specific information.

The inventory in Figure 2-7 can be used by students, parents, and teachers to find out about student behavior in the classroom (or the school). Some teachers may want to use the inventory to profile the behavior of specific students in the class. If used for this purpose, the student's name or a code is placed at the top of the inventory. If used to track a specific student, the findings are obviously confidential and should only be used as a means of providing the teacher with information to plan ways to help a particular student improve his/her behavior.

Teacher Perception Scale

A classroom teacher may want to examine his/her perceptions about a particular class. To do this a teacher may use the scale that follows:

How many students in class:	*All* 100%	*Half* 50%	*Some* 25%	*None* 0%
1. don't care about what's going on in class?	___	___	___	___
2. seem bored and uninterested?	___	___	___	___
3. leave their seats without permission?	___	___	___	___
4. don't do as the teacher requests?	___	___	___	___
5. are enjoyable to work with?	___	___	___	___
6. copy from others?	___	___	___	___
7. ask questions about the subject?	___	___	___	___
8. ask the teacher for help when they need it?	___	___	___	___
9. pay attention when the teacher is talking?	___	___	___	___
10. willingly participate in class activities?	___	___	___	___
11. are courteous and cooperative?	___	___	___	___
12. willingly assume responsibility?	___	___	___	___
13. complete assignments without complaining?	___	___	___	___
14. are prepared to discuss the topic or subject being taught?	___	___	___	___
15. enjoy coming to class?	___	___	___	___

Perceptions, however, may not be reality. A teacher should use this scale as the basis for collecting additional data about the students in class. Some ways to assess students' perceptions follow. It would be of value for a teacher to select one item on the list, i.e. "ask questions about the subject." The teacher can observe, for a week or two, whether or not his/her perceptions were accurate regarding this item and then ask the following questions: Which students ask questions most frequently? Are there reasons for this? Is there anything in my teaching behavior that causes this to happen? What strategies might I employ to improve student question-asking?

Our Class Rating Scale

Once these data are available, a teacher then knows how many students have negative attitudes. For example, suppose a teacher finds that twelve out of thirty students have negative attitudes. The task then is to determine why these twelve students have this kind of attitude. What might be causing this feeling? These and other questions may be answered by individual consultation with each student (if names were placed on the scale) or by conducting a class discussion.

The scale in Figure 2-8 is an easy way for teachers and students to

Directions: Place a check mark on the line nearest each word that describes our class in your opinion. If you have no strong feeling about the item, place the check mark on the third line.

Our Class

1. Active	___ ___ ___ ___ ___	Passive
2. Bored	___ ___ ___ ___ ___	Interested
3. Prepared	___ ___ ___ ___ ___	Unprepared
4. Restless	___ ___ ___ ___ ___	Attentive
5. Responsible	___ ___ ___ ___ ___	Obstructive
6. Uncertain	___ ___ ___ ___ ___	Confident
7. Alert	___ ___ ___ ___ ___	Apathetic
8. Thoughtless	___ ___ ___ ___ ___	Thoughtful
9. Good	___ ___ ___ ___ ___	Bad
10. Ignorant	___ ___ ___ ___ ___	Intelligent
11. Foolish	___ ___ ___ ___ ___	Wise
12. Sociable	___ ___ ___ ___ ___	Unsociable
13. Happy	___ ___ ___ ___ ___	Sad
14. Tense	___ ___ ___ ___ ___	Relaxed
15. Cheerful	___ ___ ___ ___ ___	Depressed

FIGURE 2-8
Our Class

assess their views and perceptions of the class. As you can see, the student or teacher merely checks the space near the adjective that best describes personal feelings about the class. This attitude scale takes only two or three minutes to complete. To obtain a total score, assign the value of 5, 4, 3, 2, and 1 to each of the spaces for all odd-numbered items. Reverse the numbering (1, 2, 3, 4, and 5) for all even-numbered items. Then add the numbers where a check mark has been placed. It is best not to include the third space (3) in the tabulation. The scores will range from 15 (very poor attitude) to 75 (very positive attitude). You could arbitrarily decide that students with a score ranging from 60 to 75 are those with positive attitudes and those with scores between 15 to 30 have negative attitudes.

Class Opinionnaire

Some teachers may wish to assess student feelings about the climate of the class by having them answer questions about it. Figure 2-9 is an example of an opinionnaire.

Classroom Climate Checklist

The following checklist can provide some useful data to teachers about the climate of the classroom in relation to teacher behavior, student behavior, interrelationships, and physical conditions. In the checklist, all of the odd-numbered items are negative factors; that is, factors that may contribute to a poor classroom climate. Students should merely check those items that tell about "life" in their classroom:

1. ___ students seldom study or do their work
2. ___ teacher praises us
3. ___ teacher seems to have favorite students
4. ___ students are encouraged to ask questions
5. ___ teacher calls on the same students all the time
6. ___ a lot of instructional materials are used
7. ___ teacher uses worksheets too much
8. ___ teacher has a good sense of humor
9. ___ students need to participate more in class
10. ___ teacher makes subject(s) interesting
11. ___ teacher is sarcastic
12. ___ students are not afraid to answer questions
13. ___ more students should be allowed to participate in discussions
14. ___ students are not afraid of being smart
15. ___ teacher needs to know us better
16. ___ teacher apologizes for personal mistakes

Directions: In order to voice your opinions about what makes for a good class, an enjoyable classroom, and better teaching and learning, write down your answers to the following questions. Remember there are no right or wrong answers. I want your opinion.

1. What are the good things about our class? List five.
   a. _____
   b. _____
   c. _____
   d. _____
   e. _____

2. What are some things you don't like about this class? List five.
   a. _____
   b. _____
   c. _____
   d. _____
   e. _____

3. What do you like best about our classroom? List at least three things.
   a. _____
   b. _____
   c. _____

4. What do you like least about our classroom? List at least three.
   a. _____
   b. _____
   c. _____

5. What bothers you most about the way I teach?

6. What bothers you most about your classmates?

7. What bothers you most about yourself?

8. Would you recommend a friend to become a member of this class? Tell me why you answered yes or no.

9. If you were the teacher in this classroom, what would you do to make it a better place for your students?

10. How do you feel about:
   a. Your relationship with me?

   b. Your relationship with your classmates?

FIGURE 2-9
Opinionnaire

17. ____ teacher's tests are difficult to understand
18. ____ students take care of bulletin boards
19. ____ teacher doesn't let us make many decisions
20. ____ students have a feeling of accomplishment
21. ____ assignments are generally boring
22. ____ students help each other to do a good job
23. ____ teacher doesn't give us interesting things to do
24. ____ students can work on things they like to do
25. ____ teacher has little or no control over students
26. ____ teacher lets us plan class activities
27. ____ teacher doesn't smile much; seems grouchy
28. ____ students can work together to solve problems
29. ____ teacher lectures too much
30. ____ teacher lets us plan some of the assignments
31. ____ more group activities are needed
32. ____ teacher makes us work hard
33. ____ too many students disrupt class
34. ____ teacher helps us to know each other better
35. ____ teacher talks too much
36. ____ teacher and students are well-organized
37. ____ teacher never calls on nonvolunteers
38. ____ classroom is cheerful and bright
39. ____ teacher's directions are seldom clear
40. ____ students have a good feeling about being in this class
41. ____ students don't have much respect for the teacher
42. ____ students are proud of this class
43. ____ students need to take things more seriously
44. ____ students are not afraid to ask for help
45. ____ more individual assignments are needed
46. ____ classroom is neat, clean and attractive
47. ____ students are jealous of each other's talents
48. ____ students can move about class quietly without permission
49. ____ students can leave their seats without permission
50. ____ teacher shows students are understood
51. ____ students and teacher waste a lot of time
52. ____ students can arrange their own seating plan
53. ____ teacher doesn't allow us to discuss things
54. ____ teacher doesn't shout at us
55. ____ our lessons are not very well planned
56. ____ students brag about the class outside of school
57. ____ students are seldom courteous or friendly to one another
58. ____ students are free to suggest ways to improve the class
59. ____ students do little to prevent problems in class
60. ____ teacher encourages us to discuss things in small groups

A FINAL COMMENT

Ways for evaluating and improving the culture and climate of your school and classroom have been the major focuses of this chapter. A final perspective on this discussion encompasses a thought about two important factors relating to school health and climate: the environment (in and out of school) and the student peer groups. These two factors seem to influence student academic and personal-social behavior.[19]

If schooling is to contribute to productive learning and the development of self-understanding, openness, trust, and sincerity (humanness), then it seems that principals and teachers have to employ strategies that maximize potential for students to teach one another facts, concepts, ideas, opinions, attitudes, and values that reflect the best in our cultural heritage, our democratic ideals, and our humanness. In addition, principals and teachers must "compensate or remedy environmental or peer influences which are detrimental to student development."[20]

You, the faculty, staff, students, and parents must expose students to a productive and satisfying learning environment and minimize factors that interfere with productive learning and positive human relationships. Schools should be a human and humane place to be for all personnel.

NOTES

1. Terrance Deal and Allen Kennedy, *Corporate Cultures* (Menlo Park, CA: Addison-Wesley Publishing Co., 1982).
2. Michael Rutter et al., *Fifteen Thousand Hours: Secondary Schools and Their Effects on Children* (Cambridge, MA: Harvard University Press, 1979).
3. William Firestone and Bruce Wilson, "Culture of School Is a Key to More Effective Instruction," *Bulletin of the National Association of Secondary School Principals* 68 (December 1984): 7–11.
4. William Foster, *Symposium on Transforming Leadership: Shaping the School Culture for Educational Excellence.* Paper delivered at the California Principals Conference, Anaheim, November 22, 1985.
5. William J. Furtwengler, "Implementing Strategies for a School Effectiveness Program," *Phi Delta Kappan* 67 (December 1985): 262–265.
6. Warren Bennis and Bert Nanus, *Leaders: The Strategies for Taking Charge* (New York: Harper & Row Publishers, 1985), p. 96.
7. *Ibid.*, pp. 91–92.
8. *San Jose Mercury,* May 6, 1984.
9. A. Lorri Manasse, "Effective Principals: Effective at What?" *Principal* 61 (March 1982): 12.
10. Richard D. Kimpston and Leslie C. Sonnabend, "Organizational Health: A Requisite for Innovation?" *Educational Leadership,* 31 (March 1973): 543–547.
11. Reprinted with permission from Rita King and David Meaney, San Diego County Office of Education.
12. Elizabeth Clark and Marvin Fairman, "Organizational Health: A Significant

Focus in Planned Change," *Bulletin of the National Association of Secondary School Principals* 67 (September, 1983): 109–113.

13. Bruce L. Wilson, "The School Assessment Survey," *Educational Leadership* 42 (March 1985): 50–53. A brochure is also available from Research for Better Schools, Inc., 444 North Third Street, Philadelphia, PA 19123.

14. Gordon J. Klopf et al., "A Taxonomy of Education Leadership," *National Elementary Principal* 53 (July/August 1974): 54–56.

15. Robert S. Fox et al., *School Climate Improvement: A Challenge to the School Administrator* (Bloomington, IN: Phi Delta Kappan, n.d.), p. iv.

16. *Ibid.*, pp. 7–9, 51.

17. *Ibid.*, p. 9.

18. William Wayson et al., *Handbook for Developing Schools with Good Discipline* (Bloomington, IN: Phi Delta Kappan, 1982).

19. Raphael O. Nystrand and Luvern L. Cunningham, "Organizing Schools to Develop Humane Capabilities," in *To Nurture Humaneness: Commitment for the '70s*, ed. Mary-Margaret Scobey and Grace Graham (Washington, D.C.: Association for Supervision and Curriculum Development, 1970), pp. 132–133.

20. *Ibid.*, p. 133.

REFERENCES

Alkin, Marvin C.; Daillak, R.; and White, Peter. *Using Evaluations: Does Evaluation Make a Difference?* Beverly Hills, CA: Sage Publications, 1979.

Anderson, Lorin W. *Assessing Affective Characteristics in the Schools.* Boston: Allyn and Bacon, 1981.

Berman, Martin L., and Baca, Milton L. "The School Climate Audit: A Strategy to Enhance the Voluntary Accrediting Process." *Bulletin of the National Association of Secondary School Principals* 68 (December 1984): 113–116.

Clark, David L.; Lo Ho, Linda S.; and Astuto, Terry A. "Effective Schools and School Improvement: A Comparative Analysis of Two Lines of Inquiry." *Educational Administration Quarterly* 20 (Summer 1984): 41–68.

Deal, Terrence, and Kennedy, Allan A. "Culture and School Performance." *Educational Leadership* 40 (February 1983): 14–15.

Fink, Arlene, and Kosecott, Jacqueline. *Evaluation Primer and Workbook.* Beverly Hills, CA: Sage Publications, 1983.

Levy, Joyce, ed. *The Quality of School Life.* Lexington, MA: Lexington Books, 1981.

Lezotte, Lawrence. "Climate Characteristics in Instructionally Effective Schools." *Impact on Instructional Improvement* 16 (Summer 1981): 26–31.

Zepka, William E. "Improving Your School's Climate." *Here's How* 4 (February 1986).

Zirkes, Melvin, and Penna, Robert. "Academic Competition—One Way to Improve School Climate." *Bulletin of the National Association of Secondary School Principals* 68 (December 1984): 94–97

CHAPTER 3

Evaluating for
Effective Instructional
Leadership and Supervision

The higher the value the principal places on, and behaves in, an openly communicative and collaborative style, the more teachers will be inclined to risk being open and collaborative.

Arthur Blumberg

As you know by now, another of the five correlates of effective schools is the instructional leadership demonstrated and modeled by the principal and other professionals in the schools. In this chapter, four aspects of instruction and supervision will be examined: instructional leadership, supervision, classroom observation, and staff development.

Effective school research suggests that principals in most schools have high expectations for teacher and student performance; that they possess a knowledge and understanding of the instructional program; that they hold their faculty accountable for student achievement in the basic skills; and that they are highly visible in classrooms, diagnosing classroom problems, offering advice and ways to correct instructional problems.

Effective principals seek ideas and reactions, utilize skills and talents, anticipate needs for support and information, and cooperatively monitor and plan for innovation and change with their professional staff and with personnel in the school district.[1] The effective school principal in carrying out his or her role as an instructional leader is a team builder. "On the whole, it makes more sense to consider a team approach in which critical support functions are carried out by those most able to perform them—not only the principal but supervisors, teachers, curriculum specialists, and other available personnel."[2]

INSTRUCTIONAL LEADERSHIP

Here are ten interrelated factors that highlight aspects of effective instructional leadership. You might use these ten factors as checkpoints to note your own instructional leadership efforts.

The principal, as the school's instructional leader:

1. Stresses the academics. A checklist for assessing the extent to which you and your faculty emphasize the academics follows these ten factors.
2. Supervises instruction. The remaining two-thirds of this chapter will discuss instructional supervision.
3. Evaluates teacher performance. The next chapter deals with this topic.
4. Provides and is committed to staff development. This topic is discussed later in this chapter.
5. Is a team builder and encourages cooperative decision-making. Throughout this book, teamwork, collaboration, mutual support are seen as the keys to effective school administration.
6. Establishes a student evaluation system. This topic will be discussed in the curriculum chapter.
7. Develops a standard, uniform curriculum. This topic will also be discussed in the chapter on curriculum evaluation.
8. Is a resource person for instruction. See comments in this chapter.
9. Sets standards for instruction. This topic is discussed in this chapter and in the chapter on teacher evaluation.
10. Is an effective instructional manager.

This last factor includes a variety of tasks, including time-management, record keeping, classroom visitation schedules, productive faculty meetings, providing teachers and supervisors with needed instructional materials, arranging teacher and classroom schedules, scheduling extracurricular activities, setting school rules, and arranging time for teachers to share information and plan together.[3]

STRESSING THE ACADEMICS

It has been suggested that there are three factors that help set the stage for effective schools and classrooms—the emphasis that both teachers and students place on the academics, an orderly environment, and expectations for success.[4]

Academic press is the emphasis placed on student achievement within a school as evidenced by the school's policies, the teacher's expectations and practices, and the students' beliefs in their own abilities to achieve academically. The School Effectiveness Program of Santa Clara County (California) designed a model of how academic press is created in schools.[5] The model includes four policy areas grouped under school and structure, six policy areas on student programs, and teacher practices and behaviors, all of which are conveyed to school personnel, parents, and students. The following sample questions are based on the policies necessary for creating academic press in school.

1. Are there clearly defined academic goals for academic achievement?
2. Do instructional grouping patterns promote student mastery of grade level objectives?
3. Is instructional time "protected"?
4. Are attendance and tardiness policies enforced?
5. Is there a policy on homework?
6. Is homework an integral part of classroom practices?
7. Does the principal monitor grading practices?
8. Do the teachers establish specific instructional objectives?
9. Do the teachers monitor student progress toward these objectives?
10. Do the teachers provide student feedback regarding progress in addition to the usual report cards?
11. Are retention and promotion policies based upon student mastery of basic and essential skills and content at each grade level?
12. Are students held responsible and accountable for their own work?
13. Do students have opportunities to exercise leadership in the school and classroom?

The following checklist is another way for you and your teachers to determine the extent to which there is an academic emphasis in your school.

Student Academic Emphasis

To what extent do all or most students in your classroom exhibit these behaviors? (Write one of the following words in the space provided: great/some/little/none.)

____ Work to master the basic skills.
____ Work to learn subject matter.
____ Work to attain higher order thinking skills.
____ Are ready each day to work on required tasks.
____ Have books and other materials for class.
____ Have pencils, pens, pads, paper for class.
____ Use the class and/or school library.
____ Follow school and classroom rules.

____ Perceive discipline as fair and consistent.
____ Participate in helping shape student behavior.
____ Promote school and classroom pride.
____ Participate in student activity programs.
____ Attend school regularly.
____ Set high standards for academic performance.
____ Other (specify) _____

Teacher Academic Emphasis

____ Have a clear set of instructional objectives.
____ Spend adequate time directly teaching the basic skills.
____ Set clear objectives/standards for learning.
____ Develop and teach to objectives.
____ Increase academic learning time.
____ Use formative assessment techniques before assigning students new learning tasks.
____ Control the number of interruptions to instruction.
____ Provide rewards for student achievement.
____ Assign homework regularly and grade it.
____ Plan lessons and student activities in advance.
____ Provide students feedback on their achievement.
____ Provide students and parents information regarding performance and behavior.
____ Help individual students with their problems.
____ Display student work.
____ Model behavior expected of students.
____ Demonstrate disapproval of student behavior.
____ Give student responsibilities in and out of class.
____ Encourage students to discuss their problems with you or other school personnel.
____ Involve students in ways to solve their own problems.
____ Other (specify) _____

Principal Academic Emphasis

To what extent do you exhibit the following behaviors (note that some behaviors listed for teachers are also applicable to principals):

____ Demonstrate support for the academic focus of the school.
____ Spend most of your school day on instructional matters.
____ Observe teachers teaching and students learning.
____ Confer with teachers on improving teaching and learning.
____ Develop and enforce homework and other instructional policies.
____ Organize teachers for curriculum and course planning.

___ Involve teachers in decisions for curriculum and instructional matters.
___ Reward teachers for their efforts to improve teaching and learning.
___ Help teachers who are having difficulties.
___ Press for the academic success of every student.
___ Limit the interruptions to instructional time.
___ Help teachers reach consensus on acceptable and unacceptable student behavior.
___ Apply school rules and regulations fairly and consistently.
___ Assist teachers in handling major student misbehaviors.
___ Provide staff development opportunities.
___ Other (specify) _____ [6]

Here are some ways to assess the other nine factors on the list.

ASSESSING INSTRUCTIONAL
LEADERSHIP FUNCTIONS

Daniel Duke identifies six leadership functions associated with instructional effectiveness. Four functions are identified as directly related to instructional effectiveness: staff development, which includes recruitment, inservice education, and staff motivation; instructional support, which includes a variety of activities designed to enhance teaching and learning; resource acquisitions and allocation, which includes reliance on faculty input and efforts to meet instructional needs; and quality control, which ensures that objectives are being met.[7]

The two other leadership functions are coordination, "the actions necessary to ensure that the individual units of the school do not work at cross-purposes or duplicate operation,"[8] and trouble shooting, "mechanisms for anticipating and resolving problems. . . ."[9]

Duke offers a series of representative questions that one may ask to evaluate a principal's effectiveness as an instructional leader based upon each of the six functions.

Staff Development

1. Does the principal possess a plan for recruiting the best teachers?
2. Is the staff encouraged to participate in inservice activities?
3. Does a plan exist for the regular offering of inservice opportunities?
4. Do staff members participate in decision making regarding inservice?
5. In what ways does the principal encourage teacher leadership?
6. How does the principal respond when a teacher is having trouble meeting instructional objectives?

Instructional Support

1. What does the principal do to minimize the time teachers spend on paperwork, record keeping, and classroom management?

2. What does the principal do to minimize classroom interruptions?
3. Does the principal encourage teachers to clarify their classroom management goals and to develop classroom management plans?
4. What does the principal do to minimize student absenteeism?
5. Are noninstructional activities carefully scheduled so as not to interfere with classroom instruction?
6. Are regular efforts made to keep teachers, students, and parents aware of school rules and policies?
7. Are school rules reviewed regularly and are unnecessary rules eliminated?

Resource Acquisition and Allocation

1. Are resources allocated on the basis of staff input?
2. Are efforts made to ensure that resources are allocated fairly within each classroom as well as among classes?
3. Does the principal participate in the development of the school and district budget?
4. Does the principal maintain close contact with his supervisors?
5. How does the school's operating budget for materials compare with other local schools' budgets?
6. What does the principal do to generate additional sources of revenue?
7. Do teachers have the materials they need to initiate orderly learning on the first day of school?

Quality Control

1. Does the school possess clear goals and objectives?
2. What does the principal do to see that the staff is aware of school goals and objectives?
3. What does the principal do to see that goals and objectives are being achieved?
4. What does the principal do to communicate high expectations to staff and students?
5. Does the staff have high and consistent expectations of the principal and are these communicated clearly?
6. What does the principal do to recognize staff and student achievement?
7. Does the principal regularly visit classrooms and meet with teachers?
8. What occurs when a particular student is not achieving according to expectations (i.e., Is the first reaction to assess teaching or to find reasons why the student cannot learn?)
9. Do evaluation plans include provisions for assessing unintended negative outcomes?

Coordination

1. Does the principal regularly review the operations of each department?
2. What do the principal and staff do to minimize duplication among subunits of the school?
3. What does the principal do to see that staff members are aware of each other's activities and plans?

4. Does the principal delegate authority to his assistants and chairpersons to improve coordination?
5. What does the principal do to encourage statewide, systematic planning? Is time for planning made available to staff members?

Troubleshooting

1. What does the principal do to encourage staff members to anticipate problems before they arise?
2. Do contingency plans exist for each department and class?
3. Upon what sources of information does the principal rely for accurate feedback on staff, student, and community morale?
4. Are efforts made to obtain data from as close to the source of problems as possible?
5. What does the principal do to ensure advance warning of any changes in district policy?
6. What mechanisms exist for handling problems once they arise?
7. Are staff members trained in conflict resolution strategies?
8. To what extent does the principal actively involve staff in problem solving?[10]

HOW TO EVALUATE YOUR INSTRUCTIONAL LEADERSHIP ACTIVITIES

The instructional leader attempts to improve the teaching-learning process by carrying out several specific activities related to it. For example, it is very important to seek agreement on both the purposes of instruction and the objectives of supervision. To do this requires the input and cooperation of teachers. You cannot be an instructional leader without the cooperation of the professional staff. Therefore, it is of value to assess yourself and to have the teachers assess your current attempts to improve instruction in order to improve the teaching and learning going on in your school. The rating scale in Figure 3-1 not only allows you to make such an assessment, but as you read it you will note excellent suggestions that should be part of your repertoire of activities toward the improvement of instruction.

The activities are not mere exercises. Consider whether or not you actually do anything to help teachers come together to share ideas about teaching and learning. There is evidence that they come together to decide where the bike racks will be placed or who will monitor study halls, but little evidence that teachers come together to discuss instruction. So, each activity in the list should be given serious consideration by you if you want to become the instructional leader in your school.

The Activities Rating Scale can be used as a pre- and post-assessment instrument with some conscious, directed activity in-between. For example, one principal used the scale to find out how his administrative team (himself, assistants, central office supervisor assigned to his school) rated

Principal:_____ Date:_____

School:_____

Directions for Self-Evaluation: Grade yourself on each activity using the scale below.

Directions for Teacher Evaluation: Grade your principal on each activity for improving the teaching-learning process using the scale below.

Scale: A—Excellent; B—Good; C—Fair; D—Poor; F—Does Nothing at All.

	Self-Grading	*Teacher-Grading*
1. Helps us identify the objectives/goals of instruction	A B C D F	A B C D F
2. Encourages us to share our ideas about curriculum and teaching	A B C D F	A B C D F
3. Keeps us aware of instructional materials and equipment	A B C D F	A B C D F
4. Promotes the use of self-evaluation techniques	A B C D F	A B C D F
5. Encourages us to try new methods of instruction	A B C D F	A B C D F
6. Helps us decide on the purposes of instructional supervision	A B C D F	A B C D F
7. Encourages and promotes the display of student work	A B C D F	A B C D F
8. Encourages teacher-student planning	A B C D F	A B C D F
9. Provides special funds for purchasing expendable supplies on short notice	A B C D F	A B C D F
10. Encourages us to use a variety of instructional media	A B C D F	A B C D F
11. Encourages us to use a variety of evaluative methods for assessing student learning and growth	A B C D F	A B C D F
12. Encourages us to attend workshops and visit other schools	A B C D F	A B C D F
13. Encourages our participation in in-service training programs	A B C D F	A B C D F
14. Promotes a school program that meets student needs and interests	A B C D F	A B C D F
15. Promotes our programs and progress throughout the community	A B C D F	A B C D F
16. Demonstrates and promotes the value of self-evaluation	A B C D F	A B C D F
17. Demonstrates and promotes community involvement in the school program	A B C D F	A B C D F
18. Provides instructional assistance (aides, tutors, etc.) for teachers	A B C D F	A B C D F

FIGURE 3-1
Instructional Leadership Activities Rating Scale

on each item from their own and the teachers' point of view. They discovered that their perceptions and those of the teachers differed on several activities. For example, self-evaluation (item 4) was one activity where the ratings were different—a "B" grade was the average on the administrative scale, "D" was the average on the teachers' scale.

The principal summarized the data and provided each teacher and administrative team member with a written report of the summary with a request that all be prepared to discuss discrepancies and what they could do about it at the faculty meeting.

The approach, then, is to use the scale as a pre-test; discuss results with the faculty, implement some or all of their ideas and your ideas, and then retest—find out if there is improvement. Another suggestion is to focus in on one activity that may be rated poorly by teachers. Design ways to improve poorly rated items and then design an evaluation scale similar to those found in this book and find out if the teachers changed their minds. If not, then why? If they did, your strategies paid off.

EVALUATING INSTRUCTIONAL LEADERSHIP PRACTICES

What they see will be what you get; that is, if teachers and others see little activity regarding instruction and a lot of activity doing administrative tasks, then they will probably give you a low rating on your meager efforts as an instructional leader. This section helps you examine some instructional practices. You and the faculty may wish to appraise the instructional leadership practices and the implications these have for the supervisory program in your school against a list of suggested criteria. Figure 3-2 can be used for this purpose.

HOW TO EVALUATE YOUR SUPERVISORY PROGRAM

It may be silly to ask and you may be offended, but before you can evaluate your supervisory program, you need to ask yourself if you have one. If you answer this question affirmatively, then consider these questions:

1. Is the program in writing?
2. Does it include specific objectives?
3. Does it include plans for observations, self-evaluation, and the like?
4. Does the program improve instruction?
5. How do teachers view the effectiveness of your supervisory program?

Name:_____ Date:_____

School:_____

Directions: Circle the number that represents your opinion concerning the extent to which each practice exists in the school.

In our school, the principal, faculty, and staff:	*Definitely*	*Somewhat*	*Needs Improvement*	*No*	*Not Applicable*
1. Are actively involved in defining and clarifying educational goals and objectives.	1	2	3	4	5
2. Insure that roles are clearly defined and understood.	1	2	3	4	5
3. Define and understand working relationships.	1	2	3	4	5
4. Have cooperatively defined and understand the role of specialized resource personnel.	1	2	3	4	5
5. Understand clearly the authority-responsibility-power relationships.	1	2	3	4	5
6. Share crucial rather than only routine decisions.	1	2	3	4	5
7. Hold group discussions to clarify purposes and roles.	1	2	3	4	5
8. Expect and encourage leadership to emerge from the group.	1	2	3	4	5
9. Achieve status through group acceptance and competence.	1	2	3	4	5
10. View official leaders as being helpful.	1	2	3	4	5
11. Expect leaders to help faculty/staff reassess their roles in terms of evidence from the sciences.	1	2	3	4	5
12. Expect leaders to support school program and personnel as they work to improve both.	1	2	3	4	5
13. Coordinate and support efforts for the improvement of instruction.	1	2	3	4	5
14. Believe that the main function of the principal is to provide instructional leadership for her or his staff.	1	2	3	4	5
15. Cooperatively develop rules of procedure.	1	2	3	4	5
16. Cooperatively test these procedures to determine their effectiveness in achieving goals.	1	2	3	4	5
17. Modify the school structure when this is essential to facilitate the teaching-learning process.	1	2	3	4	5
18. Cooperatively plan and decide program changes on the basis of objective data.	1	2	3	4	5
19. Evidence high morale as we work together.	1	2	3	4	5
20. Move toward mutually held goals.	1	2	3	4	5
21. Utilize human relations skills.	1	2	3	4	5
22. Who encounter teaching or other difficulties feel free to seek assistance.	1	2	3	4	5
23. Encourage one another to attempt to achieve their potential.	1	2	3	4	5
24. Establish a school climate conducive to creativeness, experimentation, and expression of individual skill and talent.	1	2	3	4	5

FIGURE 3-2
Instructional Leadership Practices Scale

	Definitely	Somewhat	Needs Improvement	No	Not Applicable
25. Are eager to explore or experiment with suggestions made by the group.	1	2	3	4	5
26. Use knowledge and data effectively in solving problems and resolving issues.	1	2	3	4	5
27. Make provisions to help each member constantly acquire new skills, understanding, and attitudes.	1	2	3	4	5
28. Have effectively established formal and informal channels of communication.	1	2	3	4	5
29. Are informed of available resources and how to use them for improving instruction.	1	2	3	4	5
30. Are encouraged to reach out beyond known resources for imaginative and creative solutions to problems.	1	2	3	4	5
31. Effectively use resources from outside the group to help clarify goals, resolve issues, gain new insights, and develop new skills.	1	2	3	4	5
32. Effectively use resources for improving instruction and contributing to faculty/staff growth inservice.	1	2	3	4	5
33. Effectively use specialized resource persons (psychologists, guidance counselors, etc.) for assistance in improving instruction.	1	2	3	4	5
34. Effectively use available instructional materials and seek new resources.	1	2	3	4	5
35. Have established procedures for evaluating the effectiveness of instructional leadership processes.*	1	2	3	4	5

*Adapted from a list of sixty-five criteria under eight categories from the Association for Supervision and Curriculum Development, *Leadership for Improving Instruction* (Washington, D.C.: National Education Association, 1960), pp. 164–168.

If you don't have a program of supervision, there are four critical questions that you must answer:

1. What are your reasons?
2. How do you improve instruction?
3. How do your teachers view you as an instructional leader/supervisor?
4. As the principal of the school, why do you neglect this important aspect of the job?

Evaluating the Effectiveness of Your Supervision Program

If a supervisory program is effective, there should be certain objective evidence that can be used to support it. Some of the following conditions may be useful to you and imply further investigation. This can be done by you, a consultant, or a committee selected from your faculty and staff. There are many techniques that can be employed by you, the consultant, or the committee. Among them are checklists, rating scales, opinionnaires, surveys, logs, records, narratives, observations, polls, meetings, conferences, and interviews, all of which should seek evidence of an increase in:

- Student achievement
- Teacher morale
- Student-teacher relationships
- Student-teacher planning
- Student-teacher self-evaluation techniques
- Student performance—morale, grades
- The use of a variety of instructional materials
- The use of a variety of teaching-learning strategies
- The use of a variety of evaluation techniques
- Teacher knowledge of subject matter
- Teacher interest and reading of research
- The improvement of student behavior
- Interest in in-service programs
- Student attendance
- Student interest and attitudes toward school and learning
- The sharing of ideas among teachers
- Discussion of teaching and learning
- The quality of questions asked by teachers and students
- Diagnostic and prescriptive teaching
- Student self-discipline and self-learning
- Classroom observations by principals, supervisors, and other teachers
- Supervisory conferences and meetings about teaching.

As principal, you should select appropriate instruments for evaluating each of these items. Following data collection, you must insure that a written report is prepared and disseminated to concerned parties. From this point on, it is important that the report be used and not filed away like many curriculum guides. The purpose of evaluation is to *do* something. The purpose of evaluating the supervisory program is to find out whether or not it is improving instruction (in the broadest sense) and to take action if it isn't or to maintain current activities if it is.

HOW TO DEVELOP AN EFFECTIVE SUPERVISORY PROGRAM

To help you supervise and actively participate in instructional improvement, it is recommended that you institute a plan called an *instructional improvement cycle* shown in Figure 3-3. This cycle contains three operational

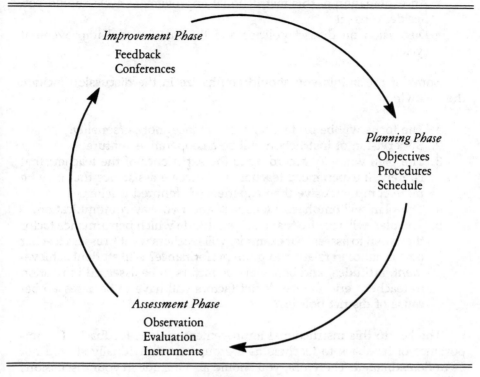

Improvement Phase
Feedback
Conferences

Planning Phase
Objectives
Procedures
Schedule

Assessment Phase
Observation
Evaluation
Instruments

FIGURE 3-3
Instructional Improvement Cycle

phases: a planning phase, an assessment phase, and an improvement phase.

The cycle is based upon communication and shared decision making by you and the faculty and by you and individual teachers. The essence of the cycle is feedback resulting from all or some methods such as self-evaluation, self-supervision, peer and student observation and evaluation, and principal/supervisor observation and evaluation.

Planning Phase

Developing plans for implementing a supervisory program in your school requires that you meet with the faculty and eventually individual teachers early in the school year. In fact, it may be best to hold a faculty meeting on the subject during orientation week. The faculty meeting should focus on the following topics:

- School district policies and procedures regarding teacher evaluation and supervision

- An explanation of this instructional improvement cycle should you decide to use it
- Discussion on district policies and the instructional improvement cycle.

Some of the points you should emphasize in the discussion include the following:

1. The focus will be on teacher performance, not personality.
2. Supervision of instruction will be a cooperative venture.
3. The plan will vary according to the experience of the teacher; that is, new, inexperienced teachers will receive assistance that may be more comprehensive than experienced, tenured teachers.
4. The plan will emphasize feedback and two-way communication.
5. The plan will require that teachers decide which performance factor they wish to assess. For example, will teachers want to assess teacher performance in relation to pupil performance? Will student achievement, attitudes, and behaviors be factors to be assessed in relation to teacher performance? What factors will have to be assessed because of district policies?

The key to this instructional improvement cycle is feedback. The importance of feedback to teachers as a group and individually should not be underestimated. Therefore, you should also include in your discussions with the faculty the value and importance of this concept. The following guidelines may be helpful to you for insuring an effective information exchange between you and the teachers:

1. Feedback should highlight the teacher's actual performance. Hearsay, assumptions, and other second-hand data should not be allowed and should be rejected by both you and the teacher.
2. Feedback should be as specific and as concrete as possible. The use of appropriate observational and self-evaluation techniques should help.
3. Feedback should not be judgmental. It does little good for a teacher to be told he or she is not doing something well. It is better to describe the teacher's performance and encourage self-examination and change.
4. Feedback should emphasize present and future behaviors. How a teacher performed in the past will do little but antagonize and create excuses. Observable, current, performance should be examined with the hope that it will contribute to change in the future.
5. Feedback must emphasize the sharing of information, honestly and openly.
6. Feedback should help the teacher examine and create alternatives

for instruction. The teacher, not the principal/supervisor, should suggest alternatives at least initially. It may be that after the teacher has had this opportunity, additional ideas could be presented by the principal/supervisor.

7. Feedback should permit the teacher to suggest changes in teaching performance.
8. Feedback should focus on specific teaching behaviors, not the entire range of possible behaviors.
9. Feedback should, first, focus upon specific behavior or performance that can easily be modified. In other words, help the teacher focus on teaching factors that can easily be changed. Successful experience in changing simple, specific factors will contribute to a feeling of success before the complex factors are considered.
10. Feedback requires summarization. Have the teacher prepare a written summary of the feedback sessions. From these, cooperatively prepare written objectives for use in the improvement phase of the cycle.[11]

In summary, the planning phase focuses upon a discussion with the faculty on the purpose of supervision and evaluation, the value of feedback, and the procedures that will best help each teacher improve performance. From this overview, you, your designee, or a supervisor meets with each teacher to determine those factors that should be observed and evaluated in relation to district requirements and the individual teacher's needs and suggestions.

Assessment Phase

This phase includes evaluation in terms of specific objectives; that is, those aspects agreed upon by faculty and individual teachers. The essence of this phase is the use of instruments that will provide teachers with information needed to improve instruction. A variety of instruments can and should be used, including self-supervision techniques, self-evaluation scales and checklists, peer and student ratings of teaching performance, and the like. Examples are provided in the improvement phase of this cycle and other chapters in this book.

Improvement Phase

This phase of the cycle requires that you, your designee, or your supervisor and individual teachers examine the data resulting from the instruments used in the assessment phase. The basis for this phase is the conference. One or more conferences with each teacher may be necessary.

The purpose of the conference(s) should be to review, analyze, and plan from the data collected during the assessment phase of this cycle.

Since the conference is seen as central to this entire process, it is apparent that crucial to the conference and discussion held between a teacher and the principal/supervisor is the "chemistry" between both parties. In other words, might previous interactions or current relationships have a bearing on the quality of the meetings to be held as a result of implementing this supervisory plan?

How would you rate the way we presently interact with one another?

Principal/Supervisor to Teacher

	5	4	3	2	1	
Open	—	—	—	—	—	Close
Honest	—	—	—	—	—	Dishonest
Respectful	—	—	—	—	—	Disrespectful
Warm	—	—	—	—	—	Cool
Friendly	—	—	—	—	—	Unfriendly
Professional	—	—	—	—	—	Non-professional
Caring	—	—	—	—	—	Indifferent
Accepting	—	—	—	—	—	Rejecting
Democratic	—	—	—	—	—	Autocratic
Rational	—	—	—	—	—	Irrational
Sociable	—	—	—	—	—	Unsociable
Cooperative	—	—	—	—	—	Uncooperative

My principal/supervisor respects/honors/encourages my:	*Always*	*Often*	*Sometimes*	*Seldom/ Never*
Ideas	A	B	C	D
Accomplishments	A	B	C	D
Creativity	A	B	C	D
Professional talents	A	B	C	D
Self-direction	A	B	C	D
Initiative	A	B	C	D

FIGURE 3-4
Principal/Supervisor/Teacher Interaction Scale

It is probably helpful to both you and each teacher to find out about this interaction. Figure 3-4 provides a scale to determine how each of you feels about the quality of interaction.

If, for example, you discover that a teacher expresses concern about your interaction with him/her, it may be best to address this point directly, rather than proceeding with a discussion of the plans for or results of the supervision/evaluation. A principal who is perceived to lack some of those qualities listed on the scale will have a very difficult time trying to establish relationships and strategies to help teachers change their behavior and improve instruction. It would be better for the principal to spend time and energy on methods to improve relationships with teachers.

Teacher Improvement Schedule

An example of a form that may be used to incorporate each of the three phases of the instructional improvement schedule is shown in Figure 3-5.

The Teacher Improvement Schedule can be used as part of the planning phase, and after a teacher proceeds through the cycle it is also useful in the improvement phase. The *objectives* are those performance items the teacher wishes to improve. They can be written as teacher objectives or in many cases as student learning objectives. In the *activities* column, the

Name:_____		Date:_____	
School:_____		Evaluator:_____	

Objectives	*Activities*	*Assessment*	*Schedule*

Constraints/Circumstances

FIGURE 3-5
Teacher Improvement Schedule

teacher describes what she or he will do to attain the objectives. The *assessment* column contains descriptions of or specific instruments to be used in evaluation of the objectives and activities. The *schedule* column will include appropriate days and dates for the use of assessment instruments, classroom visitations, videotaping of teaching, etc.; it provides a time schedule for the assessment of each objective. The *constraints/circumstances* block is designed to allow the teacher and the principal/supervisor to identify or describe conditions that should be noted when they view the results. Some of these constraints/conditions might include such things as an unusually large class, many low achievers, lack of adequate instructional supplies, excessive student absences, classroom interruptions, and the like.

PLANNING PHASE FOR
CLASSROOM OBSERVATION

"How often do you observe teachers in their classroom?" "Four times a year," responded most of the elementary principals in class. "Twice a year," responded secondary principals, "but once a year is not unusual."

"How long are your observations?" The average visit lasted thirty minutes according to these principals.

"Why do you make classroom visits?" The true answer to the question, after we were able to sort through all the verbalization, was that the superintendent required it.

Your response to these three questions may reveal your attitudes and position about classroom observation. However, regardless of the variation in practice, classroom observation remains the heart of the supervisory process. Although there are varied ways to observe teacher performance, the physical presence of an observer remains the most popular method (audiotape and videotape are the other methods). Whether the observation is done by a principal to satisfy an administrative requirement and/or to actually try to improve instruction, some practical ideas may contribute to helping you improve your observation of teachers in their classrooms.

Purpose

The planning phase must include a pre-observation conference, the purpose of which is to:

- Establish a rapport with the teacher
- Find out about the teaching-learning situation
- Dispel fears
- Develop a helping relationship
- Establish the purposes of the observation
- Allow the teacher to identify the focus of the observations
- Possibly write a contract expressing the specifics of the visitation

- Agree on instruments that will be used during the observations (observation scale, audiotape, videotape)
- Agree on an observation schedule (include both scheduled and unscheduled visits)
- Agree on post-conference dates and times.

The Principal/Supervisor/Teacher Interaction Scale suggested in Figure 3-4 would be useful during pre-conference planning since it would help you determine the teacher's perceptions of the quality of your interactions with each other before specific planning questions are answered.

Questions to Answer

The pre-conference between you and the teacher might also include a discussion of the following questions if classroom observation is to be done by you and/or a supervisor:

1. What is the purpose of the visitation(s)?
2. What is your class like?
3. What lesson(s) will you be teaching?
4. What should I know about what preceded the lesson(s) you will be teaching?
5. What should I be looking for? What specific factors would you like me to observe?
6. What factors in your teaching do you feel should be improved?
7. How will we record the observation? What instruments should we use? Construct?
8. How long should I remain in your classroom during each visit?
9. How many visits should be scheduled? Unscheduled?

These and other questions should be discussed before the actual visitations. Whether a conference is necessary before each visitation should be a factor that you and each teacher decide. Since a post-conference is recommended following each visitation, it may not be necessary to hold pre-conferences before every scheduled or unscheduled visit.

TEACHER BEHAVIOR AND EFFECTIVENESS: WHAT TO LOOK FOR

Teaching behavior that helps predict student achievement (effectiveness) in the basic skills particularly should be noted by the principal/supervisor. It is apparent that when assessing instruction, one should have a working knowledge of which teaching behaviors will influence student performance. Knowing these factors, assessment becomes less of a personality contest and more of a professional evaluation of performance. In addition, knowledge of these behaviors will help you guide the faculty towards the school's instructional objectives and it will help you plan effective staff development opportunities.

Here, then, is a list of those teaching behaviors from which you can develop assessment methods.

- Orderly, business-like classroom.
- Teacher devotes major portion of time to academic activities and tasks.
- Students are engaged in academic tasks for a major portion of the class time.
- Teacher uses a variety of instructional methods.
- Students have an opportunity to learn what is being tested; that is, the content to be learned matches the content to be tested.
- Instruction is academically focused, teacher-directed.
- Instructional objectives are made clear to students.
- Students receive feedback regarding classwork and homework.
- Student achievement is rewarded in a variety of ways.
- Teacher communicates to students high expectations regarding their learning and behavior.
- Teacher attends to the learning needs of students.
- Teacher uses a variety of ways to organize students for instruction (small groups, large groups, cooperative learning, etc).
- Teacher monitors class for inattention; keeps students attentive.
- Teacher corrects student misbehavior in a way that disruptions of learning tasks are minimized.
- Students are held responsible for their work.
- Teacher sets a brisk learning pace based on student achievement and the difficulty of the content to be learned.
- Teacher uses advanced organizers, that is, introductory materials and methods that structure the new content students are expected to learn.

You may use these factors for classroom observation but it is strongly recommended that you read the literature (see endnotes and references in this chapter and chapter four) on effective teaching, share it with your faculty, and then cooperatively, with each teacher, decide how the information will be used to assess instructional effectiveness.[12]

ASSESSMENT PHASE FOR
CLASSROOM OBSERVATION

By the time the assessment phase is implemented, you and each teacher will have decided which classroom observation method shall be used and which instruments will serve the purpose and the method. It should be noted that no one instrument alone would be used for an assessment of teacher effectiveness. Plans for using instruments that assess many facets of teaching and learning should be cooperatively developed. Three examples are described here.

Clinical Supervision

One of the more effective methods of classroom observation is known as clinical supervision. Clinical supervision is designed to improve the teacher's performance in the classroom by focusing on actual classroom events, recording what actually happens rather than using a recording form developed prior to the observation. Clinical supervision recognizes the variety of teaching styles that you will encounter in your classroom observations. Clinical supervision places the teacher in the role of generator and interpreter of events; it recognizes the professional relationship and interactions between you and each teacher; and it requires the teacher to actively participate in her or his own professional improvement.

M. Cogan[13] specifies an eight-phase process for implementing clinical supervision strategies:

Phase 1. The teacher and supervisor (principal) establish a relationship, discuss clinical supervision as well as the role, purposes, and functions of the supervisor.

Phase 2. The supervisor plans a lesson(s) or unit with the teacher.

Phase 3. The teacher and supervisor plan strategies to be used during the observation of the teacher in the classroom.

Phase 4. The supervisor observes instruction or uses other techniques for recording classroom events (videotaping).

Phase 5. The teacher and supervisor analyze the recording of classroom events; separately at first and jointly later.

Phase 6. The conference is planned by the supervisor initially and later on, if feasible, joint planning may result.

Phase 7. The conference is held between supervisor and teacher.

Phase 8. During the conference, teacher and supervisor decide on the changes to be tried in the teacher's classroom performance or behavior and the cycle begins again.

The point here is to introduce you to this method of supervision. Obviously, it is expected that should you decide to implement clinical supervision ideas you will consult the appropriate resources.

The advocates of clinical supervision suggest that the principal/supervisor describe in writing as many of the verbal exchanges that can possibly be recorded during the visit. These observation notes will become the basis for analysis and post-conference discussions. Eleven suggestions for the observation using clinical methods include:

1. Record what is said and done; record teacher-student talk verbatim.
2. Record your comments or questions on separate paper or in margins so that it is away from the raw data.
3. Record as objectively and as positively as you can nonverbal behavior.
4. Select a position in the classroom that gives you a good vantage point of the teacher but [one that] is not distracting to students.
5. Teachers should expect you to record (via note-taking) written data.
6. Do not intervene in the teaching in any manner.
7. Supplementally note the time in margins.
8. If most of the lesson is too quiet for verbatim recording, try to capture specific episodes.
9. Try a system that will allow you to identify specific students in your notes.
10. Stay for the entire lesson unless early departure has been arranged with the teacher.
11. Diagramming the teacher's and pupil's position in the classroom can be useful.[14]

Figure 3-6 is an example of an instrument that may be used for recording teacher-student behavior. You will have to duplicate several of these forms for one observation.

Interaction Analysis

One of the more popular observation scales designed to record a teacher's verbal behavior is Flanders' Interaction Analysis.[15] This system of verbal analysis will help the observer help the teacher distinguish between direct and indirect verbal interaction occurring in the classroom. The instrument can be used with audiotape as well as with direct observation by a principal/supervisor.

The results, obtained by recording a number on the matrix every three seconds (twenty per minute), can be used by you and the teacher to examine specific classroom interaction factors posed in the following questions:

1. How much talking does the teacher do in the classroom?
2. Can the teacher be classified as direct or indirect in style?
3. How does the teacher react to student verbal behavior?
4. How much time does the teacher spend lecturing in class?
5. How much time does the teacher spend expanding on and using student ideas?
6. How do students react to the teacher's influence behavior?
7. Does the teacher accept, clarify, and use student emotion (ability to empathize) in the interaction process?
8. How often and effective is the teacher's use of praise?
9. How often and effective is the teacher's use of criticism?

Observer/Principal/Supervisor:_____

Class:_____ No. of Students:_____

Teacher:_____ Date:_____

Time of Observation: From:_____ To:_____

Objectives from pre-conference:

Subject of lesson:

Description of observation (include teacher behavior, student behavior, episodes, patterns):

Additional comments:

Concerns:

Questions:

Time:

FIGURE 3-6
Sample Observation Form—Descriptive

10. How effective is the teacher in communicating subject matter to students?
11. How effective is the teacher in soliciting student participation in class?[16]

Question Approach

Several years ago, Briggs and Justman[17] suggested a procedure for observing classroom instruction that will be of value to the principal/ supervisor as well as the teacher. The questions have been categorized to correspond to the sequence of teaching a lesson. It is suggested that the observer focus upon only a few of the questions during a visit to the teacher's classroom.

Purpose

1. What is the teacher's purpose? To what extent is it worthy? Definite? Specific with regard to this class? Attainable?

2. To what extent did the pupils share in proposing this purpose? To what extent do they comprehend, approve, and adopt as their own the purpose proposed by the teacher?
3. How suitable for achieving the desired purposes is the plan of instruction which the teacher has prepared?
4. To what extent do the learning experiences proposed promise to help realize the desired purposes?

Preparation

5. Is the preparation by the teacher adequate?
6. To what extent have pupils been psychologically prepared, by assignment and otherwise, to participate in this learning experience?
7. What study was expected of the pupils? What direction was given to make it effective? What apparently did the pupils actually do in preparation for this lesson? What better could they have done?

Classroom Climate

8. What is the atmosphere of the classroom and what is the morale of the pupils as evidenced by their attitude toward each other, toward the teacher, and toward the work they are doing?

Organization and Development

9. Is the learning experience so organized as best to promote the purposes of instruction?
10. What concomitant learnings of wide educational importance does the teacher encourage and direct?
11. Are abundant and rich materials prepared by teacher or by pupils ready for use?
12. To what extent does the teacher, by recall of what has already been learned and by giving meaning to the new material by showing its relations to a large significant problem, create a readiness in the pupils?
13. Are the pupils obtaining adequate guidance from the teacher in directing their own learning? Does each pupil know what to do?
14. To what extent is the presentation of the new material adequate and clarified by explanation, by obvious order, by illustrations, by relation to the pupils' past experiences, and by application to pupils' needs, immediate or recognized as probable in the future?
15. What provisions are made for individual differences in interest, probable needs, special aptitudes, and ability? Does the teacher distribute efforts equitably among the pupils? Does he insure that every pupil is successful in something?
16. What is the amount and quality of participation by pupils? Do they demonstrate intelligent interest, the spirit of inquiry, open-mindedness, initiative, enthusiastic persistence, the ability to judge their own work, and satisfaction with nothing less than mastery in terms of the accepted purposes of the unit?
17. What are the teacher's responses to the proposals and activities of the pupils? Is he receptive, considerate, fair, tactful, and able to give them fruitful direction?

18. To what extent are pupils being trained to work both independently as individuals and cooperatively with others?
19. How ready is the teacher to modify his plan so as to seize opportunities as they appear and how resourceful is he to make the new plan effective?
20. What provisions are made to insure adequate understanding and retention of what is learned, in terms of individual needs?
21. What provisions are made to insure the ability to apply or use what is learned? To strengthen good habits of use in a new situation?
22. If tests are used, are they valid in terms of the purposes sought, significant to the pupils, and reliable in form? What is indicated for further teaching by the results?
23. What attempts are made to provide remedial instruction for those who need it?
24. What provision is made to incorporate the new learning into larger and more meaningful units?
25. To what extent is the teacher successful in revealing opportunities and direction for further growth on the part of pupils?

Results

26. Wherein are pupils better for the learning experience that they have just had?

The Teacher

27. What is outstanding in promise in the work of the teacher observed?
28. What immediate and what ultimate help does he need to strengthen his weaknesses so that his strengths may be increasingly effective?

Relation to the Unit and Other Goals

29. How is the unit of study contributory to the general purposes of education and to the special functions of the particular school?

The use of a question-type observation approach helps when the observer and the teacher discuss the subjective perceptions of the observer. For example, during a particular visit or two, the observer should have focused on two or more related questions (i.e., purpose of the lesson), then the discussion can be on what was observed via the written notations after each question, and from the teacher's point of view of what was intended (if perceived differences exist). This question method, in addition to checklists, etc., should help the supervisor and the teacher appreciate teaching styles and the fact that there is no one best method of teaching.

OTHER SUPERVISORY METHODS

Just as there is no one best method of teaching, there is no one best method of supervision or of assessing what teachers and learners do in the classroom. Just as it is your job, as principal, to know about clinical supervision, it is also important to know about other methods such as:

- Elliot W. Eisner's Artistic Approach. See Thomas J. Sergiovanni, ed. *Supervision of Reading* (Alexandria, Virginia: Association for Supervision and Curriculum Development, 1982), Chapter 4, "An Artistic Approach to Supervision."
- Thomas J. Sergiovanni's Integrated Supervisor Approach. See above reference, Chapter 5, "Toward a Theory of Supervisory Practice: Integrating Scientific, Clinical, and Artistic Views."
- Shadow Study Method, Child Study Method, Activity Log Method, Nonverbal Behavior Analysis Methods. See Charles Beagle and Richard Brandt, eds. *Observational Methods in the Classroom* (Alexandria, Virginia: Association for Supervision and Curriculum Development, 1973).

IMPROVEMENT PHASE FOR CLASSROOM OBSERVATION

It is during this phase that data collected during the assessment phase are studied and analyzed in relation to the objectives established in the planning phase. The basis for the improvement phase is to provide feedback to each teacher resulting from the observations. The vehicle for doing this is the post-conference(s). How you conduct the conference determines its success. Like the pre-conference, it is important to establish rapport with the teacher, putting the teacher at ease and developing an atmosphere that demonstrates that you are genuinely interested in helping that teacher improve classroom instruction.

One caution should be mentioned. Although post-conference appears to be singular in effect, the fact is there may be more than one observation. It is easy to become trapped by what appears to be a rather mechanical procedure of a pre-conference, an observation, a post-conference—and presto! the teacher changes behavior. Change in teaching behavior takes time, effort, energy, and a feeling of a need to change. You may have to have several post-conferences with a teacher because change takes time. The teacher will need continuous feedback, additional observation, encouragement, and a commitment on your part to assist in the change.

Guidelines and Recommendations

The content and quality of the post-conference(s) is crucial to the supervisory and change process. To help you do a better job in post-conference sessions with teachers, the following questions are presented as guidelines:

1. How can you help the teacher analyze the data from the observation(s)?

2. How can you help the teacher use the data to identify strengths and weaknesses?
3. How can you help the teacher use the data to make a commitment to change?
4. How can you help the teacher create a willingness to try new ideas, whether they be from you, from the teacher, or from others?
5. How can you help the teacher feel confident and secure during the change process?
6. How can you help the teacher develop long- and short-term objectives for changing teaching behavior?
7. How can you help the teacher develop an evaluation plan that will assess the effects of the planned change?
8. How can you help the teacher want to self-supervise (videotape and audiotape) and self-evaluate teaching behavior?
9. How can you help the teacher evaluate your supervisory methods and procedures?
10. How can you help the teacher summarize the important factors resulting from the post-conference(s)?

These questions suggest several specific recommendations for the principal/supervisor:

1. The conference requires preparation. That is, both you and the teacher should have a clear idea of the purpose of the conference and the data to be discussed.
2. The conference setting should be pleasant, informal, and free from potential interruptions.
3. The conference should focus on the data at hand. Discussion should be purposeful, sincere, and honest.
4. The conference should focus on problem solving and feedback resulting from the analysis of the data.
5. The conference should emphasize interactions that require the active participation of the teacher. In other words, the teacher should not take a passive, listening role, but should, because of your methods, be actively engaged in the discussion.
6. The conference should include outcomes, recommendations, ideas, and future plans that are designed to help the teacher improve instruction.
7. The conference should include a written record of future actions, activities, and evaluation plans.
8. The conference should conclude on a positive, encouraging note.

These questions and recommendations should be carefully considered by every principal/supervisor. The importance of what you are doing is obvious. Here is your chance to help a teacher improve performance, the result of which should be a more positive learning situation for children and young people. A convenient report form incorporating these recommendations is shown in Figure 3-7.

Post-Conference Evaluation

Every post-conference should be evaluated to insure that what was discussed, perceived, and written between the teacher and the principal/supervisor was agreeable to both parties. Figure 3-8 shows a post-conference evaluation form that may be used one or two days after the conference. This time span gives the teacher and the principal/supervisor time to think about what took place during the conference and what was recorded on the Post-Conference Report Form. It is also recommended that

---

Teacher:_____   Principal/Supervisor:_____
Date of Observation:_____   Date of Post-Conference:_____
Time of Observation:_____   Time of Conference:_____

Pre-Observation Conference Notes (see previous records):_____
Observation Conference Data (see records):_____

Instruments Used During Observation(s):

Data Discussed by Teacher and Principal/Supervisor:

Problems Identified:

Statement of Objectives:

Suggestions for Teacher Action:

Methods of Evaluating Objectives/Actions:

Schedule for Implementing Actions:

    (Teacher's Signature)   (Principal's/Supervisor's Signature)

FIGURE 3-7
Sample Post-Conference Report Form

Directions: Please rate your feelings/values of the post-conference held between_____

(teacher)

_____ and _____on_____.

(principal/supervisor)   (date)

Circle the number that best represents your rating of the item: 1 represents a low rating; 10 a high rating.

How would you rate the_____of/during/from the conference?

		1	2	3	4	5	6	7	8	9	10
1.	Climate/atmosphere	1	2	3	4	5	6	7	8	9	10
2.	Discussion/communication	1	2	3	4	5	6	7	8	9	10
3.	Openness/honesty	1	2	3	4	5	6	7	8	9	10
4.	Interaction/exchange	1	2	3	4	5	6	7	8	9	10
5.	Analysis of data	1	2	3	4	5	6	7	8	9	10
6.	Feedback you received	1	2	3	4	5	6	7	8	9	10
7.	Contributions	1	2	3	4	5	6	7	8	9	10
8.	Understanding/empathy	1	2	3	4	5	6	7	8	9	10
9.	Recommendations	1	2	3	4	5	6	7	8	9	10
10.	Suggestions	1	2	3	4	5	6	7	8	9	10
11.	Plans/objectives	1	2	3	4	5	6	7	8	9	10
12.	Plans/activities	1	2	3	4	5	6	7	8	9	10
13.	Plans/evaluation	1	2	3	4	5	6	7	8	9	10
14.	Results/outcomes	1	2	3	4	5	6	7	8	9	10
15.	Degree of your satisfaction	1	2	3	4	5	6	7	8	9	10

_____   _____

(Teacher's Signature)   (Principal's/Supervisor's Signature)

FIGURE 3-8
Post-Conference Evaluation Form

both parties complete the form, share their ratings, informally discuss discrepancies, and file these reports for use in preparation for the next observation and post-conference.

HOW TO EVALUATE YOUR STAFF DEVELOPMENT PROGRAM

Inservice programs or staff development (the two are used here synonymously) should serve to improve teacher performance and be a vehicle for helping you and the teachers plan activities resulting from post-conference meetings discussed in the previous section. Supervision of staff development programs is your responsibility and that of the supervisors and other administrators in the school and in the district. It should not be delegated.

It is clear from both research and practice that the school principal plays a major and crucial role in inservice program efforts. "Effective principals promote norms of continuous improvement and collegiality. They hold and support expectations that improving one's teaching is a collaborative rather than a solo enterprise and that analysis, evaluation, and experimentation in concert with one's colleagues set the conditions under which teachers can become more effective."[18]

Effective principals, then, can enhance teacher competence by being effective instructional leaders, providing meaningful supervision, and supporting continuous inservice education opportunities. The bottom line, once again, is that effective teaching means that students will achieve and that efforts to improve teacher performance will result in the improvement of student performance.

Given these premises, the discussion that follows will address the evaluation of three aspects of staff development programs: needs assessment, program planning and implementation, program evaluation and follow-up.

It should be noted that on the average teachers participate in only three days of inservice education opportunities each year and often these are one-shot programs on isolated topics with little, if any, follow-up.[19] It should be obvious that if this is the case in your school district, then teachers will or should conclude that professional development is a low-priority objective. It is essential that before beginning an evaluation of your school or district's staff development efforts school administrators be polled regarding their interest, support, and potential involvement. It needs to be given priority and it must focus on the needs of school personnel to advance the goals of the district, the school, and gain faculty acceptance.[20]

Needs Assessment

The first need for you, the faculty, and anyone else in the school district involved in staff development programs, is to know what research says about effective staff development programs leading to effective teaching. Here is one summary for your review.

Once you and others have read the research, the question to be asked is: Have we used this research as the basis for our school or district's inservice programs?

The second need is central to participation and pay-off. Teachers should be involved in every phase of staff development. You can determine the extent to which your school and district meets this need by reacting to the following statements:

- Teachers are involved in planning, implementing, and evaluating inservice programs.
- Inservice programs are based upon district goals, school objectives,

Highlights From Research on Staff Development for Effective Teaching

Studies comparing various models or processes of staff development are rare. While it is not possible to state conclusively that one inservice design is superior to another, we can put together the many pieces of research reviewed here to make some general recommendations about staff development programs for more effective teaching.

1. Select content that has been verified by research to improve student achievement.
2. Create a context of acceptance by involving teachers in decision making and providing both logistical and psychological administrative support.
3. Conduct training sessions (more than one) two or three weeks apart.
4. Include presentation, demonstration, practice, and feedback as workshop activities.
5. During training sessions, provide opportunities for small-group discussions of the application of new practices and sharing of ideas and concerns about effective instruction.
6. Between workshops, encourage teachers to visit each others' classrooms, preferably with a simple, objective, student-centered observation instrument. Provide opportunities for discussions of the observation.
7. Develop in teachers a philosophical acceptance of the new practices by presenting research and a rationale for the effectiveness of the techniques. Allow teachers to express doubts about or objections to the recommended methods in the small group. Let the other teachers convince the resisting teacher of the usefulness of the practices through "testimonies" of their use and effectiveness.
8. Lower teachers' perception of the cost of adopting a new practice through detailed discussions of the "nuts and bolts" of using the technique and teacher sharing of experiences with the technique.
9. Help teachers grow in their self-confidence and competence through encouraging them to try only one or two new practices after each workshop. Diagnosis of teacher strengths and weaknesses can help the trainer suggest changes that are likely to be successful—and, thus, reinforce future efforts to change.
10. For teaching practices that require very complex thinking skills, plan to take more practice, and consider activities that develop conceptual flexibility.

teacher needs, all of which are translated into student learning and achievement.
- Teachers in my school have opportunities to discuss the "what is" and "what should be" regarding staff development.

A third need relates to district and school support and resources. There is a need to determine the extent to which the district or school will:

- Provide teachers with released time or paid personal time to engage in staff development opportunities.
- Provide financial, material, and personnel resources to meet the expressed inservice needs of the district, the school, the individual teachers.
- Provide resources for effectively evaluating program efforts and planning future programs.

The major question is straightforward: Is there leadership and support from school board members and administrators for developing and promoting effective, continuous professional development programs for all school personnel?

Program Planning and Implementation

Effective inservice education programs are carefully planned and implemented with a great deal of care and concern for details. To this end, here is a checklist that may be used as criteria for evaluating program planning and implementation.

The inservice/staff development program in our school or district:

- Has a clearly written statement of goals and objectives.
- Is based upon the expressed needs of teachers.
- Is based upon research and best educational practices.
- Is related to the instructional program.
- Is on-going, continuous, long-range.
- Is designed to improve student achievement.
- Has administrative support and involvement, particularly at the school-site level.
- Promotes collegial exchanges and relationships.
- Is useful, practical, and transferable to teaching and learning problems and activities.
- Provides a variety of strategies, such as demonstrations and modeling.
- Allows teachers the time to practice and/or apply the new strategies.
- Provides opportunity for teacher feedback and follow-up assistance.
- Provides the instructional time required to achieve stated objectives.

- Provides participants with the personnel and material resources needed for successful program implementation.
- Has a budget that supports the program.
- Includes an on-going evaluation plan.[22]

As you well know, there is a variety of program options that may be used for inservice education. Among the more popular ones are workshops, seminars, independent study, teacher exchanges, visitations, professional conferences, graduate courses, and sabbaticals.

Program Evaluation and Feedback

Much of what was said in the previous two sections on needs assessment and program planning/implementation has evaluative content that can be included in this discussion of program evaluation and follow-up. Since inservice programs vary from district to district, school to school, and since districts usually provide (or should provide) a variety of inservice program opportunities for school personnel, an evaluation template will be outlined here.

This template is designed to gather data for decision making by you and district administrators but especially for those responsible for the staff development programs of the school or the school district (i.e. staff development committee). While this template represents a summative evaluation scheme, it is assumed that there is a systematic, on-going inservice education evaluation plan in your school or school district. The template has three main decision areas outlined below.

Decision Points. To evaluate an inservice education program, there are seven areas where decisions have to be made:

1. Needs assessment.
2. Program objectives.
3. Program participants.
4. Program schedule.
5. Program implementation.
6. Program outcomes.
7. Program follow-up.

Decision Data. Each of these decision points requires data/information upon which decisions can be made. The decision data aspect of the template requires:

(a) Data needs.
(b) Data suppliers.
(c) Data collectors.

(d) Data analysis.
(e) Data use.

Each of these in turn should be implemented by answering the questions—who, what, when, where, how, and why? For any decision point you (or the committee) would need data, suppliers, collection, and analysis, and you would use some or all of the six questions. Let's apply this scheme to decision point six: program outcomes.

Data Needs

What kinds of information do you need to determine the extent to which the program outcomes have been realized?
What methods are you going to use to get the data?
Why do you want this data?

Data Suppliers

Who are the data suppliers?
Who is going to provide you with the information needed about program outcomes?

Data Collection

When are you going to get the data you need?
What methods are you going to use to collect the data?
Where will the data be collected?
What procedures will you use to record the data?

Data Analysis

How are you going to interpret the information you have?
What methods will you use to study the data (i.e., statistical procedures, ethnographic categories—diaries, logs, field notes, etc.)?
Who will help you analyze the data?
When will you analyze the data?
When will you complete data analysis?
What data is missing that you now wish you had collected?

Data Use

How will the data be reported?
Who will do the report?
How will the information be reported to others?
When will the report be completed?
Where will the report be available for others to read?
What are you (the committee) going to do with the data now that you have it?

Decision Action

What does the data suggest for the future?

What are your plans for the future, for on-going inservice programs for teachers?

Who will do the work to get your plans into operation?

When will you go back to the needs assessment and repeat the decision point cycle?

Now, this template is an example. It should be coupled with the suggestions discussed in the needs assessment and program planning/implementation and other evaluation recommendations[23] before you or the committee proceed to carry out this important task. It is important to highlight the fact that "well-designed and well-executed staff development programs should leave an impact on teachers with learning becoming more exciting and significant for students."[24]

A FINAL COMMENT

Effective schools have effective principals who are effective instructional leaders. We see it in practice and we find it supported in the research—the effective principal is the school's instructional leader. That was what this chapter was all about. In summary, the principal who is the instructional leader will:

- Articulate the school's goals and objectives.
- Communicate the academic mission of the school.
- Coordinate curriculum and instruction.
- Group students for instructional purposes.
- Monitor the instructional program using a variety of supervisory methods.
- Evaluate teacher performance in the classroom.
- Monitor student progress.
- Actively promote and support staff development.[25]

NOTES

1. Suzanne M. Stiegelbauer, "Leadership for Change: Principal's Actions Make a Difference in School Improvement Efforts," *Research and Development Center for Teacher Education Review* (University of Texas) 2 (January 1984): 1–2.
2. Russell Gersten, Douglas Carnine, and Susan Greene, "The Principal as Instructional Leader: A Second Look," *Educational Leadership* 40 (December 1982): 48.
3. Jack McCurdy, *The Role of the Principal in Effective Schools: Problems and Solutions* (Arlington, VA: American Association of School Administrators, 1983): 21.

4. David A. Squires, William G. Huitt, and John K. Segars, *Effective Schools and Classrooms: A Research-Based Perspective* (Alexandria, VA: Association for Supervision and Curriculum Development, 1984).

5. Joseph F. Murphy, Marsha Weil, Philip Hollinger, and Alex Mitman, "Academic Press: Translating High Expectations into School Policies and Classroom Practices," *Educational Leadership* 40 (December 1982): 22–26. See also "Academic Press: Policy, Practice, Behavior," *School Improvement Council News* (Spring 1985), College of Education, University of South Carolina.

6. *Op. cit.*, Some of the items are based upon the materials in chapter five. The authors provide a series of questions for modeling, consensus building, and feedback that school principals and others will find useful and informative.

7. Daniel L. Duke, "Leadership Functions and Instructional Effectiveness, *Bulletin of the National Association of Secondary School Principals* 66 (October 1982): 3–7.

8. *Ibid.*, p. 7.

9. *Ibid.*, p. 9.

10. *Ibid.*, pp. 9–11. Used with permission from publisher and author. This material also appeared in *School Leadership and Instructional Improvement* (New York: Random House, 1987).

11. Bruce W. Tuckman, "Feedback and the Change Process," *Phi Delta Kappan* 57 (January 1976): 341–344.

12. See Part 2, "Effective Teaching," by Willis D. Hawley and Susan I. Rosenholtz, "Good Schools: What Research Says About Improving Student Achievement," *Peabody Journal of Education* 61 (Summer 1984): 15–52.

13. Morris Cogan, *Clinical Supervision* (Boston: Houghton Mifflin Co., 1973), pp. 10–12.

14. Robert Goldhammer, *Clinical Supervision* (New York: Holt, Rinehart, and Winston, 1969), pp. 89–90.

15. Edmund J. Amidon and Ned A. Flanders, *The Role of the Teacher in the Classroom* (Minneapolis: Association for Productive Teaching, 1967); and Ned Flanders, "Intent, Action, Feedback: A Preparation for Teaching," *Journal of Teacher Education* 24 (September 1963).

16. *Ibid.*, pp. 65–71.

17. Thomas H. Briggs and Joseph Justman, *Improving Instruction Through Supervision* (New York: Macmillan Co., 1952), pp. 339–341.

18. *Op. cit.*, Hawley and Rosenholtz, p. 68.

19. Bruce Joyce and Beverly Showers, *Power in Staff Development Through Research in Training* (Alexandria, VA: Association for Supervision and Curriculum Development, 1983), p. 1.

20. Robert Alfonso, Gerald Firth, and Richard Neville, *Instructional Supervision: A Behavior System* (Boston: Allyn and Bacon, 1983), p. 395.

21. Georgea Mohlman Sparks, "Synthesis of Research on Staff Development for Effective Teaching," *Educational Leadership* 41 (November 1983): 71. Reprinted with permission of the Association for Supervision and Curriculum Development and Dr. Sparks. Copyright © 1983 by the Association for Supervision and Curriculum Development. All rights reserved.

22. See Fred H. Wood, Steven R. Thompson, and Sr. Frances Russell, "Designing Effective Staff Development Programs," Betty Dillon-Peterson, ed., *Staff Development/Organization Development* (Alexandria, VA: Association for Supervision and Curriculum Development, 1981), Chapter 4.

23. See, for example, Daniel L. Duke and Lyn Corno, "Evaluating Staff Development," Betty Dillon-Peterson, ed., *Staff Development/Organization Development* (Alexandria, VA: Association for Supervision and Curriculum Development, 1981), Chapter 5.

24. Lloyd W. Dull, *Supervision: School Leadership Handbook* (Columbus, Ohio: Charles E. Merrill, 1981), p. 113.

25. Joan Shoemaker, *Research-Based School Improvement Practices* (Hartford, CT: State Department of Education, 1984), pp. 25–27.

REFERENCES

Educational Leadership 41 (April 1984): Theme of this issue is "The Realities of Supervision."

Goldhammer, Robert; Anderson, Robert; and Krajewski, Robert. *Clinical Supervision: Special Methods for the Supervision of Teachers* (New York: Holt, Rinehart and Winston, 1980).

Hosford, Philip L., ed. *Using What We Know About Teaching* (Alexandria, VA: Association for Supervision and Curriculum Development, 1984).

Iwanicki, Edward F., and McEachern, Lucille. "Use Teacher Self-Assessment to Identify Staff Development Needs." *Journal of Teacher Education* 35 (March–April 1984): 38–41.

Meitens, Sally. "The Basics in Inservice Education: Findings from Rand and Teacher Center Studies." *Action in Teacher Education* 4 (Spring–Summer 1982): 61–66.

National Association of Elementary School Principals. "Making Evaluation a Tool for Improvement." *Centerfold Seminars*, November 30, 1980.

Sergiovanni, Thomas J., and Starrott, Robert J. *Supervision: Human Perspectives* (New York: McGraw-Hill, 1979).

Strother, Deborah B. "Inservice Education." *Practical Applications of Research* 5 (March 1983), Bloomington, IN: Phi Delta Kappa's Center on Evaluation, Development, and Research.

Wilson, Robert M., and Blum, Irene. "Evaluating Teachers' Use of Inservice Training." *Educational Leadership* 38 (March 1981): 490–491.

CHAPTER 4

Evaluating for Effective Teaching

When an educational critic appraises in a way which is designed
to provide constructive feedback to the teacher, evaluation begins
to perform its most important function: providing the conditions
that lead to the improvement of the educational process.

Elliot W. Eisner

A single chapter is not going to do justice to such a comprehensive
topic as teacher evaluation. The content, references, and endnotes of this
chapter and the previous chapter on instructional supervision must be read
if you, as school principal, expect to implement a fair, consistent, comprehensive teacher evaluation program. Also keep in mind as you read this
chapter that there is probably a state or district-wide teacher evaluation
program currently operating that is initiated and guided by collective bargaining agreements and legal requirements. So it is within these two parameters that we examine evaluation for effective teaching.

PURPOSES OF TEACHER EVALUATION

It seems apparent that there are two purposes for evaluating teachers: the
first is to improve teacher performance, the second to provide a measure
of accountability. That's it. Everything else is a variation on the theme.

The first purpose, improvement, usually means that evaluation methods (formative) are employed to help teachers diagnose and improve their
teaching skills. By means of teacher development opportunities, efforts are
made to improve instruction. The methods for improvement vary, but they
include teacher participation in gaining insights about their teaching performance from peers, colleagues, students, supervisors and self.

The second purpose, accountability, usually means that evaluation
methods (summative) are employed by administrators to determine reten-

tion and tenure, hiring or firing, promotion or reassignment. The methods vary but usually a principal or his/her assistant visits a teacher's classroom several times, using a district rating scale or some other standardized instrument, the results of which are used to make a personnel decision.

While there are problems with many current teacher evaluation methods,[1] among the major positive aspects of teacher evaluation are that the process improves teacher-principal communication, it increases teacher awareness of instructional goals and classroom practices, it impacts instruction and classroom practices, it gives teachers a sense of pride and professionalism, and it increases public confidence in the schools.[2] So we begin by suggesting some guidelines for evaluating teacher performance.

GUIDELINES FOR EVALUATING TEACHERS

A recent task-force study recommended several guidelines that principals should follow in evaluating the performance of teachers. These guidelines were developed with one state's laws in mind, but they probably have applicability to other states as well. Not only do the guidelines have legal implications, they suggest a common sense approach to teacher evaluation. The guidelines fall into two categories: procedural considerations and the contents of the evaluation form.

Procedural Considerations

The teacher performance evaluation process must:

- Involve the superintendent, principals, and teachers
- Identify the number (of teacher evaluations per year) and area of emphasis (personal characteristics, instructional role, etc.)
- Clearly state the purposes for the evaluation
- Include pre- and post-conference regarding the evaluation
- Fully inform teachers about the scope of the evaluation process; i.e., classroom observation, conferences, other documentation to be gathered by the principal (daily journals, memorandums, etc.)
- Spell out causes for termination of a teacher contract following state law and local collective bargaining agreements
- Be based on factual descriptions, not interpretations or conclusions; that is, the use of evaluative information other than the performance evaluation (or principal's daily journal, etc.) must be complete, objective, and defensible
- Be open to teacher review
- Represent a fair sampling of the teacher's performance; i.e., show a pattern of performance over a period of time

- Inform the teacher, as early as possible, about any deficiencies in performance
- Provide the teacher with opportunities to correct deficiencies
- Guarantee equal treatment regardless of personal status, race, sex, and age.

Evaluation Form

Several suggestions were outlined regarding the evaluation form itself. In summary, the evaluation form must:

- Define incompetency; causes for which a teacher contract can be terminated
- Define the values on the scale used; i.e., which end is high or low on a 1 to 5 scale
- Rate single characteristics only; don't combine two terms in a single statement
- Include a written glossary defining the characteristics, attitudes, and behaviors to be evaluated
- Be cautious about cumulative numerical ratings; that is, assigning equal weight to all evaluative items
- Not be based solely on open-ended statements
- Include a comment section where the principal's comments reflect the strengths and shortcomings already listed on the rating scale
- Provide explicit instructions on how the form is to be used
- Have a clear statement of the purpose of the evaluation
- Include space for a teacher review statement and teacher signature.[3]

Using these guidelines as the basis for evaluating teacher performance, a three-phase evaluation plan will be outlined.

Basic Questions for the Faculty

Wise and his colleagues say that their "preliminary assessment (of teacher evaluation practices) led us to conclude that school authorities do not agree on what constitutes the best practices with regard to instrumentation, frequency of evaluation, the role of the teacher in the process, or how the information could or should inform other district activities."[4] Given this observation and my experiences with teachers and administrators, it would make sense for each school principal to engage in discussions with teachers regarding the district's evaluation program and teacher evaluation in general—a good topic for faculty meetings. For some reason, this very important topic is seldom discussed at local school sites and may only be discussed at the district level during union-district negotiating sessions.

Here are some questions you and your teachers may wish to discuss:

1. Why should teachers be evaluated?
2. How do teachers feel about the district's current teacher evaluation program?
3. What does the literature say about teacher evaluation?
4. Which school districts have exemplary teacher evaluation programs? Why are these considered exemplary?
5. What are the factors that should be evaluated in an effective teacher evaluation plan?
6. Should there be differences in the way non-tenured and tenured teachers are evaluated?
7. Who should do the evaluating?
8. How should evaluation be done?
9. What should be done with the results of the evaluation?
10. What training is necessary to insure that those who evaluate teaching performance do it competently?

You will recall that the instructional improvement cycle discussed in the previous chapter included three phases—a planning phase, an assessment phase, and an improvement phase. This same pattern will be used for the discussion about teacher evaluation. Before examining the teacher evaluation plan of the instructional improvement cycle, however, it is more appropriate to say a few words about evaluating beginning teachers.

EVALUATION AND THE NEW TEACHER

In view of the current teacher shortage, we can expect many new teachers to come to schools enthusiastic, idealistic, and fearful about their first year as a teacher. It is a difficult time for them and unless you, as school principal, attend to beginning teacher needs, it can be a difficult time for you as well. It also can lead to a loss of teacher talent. It has been estimated that "approximately 15% of new teachers leave after their first year of teaching compared to the overall teacher turnover rate of 6%. Of all beginning teachers who enter the profession, 40–50% will leave during the first seven years of their career, and two-thirds to three-fourths of those will do so in the first four years of teaching."[5] Couple this information with the fact that research indicates that the most academically talented teachers leave in the greatest numbers and one can easily conclude that attention has to be given to the needs of the beginning teachers.[6]

The topic of evaluating beginning teachers is placed in this chapter rather than in the chapter on instructional supervision because it is during a new teacher's probationary period that a school principal must attend to both the need for improvement (formative evaluation) and the need for reappointment and/or tenure (summative evaluation). The two are also in the right order, for most if not all beginning teachers will have instructional improvement needs and it is the principal's task to determine, after a given period of time, whether that improvement is sufficient to indicate that the new teacher has become an acceptable teacher in the school district (awarded tenure). In other words, the evaluation program can give a new teacher the chance for success, but it may also be a vehicle for screening out the least promising teachers (although in reality this seldom happens). An effective, meaningful teacher evaluation program must include the evaluation of the district's and the school's induction program, the resources provided to assist beginning teachers, and the extent to which the program improves the performance, self-confidence, and self-esteem of beginning teachers.

EVALUATING GOALS

The assumption here is that your district has an induction program for beginning teachers. If it does, then what follows should be used as a means of evaluating the existing program. If the district needs a program, then the content can be used by you to encourage the creation of a district-wide beginning teacher induction program.

We begin by examining goals. The question is: What are the goals of your school district's beginning teacher induction program? It might be interesting to compare them to the goals recommended by others. For example, Leslie Huling-Austin recommends four generic goals for induction programs:

1. To improve teaching performance;
2. To increase the retention of promising teachers during the induction years;
3. To promote the personal and professional well-being of beginning teachers;
4. To satisfy mandated requirements related to induction and certification.[7]

EVALUATING PRACTICES

Odell suggests seven categories of support that should be made available to beginning teachers:

1. "System information—giving information related to procedures, guidelines, or expectations of the school district;
2. Resources/materials—collecting, disseminating, or locating materials or other resources for use by the new teacher;

This form is designed to evaluate the practices in our current beginning teacher induction program. Its purpose is to find out whether the suggested practice exists (status) and, if so, how you rate the practice (value). To determine your relationship to the program, please check one of the following:

_____ a beginning teacher in the program   _____ a mentor teacher in the program   _____ a school site administrator

_____ involved in the program as a

	Status		Practice	Value			
	Included	Excluded		Great	Some	Little	None
1.	____	____	1. The program involves the local teachers' union in planning and implementing the program.	1. ____	____	____	____
2.	____	____	2. Policies and procedures of the school district and school site are reviewed.	2. ____	____	____	____
3.	____	____	3. Administrators provide a clear statement of effective, successful teaching.	3. ____	____	____	____
4.	____	____	4. Assistance is provided with regard to lesson planning and implementation.	4. ____	____	____	____
5.	____	____	5. Coaching techniques are used.	5. ____	____	____	____
6.	____	____	6. Classroom management techniques are part of the program content.	6. ____	____	____	____
7.	____	____	7. General information about the school district, the community, and the assigned school is provided.	7. ____	____	____	____
8.	____	____	8. Observation and feedback about teaching performance are provided.	8. ____	____	____	____
9.	____	____	9. Opportunities to visit other teachers and observe their teaching are part of the program.	9. ____	____	____	____
10.	____	____	10. Released time is provided for staff development and additional training.	10. ____	____	____	____

			11.	There is a buddy system for the mentor relationship aspect in the program.
			12.	Special assistance is provided by central office supervisors.
			13.	The principal keeps in frequent contact with beginning teachers.
			14.	Access to instructional materials is provided.
			15.	New teachers have fewer responsibilities than the tenured/experienced teachers.
			16.	New teachers are assigned to classes for which they were trained. (There are no misassignments.)
			17.	Resources and materials that relate directly to the curriculum being taught are provided.
			18.	Assistance is provided to help new teachers with "problem" children.
			19.	There are opportunities for new teachers to interact with the other teachers in the building.
			20.	New teachers are helped to manage their personal and professional time appropriately.

FIGURE 4-1

Evaluation of Induction Program Practices

3. Instructional—giving information about teaching strategies in the instructional process;
4. Emotional—offering new teachers support through empathetic listening and by sharing experiences;
5. Classroom management—giving guidance and ideas related to discipline or to scheduling, planning, and organizing the school day;
6. Environment—helping teachers by arranging, organizing, or analyzing the physical setting of the classroom; and
7. Demonstration teaching—teaching while new teachers observe (preceded by conference to identify focus of observation and followed by analysis conference)."[8]

Within the framework of these seven categories, the scale in Figure 4-1 enables you to determine whether or not the induction program includes the suggested practices and, if it does, its value as viewed by beginning teachers, school site administrators, and others.

Obviously there are other practices that can and should be added to the list. The practices in Figure 4-1 are illustrative. Teacher evaluation practices should be closely allied to the goals of the program. The practices should reflect what is suggested in the research as well as exemplary induction programs in other school districts.

EVALUATING OUTCOMES

The evaluation of the teacher induction program in your school district must be based upon its goals and practices. There are many informal and formal ways to assess such a program. The recommendation here is to employ evaluation methods that are best for the program in your district but provide evidence that the program

- Improves teaching performance
- Increases the selection of promising beginning teachers
- Screens out less promising teachers
- Promotes beginning teachers' self-confidence and self-esteem
- Satisfies collective bargaining agreements
- Improves communication and relationships between beginning teachers and the school faculty as well as other teachers in the district
- Improves communication and relationships between beginning teachers and school administrators
- Is periodically evaluated to determine its strengths and weaknesses.

An effective teacher induction program can be helpful in setting the conditions for a successful teacher evaluation program and for successful teaching. "Without such an approach, and without sufficient attention to conditions of the workplace, the U.S. system of education risks producing yet another cadre of individuals who entered teaching with a strong desire to serve students—but who find, after exposure to the working conditions of their profession, that they can't and won't teach."[9]

The previous chapter outlined an instructional improvement cycle for use in the supervision of instruction. This cycle is also applicable for evaluating the performance of teachers, since supervision and evaluation of instruction go hand in hand.

PLANNING PHASE FOR TEACHER EVALUATION

The following guidelines are worthy of consideration as you, the subcommittee, and/or faculty plan the teacher evaluation program.

1. The first step in designing your teacher evaluation program is to insure that the faculty understands the two purposes for evaluating teacher performance from the principal's point of view:
   a. Instructional improvement is dependent upon the willingness of teachers to improve their teaching, which essentially means helping them change their behaviors.
   b. Teachers must be evaluated for administrative purposes.
2. The plan is based upon democratic processes:
   a. A sharing of ideas and problems
   b. Open communication
   c. Fairness and justice
   d. Desire for objectivity.
3. The plan requires the principal and teachers to identify performance standards and/or objectives.
4. The plan is shared with the community and is subject to review, at any time, by principals and teachers.
5. The evaluation plan is designed to help teachers improve professionally and enhance the quality of instruction.
6. The evaluation plan is a continuous process.
7. The plan is shared and discussed with new teachers and published in the teachers' handbook.
8. The plan is based upon self-appraisal techniques as well as appraisal by others (principal, supervisor, students, peers).
9. The plan focuses upon the quality of human relations—understanding, concern, care, self-respect, and the like.
10. The evaluation plan provides information about the faculty as a whole and individual teachers specifically; information on the individual teachers is confidential.
11. The evaluation plan does not permit comparison of one teacher with another.

12. The evaluation plan uses multiple evaluations, several kinds of instruments, and includes a variety of supervisory techniques (direct observation, audiotape, videotape).
13. Conferences follow most, if not all, the evaluation strategies.

These guidelines can be helpful to you and the faculty when initiating a teacher evaluation program.

Characteristics of Successful Programs

Those who have a teacher evaluation program may wish to consider A. Brighton's suggestion that there are certain characteristics present in successful teacher evaluation programs, and the absence of one or more of the characteristics greatly diminishes the chance of success. The following checklist is designed to help you determine which characteristics are present in your current teacher evaluation program. Place a checkmark before one of the two statements for each item that best describes your teacher evaluation program.

1. ___ (A) Teachers, principals, and supervisors are actively involved in planning and reviewing our program.
   ___ (B) Administrators institute the program with little or no participation by teachers.
2. ___ (A) There is little or no preparation by faculty and administrators before implementing our teacher evaluation program.
   ___ (B) We plan, study, and prepare professional personnel before instituting our teacher evaluation program.
3. ___ (A) This school's education goals and objectives have been established and generally accepted.
   ___ (B) Educational goals and objectives are unpublished, generally unknown, and not clear.
4. ___ (A) Teaching has been defined and job descriptions developed.
   ___ (B) Teachers are not clear or at least vaguely aware of their responsibilities.
5. ___ (A) We rate teachers primarily for administrative purposes.
   ___ (B) We rate teachers primarily to improve instruction and help teachers succeed.
6. ___ (A) It is clear to all personnel who will make the evaluations.
   ___ (B) Personnel are generally not clear on who has the responsibility for evaluation.
7. ___ (A) Teacher evaluation is based on nonclassroom activities, teacher traits, hearsay, or conformity to raters' values.
   ___ (B) Teacher evaluation is based on observation of teachers' classroom performance.

8. ___ (A) Teacher evaluation is recorded on a cooperatively developed or selected instrument.

___ (B) Teacher evaluation is recorded on an instrument selected by the administration.

9. ___ (A) Teacher evaluation records are not readily available to teachers.

___ (B) Teacher evaluation records are available to teachers.

10. ___ (A) The teacher evaluation program includes informal conferences between the evaluator and teacher.

___ (B) The teacher evaluation program includes no conferences, or, if there is one, it is a formal, administrator-controlled one.

11. ___ (A) Administrator's rating is final with no provision for reviewing ratings of observations.

___ (B) Disagreement on any item provides for conferences, reviews, and provision for other observers or evaluators.

12. ___ (A) Provisions are made for developing supervisors'/principals' skills and competencies in teacher evaluation.

___ (B) Teacher evaluation is conceived as an addition to the principals' task without concern for qualifications or work load.

13. ___ (A) No provisions are made for assessing the effectiveness of principals/supervisors in the teacher evaluation program.

14. ___ (A) The teacher evaluation program itself is evaluated periodically.

___ (B) The teacher evaluation program is seldom evaluated.

15. ___ (A) The teacher evaluation program is changed whenever the evaluation suggests it should be changed.

___ (B) The teacher evaluation program as implemented continues unchanged or with minor administrative changes from year to year.[10]

These guidelines and characteristics serve as a foundation upon which an effective, reliable teacher evaluation program can be developed. The next step in the planning phase is to decide which aspects of a teacher's performance should be evaluated.

Deciding What to Evaluate

To be straightforward about it, you and your teachers can evaluate many aspects of teaching and instruction. Here are some factors that can be evaluated:

- Teacher's characteristics
- Teaching techniques and methods
- Teacher's performance

- Teacher's relationships with students
- Teacher's use of instructional media
- Teacher's instructional methods, i.e., grouping, teacher-centered, student-centered, individualizing
- Teacher talk, verbal interactions
- Teacher's questions—kind, quality
- Teacher's knowledge of learning principles
- Teacher's knowledge of child and adolescent growth and development
- Teacher's ability to write instructional objectives
- Teacher's evaluation procedures—testing, grading
- Teacher's classroom climate
- Teacher's classroom management skills
- Teacher's ability to handle discipline problems
- Teacher's ability to teach concepts of the subject.

The question before you and your teachers is what should be evaluated. Part of the answer to this question will depend upon your district's policies and union negotiation regarding teacher evaluation. The teacher performance evaluation instrument will contain items that teachers and administrators feel are important to the instructional process. This means that you and the faculty must decide together what factors, performance objectives, and characteristics are worthy of evaluation with the intent that the effort will contribute to the improvement of instruction.

Deciding Who Should Evaluate

There are seven potential evaluators that you and your faculty should consider:

- The principal
- The teacher
- The students
- The teacher's peers
- The school district's supervisor and/or coordinator
- The department chairperson, unit leader, master teacher
- Review team of master teachers.

Your evaluation plan should include a description of the role of all seven of these potential evaluators. The case has been made for the role of the principal as an evaluator of teacher effectiveness. While the supervisor (central office) can be of assistance in the evaluation of teachers and teaching, many prefer that the role be one outside of evaluation; namely, a consultant role, helping teachers with methods, procedures, and materials of instruction, serving as a master teacher by demonstrating methods and techniques that may be of value to a teacher or group of teachers. Supervisors should help both principals and teachers by engaging in the evaluation process as an important third party who serves as a consultant to both the teacher(s) and the principal. A similar role can be assumed by department chairpersons, unit leaders, and/or master teachers working as a team. In other words, if the situation allows it, four parties could be engaged in the evaluation process: principal, supervisor, department-unit leaders, and an evaluation team.

A few words about the review team are in order before proceeding further. The ideas come from an article by W. James Popham, who makes a case that we do not know how to evaluate teachers. He contends that methods used (ratings, observations, pupil test performance, self-evaluators, etc.) are useless as summative approaches, but by employing a "multidata professional judgment model," a review team with experienced master teachers using a formative evaluation format could, with training, collect evidence from a variety of sources and improve the quality of teaching.[11]

Now, it's one thing to say that there are three or four sources for teacher evaluation and another to determine the competency of those about to do the evaluation. If there is one weakness in the evaluation process, a weakness that is of major concern to those being evaluated, it is the extent to which evaluators are competent to evaluate teaching. Training administrators, supervisors, and peers to know what good teaching is, to observe competently, and then to evaluate effectively is essential if the evaluation process is to be valued by teachers. Evaluators need to be trained to know what to look for, how to record what they observe concisely and precisely, and how to communicate their observations to the teachers both orally and in writing.

Let's take an example of how one small school district does the job of evaluating teachers. First, the district, from school board members to teachers, has made it clear to the public and school personnel that instruction is the central focus and that principals should spend most of their time in classroom observation and in supervising instructors. Second, each principal plans and implements a school site professional development program. Third, principals are trained to write effective observations and evaluations. That is, they are trained to write concise observations of two or three paragraphs. Fourth, principals are required to write four brief observations and one clinical supervision per week. Fifth, guidelines are provided to administrators for feedback and communication with the teacher that include such things as: address teacher by first name, indicate accomplishment of objectives, follow contractual timetables, make suggestions for improvement, encourage the teacher to respond in writing, and "don't always document the first problem incident, but keep an anecdotal file in your desk of problems that could be accumulated if they continue or disregarded if not."[12]

The reason for citing this example is that it attempts to do five essential things with regard to teacher evaluation:

1. It focuses on the fact that the school principal is the key to instruction and to teacher evaluation.
2. It highlights the need for training principals in clinical supervision and evaluation methods.
3. It requires principals to write concise observations regularly, thus getting principals into the classroom.
4. It provides guidelines for following up the observations.
5. It probably improves communications and expectations between the principal and the teachers.

ASSESSMENT PHASE FOR TEACHER EVALUATION

Once you and your faculty have implemented the suggestions in the planning phase for teacher evaluation, you should have settled on the why, what, who, and when aspects of the plan. The recurring issue is how to evaluate teachers.

In this section, a sampling of ideas for assessing teacher performance will be described, including classroom observation, teacher evaluation profile, student evaluation, peer evaluation, self-evaluation, evaluating specific aspects of teaching, and other assessment resources. We begin with a few comments about classroom observations.

CLASSROOM OBSERVATION

Despite its weaknesses, classroom observation is still the most frequently used method of teacher evaluation. Regardless of the criticism leveled at the practice, classroom observation provides a panorama of classroom life that other methods of evaluation are unable to offer.

The discussion of classroom observation in the last chapter focused on a three-phase supervisory approach—a planning phase, an assessment phase, and an improvement phase. What was said under these headings is also applicable to classroom observation for evaluation purposes. Thus, a few more suggestions, stated in question form, will summarize major concerns:

1. Is the emphasis in your teacher evaluation program on the teacher's classroom performance? On generic teaching skills?
2. Does the teacher evaluation program require frequent classroom observations (4 or more)?

3. Is the plan cost effective?
4. Does the plan provide training opportunities for those doing the observation?
5. Are the instruments valid and reliable?
6. Do the instruments lend themselves to specific standards for interpretation?
7. Does the plan provide classroom observation options for the principal? That is, does the plan allow the principal to use the talents of department chairs, mentor teachers, supervisors to assist in classroom observations?
8. Does the plan require the observation of all teachers or does it provide an opportunity for scheduling specific teachers during a specific year?
9. Does the plan require the input from teachers to be observed?
10. Is the plan evaluated regularly?

Answers to these questions and those posed in Chapter 3 will enable you and your colleagues to make classroom observations less of a chore and more of a worthwhile endeavor designed to improve teaching and learning. In conclusion, it may be of value to review the tenets of classroom observation posed by Thomas McGreal:

> One, the amount and kind of information you have beforehand the more reliable and useful will be the observation.
> Two, the narrower your focus of observation, the more accurate the observation will be.
> Three, your method of recording the information affects your relationship with the teacher and his/her willingness to improve instruction.
> Four, your method of feedback affects your relationship with the teacher and his/her willingness to improve instruction.[13]

Teacher Evaluation Profile

The evaluation profile in Figure 4-2 uses factors found in the research regarding successful, effective teaching and basic principles of learning. This profile is to be completed by the principal/supervisor. Directions would require the evaluator to shade in the bar graph under each personal characteristic and to place a check along the line for each item under Methods, Learning Environment, and Learning Processes. The checks can then be connected with a line that will provide a "picture" profile of the teacher. The profile is designed to be used by the principal but, with some adaptation, it can serve as a self-evaluation and/or student evaluation instrument. If this is done, the bar graphs can be shaded in with colored pencils to reflect the ratings of the teacher, the principal/supervisor, and the students. Lines of different colors could be used on the other items of the profile.

Personal Characteristics

Enthusiasm	*Rapport*	*Warmth*	*Friendly*	*Responsible*	*Systematic*

Much
100

Some
50

Little
0

Stimulating	*Imaginative*	*Positive Self-Image*	*Understanding*	*Businesslike*	*Sense of Humor*

Much
100

Some
50

Little
0

Teaching Performance: Methods

	Never/ Limited		Sometimes/ Moderate		Always/ Extensive
1. Objectives of each lesson are clear.	0	25	50	75	100
2. Uses multiple texts.	0	25	50	75	100
3. Uses a variety of instructional methods.	0	25	50	75	100
4. Assesses student progress frequently.	0	25	50	75	100
5. Uses diagnostic evaluative methods.	0	25	50	75	100
6. Uses a variety of instructional resources.	0	25	50	75	100
7. Assignments are interesting.	0	25	50	75	100
8. Presents subject matter interestingly.	0	25	50	75	100
9. Lessons are presented clearly.	0	25	50	75	100

FIGURE 4-2
Teacher Evaluation Profile

Teaching Performance: Methods

	Never/ Limited		Sometimes/ Moderate		Always/ Extensive
10. Methods include a review of what is to be taught and learned.	0	25	50	75	100
11. Questions asked of students are more than memory/recall.	0	25	50	75	100
12. Focuses instruction on student learning.	0	25	50	75	100
13. Asks student opinion on difficulty of lesson.	0	25	50	75	100
14. Methods require students to think about their ideas, opinions, and answers.	0	25	50	75	100
15. Methods require students to try to attain teacher-student objectives.	0	25	50	75	100
16. Methods are task-oriented and well-planned.	0	25	50	75	100
17. Methods encourage student discussion and debate.	0	25	50	75	100
18. Demonstrates flexibility in teaching.	0	25	50	75	100
19. Methods reflect that teacher sees things from student point of view.	0	25	50	75	100
20. Utilizes an informal, easy teaching style.	0	25	50	75	100
21. Methods reflect a sound knowledge of subject matter.	0	25	50	75	100
22. Personalizes teaching.	0	25	50	75	100
23. Is willing to experiment; to try new things.	0	25	50	75	100
24. Methods are democratically oriented.	0	25	50	75	100
25. Methods emphasize productive learning.	0	25	50	75	100

Teaching Performance: Learning Environment

	Never/ Limited		Sometimes/ Moderate		Always/ Extensive
1. Maintains an aesthetically pleasant classroom.	0	25	50	75	100
2. Involves students in helping with classroom decor.	0	25	50	75	100
3. Involves students in classroom cleanliness.	0	25	50	75	100
4. Involves students in creating a positive learning environment.	0	25	50	75	100
5. Provides areas for quiet study; independent work.	0	25	50	75	100
6. Provides areas for small group discussions and work.	0	25	50	75	100
7. Uses classroom space and equipment effectively.	0	25	50	75	100

(cont.)

Teaching Performance: Learning Environment

	Never/ Limited		Sometimes/ Moderate		Always/ Extensive
8. Involves students in classroom managerial tasks.					
	0	25	50	75	100
9. Involves students in daily clerical tasks.					
	0	25	50	75	100
10. Demonstrates concern for safety and security of students and materials.					
	0	25	50	75	100

Teaching Performance: Learning Processes

	Never/ Limited		Sometimes/ Moderate		Always/ Extensive
1. Encourages creative, imaginative work from students.					
	0	25	50	75	100
2. Encourages independence in student learning.					
	0	25	50	75	100
3. Provides opportunities for students to learn the material.					
	0	25	50	75	100
4. Encourages and uses students' ideas and suggestions.					
	0	25	50	75	100
5. Encourages and uses students' questions.					
	0	25	50	75	100
6. Promotes and uses students' curiosity.					
	0	25	50	75	100
7. Capitalizes on students' interests.					
	0	25	50	75	100
8. Plans motivational activities for students.					
	0	25	50	75	100
9. Uses problem-solving techniques.					
	0	25	50	75	100
10. Involves students in unit and lesson planning.					
	0	25	50	75	100
11. Promotes cooperation in group learning.					
	0	25	50	75	100
12. Works with students in developing long- and short-term objectives.					
	0	25	50	75	100
13. Involves students in arranging groups.					
	0	25	50	75	100
14. Promotes cooperation and responsibility in group work.					
	0	25	50	75	100
15. Encourages students to respect each others talents, abilities, interests, and needs.					
	0	25	50	75	100
16. Involves students in the evaluation of their work.					
	0	25	50	75	100
17. Promotes self-evaluation methods.					
	0	25	50	75	100
18. Helps students assess progress toward specified objectives.					
	0	25	50	75	100
19. Helps students identify barriers to achieving objectives.					
	0	25	50	75	100

FIGURE 4-2 *(cont.)*

Teaching Performance: Learning Processes

	Never/ Limited		Sometimes/ Moderate		Always/ Extensive
20. Helps students identify barriers to learning subject matter content.					
	0	25	50	75	100
21. Helps students develop effective study skills and habits.					
	0	25	50	75	100
22. Praises more than criticizes students.					
	0	25	50	75	100

FIGURE 4-2 *(cont.)*

It should be noted that other items may be added to the profile. For example, methods of instruction could be detailed. Items from the chapter on classroom climate might be added to the section on learning environment.

It would only be fair to point out that some authorities feel that rating scales as the one above, "lack the minimum properties necessary for accurately measuring the performance of teachers . . . lack validity . . . and are highly susceptible to the halo effect."[14] This caution should be heeded and applied to any rating scale you or your school district uses to evaluate teaching performance.

Student Evaluation

A poll by the National Education Association showed that 50 percent of the elementary and secondary teachers surveyed favored formal student evaluation of teachers, while the remaining 50 percent were opposed. Students can and should evaluate their teachers for the following reasons:

1. Students are the continual recipients of what the teacher does.
2. Students are exposed to methods, styles, and procedures that they can react to, and, within limits, they can provide valuable feedback to the teacher.
3. Teachers are in the learning business, and it makes sense to find out from learners how well this business is being transacted.
4. Student evaluation of teachers will demonstrate to students the value of feedback, and of knowing strengths and weaknesses.
5. Feedback from student evaluations will provide additional data to the teacher that may help improve teaching performance.

There are several guidelines that should be followed when and if you and your teachers decide to have students evaluate instruction:

1. Student evaluation of teachers should be on a volunteer basis only.
2. Student evaluation of teachers should be anonymous.

3. Student evaluation of teachers should be on a continuous-periodic basis throughout the school year.
4. Student evaluation of teachers should be promoted as a sense of self-improvement.
5. Student evaluation of teachers should not be used for administrative decisions about the teacher.
6. Data collected from student evaluation remain with the teacher.
7. The teacher decides whether to share the results with you during conferences.
8. Teachers should be given opportunities to share their experiences using student evaluation with the faculty should they desire to do so.
9. Teachers should be encouraged to use a variety of instruments, at different times throughout the year, to obtain student reaction to their methods, assignments, and the like.

Many of the instruments already suggested in this and other chapters can easily be adapted and used as student evaluation instruments, at least for students who can read. Since reading ability in the primary grades limits the use of instruments previously described, some alternate examples may be helpful.

Michael Scriven says that "the student questionnaire should be a key component in the evaluation from above grade six. . . . Below the sixth grade, student evaluations require more preparation of the class and perhaps can best be done in group discussion."[15]

Teacher Evaluation—Primary Grades. Can students in the primary grades evaluate teachers? Listen to children as they leave school each day, or on the last day of school you can hear them shouting to one another, "Who did you get?" In some cases, you can hear a teacher's name mentioned—groans! Another is named—cheers! Yes, primary grade children (and their parents, for that matter) can evaluate (some authorities prefer the word *rate*) teachers, however informally and impressionistically.

To formalize the process somewhat, one instrument is presented as an illustration of what might be used by primary grade teachers. Obviously, the results are to be treated cautiously. Nevertheless, they can reveal information that will be useful to primary grade teachers.

Figure 4-3 shows a form that has been used successfully with primary grade students. The teacher can read the directions and items to the children. Students place an X on the face that best describes how they feel.

Other aspects of teaching and learning may be added to the categories in Figure 4-3, such as: The worksheets we use? The workbooks we use? Answering in class? Your reading groups? The time I give you to do things? The way I talk to the class? The way I test what you have learned?

How do you feel about:

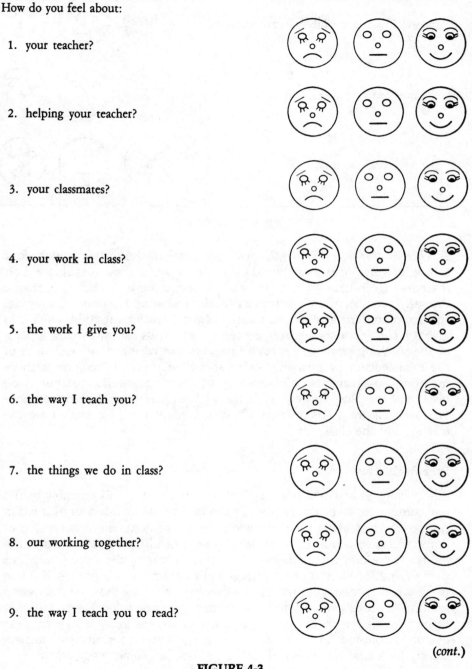

1. your teacher?

2. helping your teacher?

3. your classmates?

4. your work in class?

5. the work I give you?

6. the way I teach you?

7. the things we do in class?

8. our working together?

9. the way I teach you to read?

(cont.)

FIGURE 4-3
Primary Grade Student Evaluation of Teacher/Class

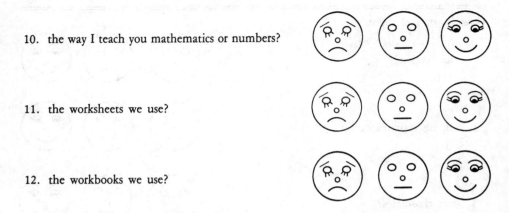

10. the way I teach you mathematics or numbers?

11. the worksheets we use?

12. the workbooks we use?

FIGURE 4-3 (*cont.*)

Teacher Evaluation—Upper Grades.   Students in the upper grades (four through twelve) can and should be given opportunities to evaluate their teachers. To initiate such a program would require teacher volunteers. Properly promoted, with volunteer teachers sharing the benefits they derive from student evaluation, many skeptical teachers may be willing to give it a try. Students are very perceptive and thus can rate many aspects of the teaching-learning process. Students can be effective evaluators of the total teacher performance or of specific aspects of teaching such as methods, assignments, effectiveness of learning results, teacher-made tests, and the like. Student evaluation of teachers should be done anonymously. Figure 4-4 is an example of a student form for evaluating the teacher and the class.

Peer Evaluation

Realistically, peer evaluation, regardless of its merits, will probably be the one component to be questioned by the faculty. Although peer evaluation can be of great value for instructional improvement, the concerns, cautions, and fears it may generate among your faculty may not be worth the effort. Therefore, for experienced-tenured teachers, the opportunity for peer evaluation should be encouraged but left on a volunteer basis. If one teacher wants colleagues to observe the way she or he uses the discussion method, then you should do what needs to be done to enable that teacher to be provided with assistance, ideas, and suggestions. However, peer evaluation should, in my opinion, be a requirement for all new teachers during their first two years of teaching. Here are some suggestions:

1. All new teachers should be told about peer evaluation before they are employed.

	Yes	No	Sometimes
1. Do you always know what I want you to do?	___	___	___
2. Is reading easy for you?	___	___	___
3. Do you have many different things to do?	___	___	___
4. Do I like you?	___	___	___
5. Do you like me?	___	___	___
6. Do your classmates like you?	___	___	___
7. Do you like your classmates?	___	___	___
8. Do you like the way I teach reading?	___	___	___
9. Do you like the way I teach math or numbers?	___	___	___
10. Do you like the way I teach you other subjects?	___	___	___
11. Do you like the way I discipline your classmates?	___	___	___
12. Do you like the tests I give you?	___	___	___
13. Do you always know what I want you to do?	___	___	___
14. Do you like the assignments I give you?	___	___	___
15. Do you like my voice?	___	___	___
16. Do I make school work interesting for you?	___	___	___
17. Do I help you when you need it?	___	___	___
18. Do I give you enough of my time?	___	___	___
19. Do you like to help me?	___	___	___
20. Do you like to help your classmates?	___	___	___
21. Do you like to share your ideas?	___	___	___
22. Do you understand my directions?	___	___	___
23. Do you feel good about being in this class?	___	___	___

FIGURE 4-4
Upper Grade Student Evaluation of Teacher/Class

2. Experienced teachers on your faculty should be selected by you from a list of recommended teachers that is submitted by the faculty.
3. You and the selected teachers (two or three depending on the size of the school) should meet and plan the evaluation process—the what, when, where, and how.
4. Peer evaluators should be given time to do the job; therefore, substitute teachers or teacher aides should be utilized to relieve class assignments at the appropriate time.
5. Peer evaluation should take place once a month for two years between October and May.
6. Classroom observations should be scheduled for at least one-half hour.
7. Conferences should be held before and after the peer evaluator observes the new teacher.
8. Conferences between the principal and peer evaluator should be held regularly to compare data, schedule meetings with the new teacher, and make recommendations.

In summary, "perhaps the most highly qualified evaluators of teacher performance are other teachers. Peer evaluation offers several important advantages . . . : "Teachers often perceive more clearly than others the strengths and weaknesses of colleagues; peer evaluators and teachers benefit professionally from preparing for and conducting evaluations; and . . . peers have a realistic sense of what can be accomplished in classrooms and can therefore make practical, reasonable suggestions for improvement."[16]

Self-Evaluation

Like self-supervision, self-evaluation can be a powerful method for changing behavior and improving instruction. "Do as I do, not as I say." Therein lies the strategy for implementing teacher self-evaluation methods. You, as principal of the school, must demonstrate the value you place on self-evaluation. Several administrator self-evaluation methods have been described in previous chapters. It would be foolhardy to promote self-evaluation methods among your teachers without using self-evaluation as part of your plan for evaluating how you administer the school.

Purposes of Self-Evaluation.   The purposes of teacher self-evaluation are:

- To change teacher behavior
- To improve instruction
- To improve specific aspects of a teacher's performance
- To initiate experimentation; to get teachers to try new things, new ideas
- To promote an attitude that "we can do it better."

Self-evaluation, although effective for new and inexperienced teachers, may be the most significant part of a teacher evaluation plan for experienced, tenured teachers.

There is a multitude of behaviors, performances, and activities that can be evaluated through self-evaluation methods. For example, some teachers use self-evaluation methods to determine

- Time on task
- Student attitudes, interests, self-concepts, etc.
- Instructional methods
- Value, purpose, importance of student assignments
- Testing procedures
- Student knowledge of instructional goals and objectives
- Classroom climate
- Independent learning activities (learning centers, etc.)
- Student reaction to texts and other materials

- Time spent with individual students, groups, whole class
- Teacher-pupil relationships
- Teacher behavior as perceived by students
- Parent attitudes about the teacher
- Relationship with the administration
- Relationship with teachers in the building.

Self-evaluation techniques have also been used to assess out-of-class activities and professional activities such as:

- College courses
- Independent readings, professional readings
- In-service programs, workshops attended
- Trips of an educational nature
- Extra-school activities (chaperone, class-supervisor, etc.).

A Procedure for Self-Evaluation. The principal and faculty should give some attention to the procedures used for implementing self-evaluation plans. For example, it would be helpful to have teachers:

- Read about self-evaluation procedures (see references)
- Learn to write objectives as specifically as possible
- Examine existing self-evaluation instruments
- Learn to construct their own self-evaluation instruments
- Learn to use observational techniques (see self-supervision in previous chapter)
- Plan self-evaluation methods for the entire faculty, groups within the faculty, as well as individual teachers.

A suggested procedure for implementing self-evaluation plans, whether for groups or individuals, follows.

1. Self-Evaluation Objective:
   a. I(We) would like to self-evaluate . . .
   b. Therefore, my(our) objective(s) is (are) . . .
2. Self-Evaluation Methods:
   a. To self-evaluate this objective(s), I(we) will . . .
3. Self-Evaluation Instrument(s):
   a. To self-evaluate this objective(s), I(we) will use the following instruments(s) . . .
4. Self-Evaluation Schedule:
   a. To self-evaluate using this instrument(s), I(we) will utilize the following schedule . . .
5. Self-Evaluation Results:
   a. The results of this self-evaluation are summarized as follows:

6. Change:
   a. Based upon the results, I(we) plan to take the following action(s)
      . . .

   b. Therefore, my(our) new objective(s) for self-evaluation is(are)
      . . .

Audio and Video Taping

As J. Gregory Carroll points out, "one of the potentially most powerful forms of self-assessment is the opportunity to 'see ourselves as others see us' through video and/or audio recordings."[17] Videotaping is an excellent and effective technique for assessing one's teaching performance provided one knows what to look for during the viewing session. While audiotaping is not as dramatic as seeing oneself in action, it can be an effective means of assessing teacher-student verbal interactions. Use of both mechanisms requires training so that some of the anxiety about using these tapes can be reduced. Training is also required to help teachers focus on what they want to observe and to try to do it with some objectivity. Within the context of the value of these two mechanical means for recording teaching performance and the cautions regarding their use, self-appraisal leads to self-awareness, which, one hopes, leads to self-improvement.

Evaluating Specific Aspects of Teaching

Not all evaluating instruments have to assess the broad range of teacher-teaching behaviors. Instruments can be designed to evaluate specific aspects of teaching. In fact, it may be more helpful to teachers to focus in on certain aspects of teaching and instruction so evaluation can be more specific and concrete. For these reasons, two examples follow. I have used several of the instruments with principals and teachers as they work toward the goal of improving instruction. The first example is designed to help teachers evaluate instructional methods, the second helps them examine processes they use in their teaching. These examples are presented here to help your teachers evaluate themselves on the many factors than influence teaching and instruction.

Instructional Methods. In this example, a competency statement will be the focus of the evaluation. The competency is stated as follows: A competent teacher uses a variety of instructional methods. An instrument was designed to help teachers determine the extent to which various instructional methods are used (Figure 4-5).

The instrument serves as a self-evaluation tool initially. Some teachers have used the instrument as a student evaluation tool as well. In this case, the question on the form can be changed to: "How often does your teacher

Teacher's Name:_____

Grade Level or
Subject Taught:_____

Competency: Effective teachers use a variety of instructional methods. Therefore, a competent teacher will plan and use a variety of instructional methods.

Question: How often do you use each of the following in your classes?

Methods	Very Often	Often	Some-times	Seldom	Never	Example of How and When It Was Used
1. Cassette tapes	___	___	___	___	___	
2. Demonstration by teacher	___	___	___	___	___	
3. Differentiated assignments	___	___	___	___	___	
4. Discussion	___	___	___	___	___	
5. Display of student work	___	___	___	___	___	
6. Flexible grouping	___	___	___	___	___	
7. Field trips	___	___	___	___	___	
8. Films	___	___	___	___	___	
9. Filmstrips	___	___	___	___	___	
10. Game-type activities	___	___	___	___	___	
11. Peer teaching	___	___	___	___	___	
12. Independent study	___	___	___	___	___	
13. Inquiry techniques	___	___	___	___	___	
14. Learning centers/stations	___	___	___	___	___	
15. Learning packets	___	___	___	___	___	
16. Lecture	___	___	___	___	___	
17. Multilevel materials	___	___	___	___	___	
18. Newspapers, magazines, etc.	___	___	___	___	___	
19. Outside speakers	___	___	___	___	___	
20. Group projects	___	___	___	___	___	
21. Individual projects	___	___	___	___	___	
22. Role playing	___	___	___	___	___	
23. Small group instruction	___	___	___	___	___	
24. Student aides (tutorial)	___	___	___	___	___	
25. Student demonstrations	___	___	___	___	___	
26. Videotapes	___	___	___	___	___	
27. Debate	___	___	___	___	___	
28. Student self-evaluation	___	___	___	___	___	
29. Student-teacher planning	___	___	___	___	___	
30. Other	___	___	___	___	___	

FIGURE 4-5
Instructional Methods Questionnaire

use the following methods in class?'' If the form is to be used by a principal/supervisor, the question may read: "How often have you observed each of these methods being used by the teacher?''

Using this instrument, the teacher can analyze the data and then write an objective (e.g., I will attempt to use more group-type activities during the next term). The teacher designs procedures for implementing this objective and may have to develop a new instrument to determine whether or not he or she attained the objective. A similar procedure can be used by teachers to evaluate the processes of teaching and learning.

School: _____ Subject(s) and Grade: _____

As a teacher, how often do you use and teach each of the following processes in your class(es)?

	Very Often	Often	Sometimes	Seldom	Never	Process Taught: Specifically	Indirectly	Not at All
Process								
1. Questioning	—	—	—	—	—	—	—	—
2. Reading	—	—	—	—	—	—	—	—
3. Discussing	—	—	—	—	—	—	—	—
4. Observing	—	—	—	—	—	—	—	—
5. Collecting Data	—	—	—	—	—	—	—	—
6. Identifying Variables in the Data	—	—	—	—	—	—	—	—
7. Listening	—	—	—	—	—	—	—	—
8. Conferring, Reporting, Interviewing	—	—	—	—	—	—	—	—
9. Classifying Data	—	—	—	—	—	—	—	—
10. Discovering Principles	—	—	—	—	—	—	—	—
11. Making Hypotheses	—	—	—	—	—	—	—	—
12. Drawing, Photography, Lettering, etc.	—	—	—	—	—	—	—	—
13. Analyzing the Material	—	—	—	—	—	—	—	—
14. Displaying, Exhibiting, Graphing, Mapping	—	—	—	—	—	—	—	—
15. Generalizing from Data	—	—	—	—	—	—	—	—
16. Recognizing the Material	—	—	—	—	—	—	—	—
17. Making Relationships	—	—	—	—	—	—	—	—
18. Testing Data for Social and Personal Use	—	—	—	—	—	—	—	—
19. Creating and Imagining	—	—	—	—	—	—	—	—
20. Other	—	—	—	—	—	—	—	—

FIGURE 4-6
Teacher's Process Scale

Teaching Processes. Teachers have voiced concern and confusion about teaching processes as they relate to the teaching of content. As a means of self-evaluation and a procedure to generate discussion at faculty and in-service meetings, the Teacher's Process Scale was used (Figure 4-6). The purpose of the scale is to help teachers identify teaching processes and then to determine the extent to which they use the process in their teaching (directly or indirectly). One of the interesting findings, for example, and one that creates a dilemma for teachers, is that many will say they use a particular process (i.e., questioning, listening, etc.), but they seldom teach it directly; that is, they do not have lessons on helping students learn to question, to listen, to clarify data, to make generalizations, and so on. Asked if they expect youngsters to learn these processes indirectly usually brings a resounding "no." Asked why they don't teach most of the processes directly usually leads to interesting discussions, rationales, and eventually a request to be helped to do it.

IMPROVEMENT PHASE FOR TEACHER EVALUATION

The major purpose of the planning and assessing phase of this teacher evaluation plan is to obtain information that can be utilized in the improvement phase where plans are established to improve teaching and learning. Post-conferences are as important in the teacher evaluation phase as they are in the observation phase described in the previous chapter. In the previous chapter, guidelines for conferences between the principal and teacher were identified. These guidelines are applicable to post-conference plans in the teacher evaluation phase as well. A few additional suggestions may be helpful:

1. You and each teacher should agree, within the parameters of union/association rules and school board policies, on what evaluative data are to be retained in the teacher's file, both at school and at the central office.
2. Post-conferences, like those recommended in the previous chapter, should focus on the results of the data collected and what the data reveal about teacher behavior and performance.
3. Teacher evaluation data usually have an administrative purpose as well as an instructional purpose, and this should be reemphasized during the post-conference. In other words, teachers should know how the evaluation data will be used by the principal.
4. All instruments as well as records of post-conference results should be cosigned by both the teacher and principal.
5. Teacher evaluation should result in the improvement or maintenance of instruction. To accomplish this, it is recommended that a

plan of action be implemented that would include the following procedures:

a. Objectives—Based upon the evaluative data, the principal helps the teacher write some specific objectives for improving concepts of the teacher performance.

b. Methods—The principal helps the teacher decide what methods might best lead to the accomplishment of objectives.

c. Instruments—The principal helps the teacher select or construct evaluation instruments that will help assess progress in attaining the objective.

d. Schedule—The principal helps the teacher develop a schedule for trying out the methods, evaluating progress, and recording and reporting results.

e. Results—The principal helps the teacher analyze and interpret the results of the evaluation and other aspects of the situation that the teacher brings to the conference in relation to the objectives.

f. Change—Based upon an interpretation of the results, the teacher and principal make judgments about the teacher's performance relative to the objectives and decide whether new objectives should be identified or existing objectives should be retained for further pursuit.

These suggestions for improvement focus on individual teachers. It is also possible to plan, evaluate, and improve instruction on a faculty-wide basis. An example will illustrate the point. Teachers in a particular high school, in the middle of the year, decided with the principal's help and suggestions to evaluate student perceptions of teaching methods and assignments. Two instruments were selected; one instrument was actually designed by a group of teachers. The two instruments were administered to all students and codified in such a way that results could be analyzed for each teacher and for the faculty as a group. The results were given to the principal, who, with the help of a central office supervisor, developed a profile for the staff and for each teacher. The profile was discussed at one faculty meeting. Each teacher's profile was discussed with that teacher only if she or he wished to do so. Teachers with low ratings were offered specific assistance. At two faculty meetings, the principal and supervisor led the teachers in discussing the faculty profile and ways to improve areas of weakness. It was easy for the principal and supervisor to give examples of areas of low ratings (based on actual individual teacher performance without identifying the teacher). They asked the faculty to ''brainstorm'' ways to improve in a particular area. The teachers' list of ideas was recorded, typed, and distributed to each teacher. The supervisor and teachers with low ratings selected items that might be tried in the classroom. One point of this improvement idea is that not only did the teachers with low ratings get individual help from the principal and the supervisor, but they, like their colleagues, also benefited from the collective ideas of the faculty.

Evaluating the Evaluation Plan

Obviously, there is no one best teacher evaluation plan. There are limitations because of time, personnel, and the instruments used. A school's teacher evaluation plan should be evaluated periodically. One way to accomplish this task is to use an incomplete sentence format. The following incomplete sentences are designed for teachers. The results should be given to the principal, summarized by him or her, distributed to the teachers, and discussed at faculty or inservice meetings:

1. Teacher evaluation . . .
2. Because of the teacher evaluation plan, morale at this school is . . .
3. The principal's part in teacher evaluation . . .
4. The instrument we use . . .
5. Our teacher evaluation procedures . . .
6. Evaluation of my teaching . . .
7. One major problem with our teacher evaluation program . . .
8. Our school's teacher evaluation program needs . . .
9. One major strength of our teacher evaluation program . . .
10. Experienced teachers feel that the teacher evaluation program . . .

TEACHER EVALUATION AND IMPROVEMENT: A SUMMARY

The instructional improvement cycle for both the supervision and evaluation of instruction has, as its goal, the improvement of teaching and learning. As suggested earlier, the planning phase should include time for both you and your faculty to come together to discuss:

- Guidelines for successful teacher evaluation programs
- The characteristics of successful teacher evaluation programs
- The characteristics of effective teaching
- Who should evaluate teachers in your school.

The need to engage in discussions on these very important topics cannot be underscored enough. When you, supervisors, teachers, and others appreciate the value of diagnosing teacher strengths and weaknesses, only then can each take steps towards the improvement of instruction.

The assessment phase will flow naturally from discussions held during the planning phase. In the assessment phase, you and your teachers can cooperatively plan who will evaluate teaching; how will it be done; when will it be scheduled; what kind of evaluation instruments will be used; what factors, characteristics, methods will be evaluated; and what will be done with the results of the assessment.

A FINAL COMMENT

The Center for Performance Assessment (Northwest Regional Educational Laboratory) studied the role of performance evaluations in promoting teachers' growth and development. Teachers in the Center's four case study school districts noted that:

- Evaluation was based on only one or two formal classroom visits.
- Observations were too infrequent.
- Feedback was superficial.
- Constructive criticism was lacking.
- Strategies for improvement were not offered.
- Supervisors lacked training.
- There was no monitoring of supervisors' skill in conducting evaluations.

Administrators in this study expressed these concerns:

- Quality evaluation is time-consuming.
- Teachers seem to lack trust.
- Contractual requirements distracted from collaborative efforts.
- Meeting timelines and paperwork was a distraction.
- Lack of training to evaluate teaching performance.
- Need to place priority on evaluation for improvement.
- Need for closer organizational links between evaluation and staff development.

The Center concludes that "success in developing an evaluation program to support teacher improvement appears to hinge on a number of important factors:

- Principals and teachers must be open to change and committed to improvement.
- Teachers and supervisors must agree on priorities, sharing decisions on what needs to be accomplished and when.
- Success requires that teachers and administrators work together cooperatively. . . . "[18]

This study adequately summarizes the intent of this chapter. We said it at the beginning of the chapter and it's worth repeating in the summary: evaluating teaching performance is and must always be a collaborative effort, whether the purpose be for development or for personnel decisions.

Wise and his colleagues provide the final comment for this chapter, stating that an evaluator of instruction (you, peers, students, supervisors, self) needs two qualities: One, "the ability to make sound judgments about teaching quality," and two, "the ability to make appropriate, concrete recommendations for improving teacher performance." They also suggest that there should be some strategy in an evaluation plan for verifying the accuracy of evaluators' reports about teachers.[19]

NOTES

1. Robert S. Soar, Donald M. Medley, and Robert Coker, "Teacher Education: A Critique of Currently Used Methods," *Phi Delta Kappan* 65 (December 1983): 239–246.

2. Arthur E. Wise, Linda Darling-Hammond, Milbrey W. McLaughlin, and Harriet T. Bernstein, *Teacher Evaluation: A Study of Effective Practices* (Santa Monica, CA: The Rand Corporation, 1985), p. 23.

3. "15 Things to Remember Evaluating Teachers," *The Executive Educator* 2 (January 1980): 18–19.

4. *Op. cit.*, p. VI.

5. Leslie Huling-Austin, "Teacher Induction Programs: What Is and Isn't Reasonable to Expect," *The Newsletter of the Research and Development Center for Teacher Education* (University of Texas, Austin) 3 (Fall 1985): 2.

6. Phillip C. Schlechty and Victor Vance, "Recruitment, Selection, and Retention: The Shape of the Teaching Force," *The Elementary School Journal* 83 (April 1983): 469–487.

7. Leslie Huling-Austin, "What Can and Cannot Be Reasonably Expected from Teacher Induction Programs," *Journal of Teacher Education* 37 (January/February 1986): 2–5.

8. Sandra J. Odell, "Induction Support of New Teachers: A Functional Approach," *Journal of Teacher Education* 37 (January/February 1986): 27.

9. Milbrey W. McLaughlin, R. Scott Pfeifer, Deborah S. Owens, and Sylvia Yee, "Why Teachers Won't Teach," *Phi Delta Kappan* 67 (February 1986): 426.

10. Staynor Brighton, *Increasing Your Accuracy in Teacher Evaluation* (Englewood Cliffs, NJ: Prentice-Hall, 1965), pp. 36–37.

11. W. James Popham, "Teacher Evaluations: Mission Impossible," *Principal* 65 (March 1986): 56–58.

12. James Fleming, "Improving Quality Through Effective Evaluations," *Thrust for Educational Leadership* 15 (February/March, 1986): 37–39.

13. Thomas L. McGreal, *Successful Teacher Evaluation* (Alexandria, VA: Association for Supervision and Curriculum Development, 1983), pp. 98–117.

14. Soar, et al., *op. cit.*, p. 243.

15. Michael Scriven, "Summative Teacher Evaluation," in *Handbook of Teacher Evaluation*, ed. by Jason Millman (Beverly Hills, CA: Sage Publications, 1981), pp. 254, 257.

16. Nancy J. Bridgeford, ed., *Captrends* (Portland, Oregon: Center for Performance Assessment) (September, 1982): 4.

17. See J. Gregory Carroll, "Faculty Self-Evaluation," in *Handbook of Teacher Evaluation*, p. 193.
18. Nancy J. Bridgeford, ed. *Captrends* (September 1984): 6.
19. Wise, et al., *op. cit.*, p. viii.

REFERENCES

Ellis, T. R. "Teacher Evaluation is Hard Work—And It Should Be." *Principal* 64 (May 1985): 22–24.

Goodwin, Harold, and Smith, Edwin R. *Faculty and Administrator Evaluation: Constructing the Instruments.* Morgantown, WV: West Virginia University, 1985.

Intern, Intervention, Evaluation: A Professional Development Plan For Classroom Performance. Toledo, OH: Toledo Public Schools, 1985.

National Association of Secondary School Principals Bulletin 66 (December 1982). Teacher Evaluation is the theme of this issue.

Teacher Incentives: A Tool for Effective Management. Reston, VA: National Association of Secondary School Principals, 1984.

Zumwalt, Karen K. *Improving Teaching.* Alexandria, VA: Association for Supervision and Curriculum Development, 1986.

CHAPTER 5

Evaluating Curriculum Effectiveness

> There is no ONE BEST CURRICULUM for all schools . . . No two
> schools will or should have precisely the same characteristics;
> wide diversity is essential for equality.
>
> *Theodore Sizer*

Contrary to Sizer's view, the Carnegie Foundation for the Advancement of Teaching urged in its study of secondary education that there be a core curriculum for all students.[1] Several national reports and state departments of education echoed the conviction that all high school students experience a challenging core of academic courses. In 1980, for example, the Association for Supervision and Curriculum Development formed a network of high schools across the United States to begin redefining general education. The Association has suggested several models and ways for school leaders to conduct studies of general education in their school districts.[2] The effect of these changes on the curriculum in elementary and middle schools is yet to be determined. The need for an articulated, coordinated K-12 curriculum will certainly be influenced by changes at any level. The current trend is clear and unequivocable; there will be state-wide and district-wide mandated curricula.

Curriculum evaluation and improvement will have to include the mandates of the state and the district and within this framework local teachers and administrators will have to attend to such factors as articulation, scope and sequence, objectives, and coordination.

CURRICULUM EVALUATION AND IMPROVEMENT CYCLE

It has been suggested that there are three major models of curriculum evaluation:

1. The Achievement of Designed Outcomes Model is useful for finding out the extent to which students are achieving or performing according to specific behaviors or objectives.
2. The Assessment of Merit Model is useful for finding out whether or not "a given entity" has met a particular standard.
3. The Decision-Making Model is useful for those who wish to make future decisions based upon evaluation results.[3]

In reality, it appears that program and personal evaluators use components of all three models to deal with specific curriculum problems. The suggestions in this chapter do just that. So, we begin the quest for curriculum improvement through the process of evaluation.

Step 1: Acknowledge the Presence of a Curriculum

This means that you and your faculty have a statement of the district's goals and objectives; that you have tried and are trying to implement these through the curricular and cocurricular programs; that these have been translated into specific objectives relating to student behaviors; that these objectives, competencies, and performance standards are implemented by the teachers in your school; that the resources are available to teachers to implement the curriculum; and that you and your teachers, either formally or informally, continually evaluate the curriculum.

Some questions you and your faculty may want to ask and answer about the objectives of your current curriculum include the following:

1. What are the state curriculum requirements?
2. Does our district curriculum complement state recommendations and mandates?
3. Does the faculty know and understand the rationale and need for state- and district-wide standards/requirements?
4. At the school level, how does the current curriculum compare with the state and district curriculum standards/requirements?
5. What changes need to be made to make a better match between the curricula of the state/district/school?

For example, California instituted state-wide high school graduation requirements. To receive a diploma, a student needs to complete three years of English, three years of history-social science, two years of mathematics and two years of science, one year of either a foreign language or visual and performing arts, and two years of physical education. To assist local school districts, model curriculum standards were developed and school districts, by law, must compare their curriculum (content and sequence), to the model standards once every three years.[4] In conjunction with these changes, California implemented an accountability program that broadens the criteria by which schools are measured (test scores alone are insufficient). The program allows local district administrators to determine how to measure their schools' progress. The State Department of Education also created a plan to recognize schools for their progress and achievements. Thus, California combines state-wide quality indicators with local quality indicators, and a recognition program for schools showing improvement or exhibiting exemplary achievement.[5]

Step 2: Survey of Curriculum Practices

To determine whether the school's existing curriculum stands up to the test of some of the basic principles of curriculum improvement, the curriculum practices survey form shown in Figure 5-1 will be useful.

School:_____
Subject or Grade:_____
Position:_____

Directions: Please give us your opinion of each of the statements below. Circle the number that indicates your general reaction and use the comment space for specific opinions. Thank you for your time and cooperation. Your name is not necessary.

Item	*Not Applicable*	*No Opinion*	*Definitely*	*Sometimes*	*Not at All*
1. There is a rationale for our present curriculum. Reason/Comment:	0	1	2	3	4
2. Our curriculum is evaluated regularly. Reason/Comment:	0	1	2	3	4
3. There is evidence of curriculum innovation and change in our school. Reason/Comment:	0	1	2	3	4
4. Our curriculum is designed to promote an interest in learning. Reason/Comment:	0	1	2	3	4
5. In general, the curriculum is based upon the content of the textbooks we use. Reason/Comment:	0	1	2	3	4
6. Administrators encourage teacher innovation and experimentation. Reason/Comment:	0	1	2	3	4

(cont.)

FIGURE 5-1
Survey of Curriculum Practices

Item	Not Applicable	No Opinion	Definitely	Sometimes	Not at All
7. In our school, most teachers feel they have to cover the material by the end of the year/semester. Reason/Comment:	0	1	2	3	4
8. Meetings to discuss the educational program are held regularly. Reason/Comment:	0	1	2	3	4
9. In most cases, teachers are encouraged to cooperatively plan for instruction. Reason/Comment:	0	1	2	3	4
10. In general, the curriculum is planned partly on the needs and interests of the students. Reason/Comment:	0	1	2	3	4
11. There is a flexible time schedule for the educational program. Reason/Comment:	0	1	2	3	4
12. Our educational program is based upon written instructional objectives. Reason/Comment:	0	1	2	3	4
13. There is evidence of teacher-pupil planning. Reason/Comment:	0	1	2	3	4
14. There is evidence that a variety of teaching methods are being used. Reason/Comment:	0	1	2	3	4
15. In general, our educational program promotes special talents of students. Reason/Comment:	0	1	2	3	4
16. In general, our educational program meets the individual needs of the students. Reason/Comment:	0	1	2	3	4
17. Our grouping procedures are based upon a sound educational rationale. Reason/Comment:	0	1	2	3	4
18. In most cases, instructional materials are selected according to the purposes of the program. Reason/Comment:	0	1	2	3	4

(cont.)

Item	Not Applicable	No Opinion	Definitely	Sometimes	Not at All
19. There is evidence that the curriculum is designed to promote the intellectual and social needs of students. Reason/Comment:	0	1	2	3	4
20. There is evidence that the curriculum is designed to promote physical and aesthetic needs of students. Reason/Comment:	0	1	2	3	4
21. The scope and sequence of the curriculum is a result of careful study. Reason/Comment:	0	1	2	3	4
22. There is evidence of curriculum articulation from kindergarten through grade twelve. Reason/Comment:	0	1	2	3	4
23. Teachers representing various levels meet regularly to discuss curriculum practices. Reason/Comment:	0	1	2	3	4
24. In our instructional program, most subjects are taught in isolation; that is, there is little effort to develop interrelationships. Reason/Comment:	0	1	2	3	4
25. Most teachers know what study habits and attitudes should result because of the educational program. Reason/Comment:	0	1	2	3	4
26. Most supporting services (library, guidance, remedial, etc.) help teachers and learners to achieve the objectives of the educational program. Reason/Comment:	0	1	2	3	4
27. Others (specific): Reason/Comment:	0	1	2	3	4

FIGURE 5-1 (*cont.*)

The purpose of the survey is to generate analysis and discussion about its results. For example, in using the scale with a school's faculty, one would ask for evidence regarding a rationale for the existing curriculum, innovation, and articulation (continuity for learning experiences from one grade to another). In another example, teachers usually have great difficulty specifying the needs and interests of students. In several cases, additional meetings and some in-service opportunities have been provided to meet this and another need, namely, examination of curriculum trends and innovations.

Some additional questions include:

1. Are the objectives/content/skills of the curriculum based on district and state goals, objectives, mandates?
2. Does the curriculum appear likely to contribute to the achievement of the objectives?
3. Is the curriculum (process and content) well planned, with concern for articulation, scope and sequence?
4. Is the curriculum clear and understandable to those who must implement it?
5. Is the curriculum designed in such a way that it can be reasonably evaluated?

Step 3: Survey of Student Needs

Taking into account that, like California, your state and school district has established specific curriculum requirements, it may be of value to compare the "mandates" to teachers' views of the needs of the students and to design content and processes to meet the needs that may be lacking in the current and/or mandated curriculum.

It is obvious that the educational program (curriculum) should be evaluated to determine the extent to which it is meeting the needs of students and of the community (and state). There may or may not be differences between the needs of students and the needs of society. Societal needs are usually reflected in educational legislation (and often based upon what some feel students need). The needs of students at a school site are no less important and should be evaluated periodically.

The scale shown on Figure 5-2 may be helpful. The scale requires teachers to judge the extent to which the current program meets the needs listed.

The result of steps one, two, and three is to help teachers identify areas of dissatisfaction, concern, and need for change in the existing curriculum. Some questions in this regard would be:

1. Have you and your teachers identified real problems or are they pseudo-problems?

School:_____ Grade or Subject:_____ Position:_____

Directions: Using the scale below, rate how you feel the educational program is meeting the needs of students. Thank you for your time and cooperation.

0—Does not apply   3—Program *sometimes* meets this need
1—Cannot judge; no opinion   4—Program *seldom* meets this need
2—Program *definitely* meets this need   5—Program *never* meets this need

1. Need for proficiency in basic skills	0	1	2	3	4	5
2. Need to recognize and appreciate people of all races, nationalities, and creeds	0	1	2	3	4	5
3. Need to be concerned about the welfare of others	0	1	2	3	4	5
4. Need to live and work cooperatively with others	0	1	2	3	4	5
5. Need to develop one's creative and critical thinking habits	0	1	2	3	4	5
6. Need to learn about one's environment	0	1	2	3	4	5
7. Need to learn about the interrelationship which exists in the environment	0	1	2	3	4	5
8. Need to use leisure time effectively	0	1	2	3	4	5
9. Need to find satisfaction and success in learning	0	1	2	3	4	5
10. Need for physical and mental health	0	1	2	3	4	5
11. Need to find affection and approval from adults and peers	0	1	2	3	4	5
12. Need to assume individual responsibility for behavior	0	1	2	3	4	5
13. Need to be independent	0	1	2	3	4	5
14. Need for a positive self-concept	0	1	2	3	4	5
15. Need to promote activities and/or musical talents	0	1	2	3	4	5
16. Need to learn at his or her own rate	0	1	2	3	4	5
17. Need to develop special interests and abilities	0	1	2	3	4	5
18. Need to understand and appreciate living in a democracy	0	1	2	3	4	5
19. Need to learn about various occupations	0	1	2	3	4	5
20. Need to learn about marriage and family life	0	1	2	3	4	5

Comments or reasons may be noted on the back of this sheet.

FIGURE 5-2
Scale for Evaluating the Curriculum: Student Needs

2. Are the areas of concern or dissatisfaction worthy of further study?
3. Do these areas of concern need further clarification?
4. Have you and the faculty defined the problems in writing for all to react to?
5. Is the dissatisfaction a concern of most of the faculty or a small part thereof?

Step 4: Objectives and Content Defined

As a result of dissatisfaction with all or part of the curriculum, this step requires that you and the teachers do one or all of the following:

- Write new objectives for a specific (new/old) program.
- Write additional objectives for a specific program.
- Modify existing objectives.
- Identify the content of the program.

Whether the objectives call for a modification, addition, or a completely new program, they should be defined to meet the guidelines implied in the following questions:

1. Are the objectives written in behavioral, operational, or other specific terms?
2. Do the objectives state the evidence that will be accepted to determine achievement?
3. Do the objectives include an acceptable minimal level of performance/achievement?
4. Do the objectives suggest methods of evaluation?
5. What content is necessary for the implementation of these objectives?

One of the major problems a principal or committee may encounter in this area is that the objectives do not exist, or, if they do, they are stated in terms that defy evaluation. Teachers may not be skilled in writing clearly defined objectives. One effective way to encourage teachers to write clearly defined, operational objectives is to have them examine their course-instructional objectives. One example that has proven to be of some value is shown in Figure 5-3. Using this instrument, you, your department chairperson, or a committee would assume responsibility for collecting course objectives from each teacher.

All questionnaires would be returned to the appropriate party, who would assume responsibility for analyzing and collating the objectives as follows:

1. The objectives should be analyzed to determine whether the objectives are well written.
   a. Does each objective tell about what the learner will be doing?
   b. Does the objective indicate the kind of performance expected of the learner?
   c. Does the objective tell how the learner will be evaluated?
2. The analysis should also show whether the objectives for one subject taught by several teachers at the same grade level are similar, or differ among teachers. To find this out, a committee or the teachers themselves can collate the objectives for each subject by listing all of the objectives that are common to most teachers in one column; and, in a second column, list the objectives that were not commonly stated by most teachers. In this way, teachers can note and maybe establish some priority objectives for the subject(s) they teach.

Once the objectives have been determined for each subject and for each grade, teachers (or the Curriculum Evaluation Committee) should attend

Directions: This survey is designed to determine the objectives for each subject matter area taught in this school. Please answer each question carefully. The information you provide will be of great value to the Subcommittee on Curriculum Evaluation.

1. School:_____ Grade(s):_____
2. Subject(s) that you currently teach:_____
3. Write the *major objectives* for each subject you teach.

Subject/Course	Objectives
A. _____	_____
	_____
	_____
	_____
B. _____	_____
	_____
	_____
	_____
C. _____	_____
	_____
	_____
	_____
D. _____	_____
	_____
	_____
	_____

FIGURE 5-3
Survey of Instructional Objectives

to the curriculum content. To better coordinate the curricula, principals and teachers have to know what the subject matter objectives are, what the content is, the extent of content overlap, and the content that may be missing for each subject and for each grade.

Sharon and Weldon Zenger offer a procedure that uses a "content coordination matrix," which requires teachers to (a) compare the topics they teach in a particular course with a standardized list representing a majority of public schools in America; (b) coordinate what is taught in one grade with what is taught in the next higher grade; and (c) compile a comprehensive matrix showing the final placements of content and skills for each grade level in all subjects. In this third phase of the process, teachers identify and list the content, critical skills, and topics (related directly to the objectives discussed above), and then on a scale from K-12 or K-6 (whatever the school organization) decide where these are "introduced" (formally presented for the first time), "developed" (stressed thoroughly), and "reviewed" (reviewed, reinforced or stressed lightly again). The process according to the authors highlights some unnecessary repetitions and some glaring omissions.[6]

Step 5: Program Design

As a result of the statement of objectives, a program should be created. You and the teachers must decide whether the program will be a new one and/or an addition or modification to the existing program. Answers to the following questions should serve as the foundation for each program:

1. Is the program based upon the objectives stated?
2. What learning experiences will best achieve these objectives?
3. Is the program developed in enough detail to insure that it will be implemented, if approved?
4. Does the program include learning experiences, activities, and opportunities that may make a difference?
5. Does the program identify needed financial and personnel resources?
6. Does the program include a list or description of alternatives?
7. Does the program include methods and procedures for ongoing evaluation?
8. Does the program include the knowledges, skills, and attitudes students will be learning?
9. Does the program consider problems of articulation, scope and sequence, and organizing experiences for teaching and learning?

Step 6: Controls and Constraints

You are well aware of "the best laid plans of mice and men." The realities of a situation are not something principals and teachers can ignore. Curriculum evaluation and improvement in individual schools and school districts require a realistic look at possible controls and constraints. It would be best for you and your teachers to examine the program with regard to the following possible control or constraint factors:

- Instructional time and scheduling
- Finances
- Facilities
- Administrative or board of education
- Political
- Parental
- Professional (Do the teachers have the expertise, training, skills to carry out the program?)
- Special interest groups
- Resources and personnel
- Other

Step 7: Alternatives—Projects

This step requires that you and the faculty identify and select possible alternatives. These alternatives should be ready when and if one or more of the constraints prohibits implementation of the entire program. It may also be helpful to have the alternatives accurately described so that one or more may be selected for a trial implementation. For example, rather than implement a school-based career education program, you and the faculty may wish to "test" components of the program in the different grades or subject matter areas for a period of time with appropriate evaluation strategies. Should the entire program be approved, then you can proceed to the next step of this cycle regarding program evaluation.

The alternatives selected are tried and tested by creating projects and pilot programs. The projects must be based on one or more objectives of the entire program. In other words, the projects are an attempt to arrive at promising solutions to curriculum improvement. The projects are selected as a result of the constraints placed upon the possibility of implementing the entire program.

Step 8: Project Evaluation

In essence, you want to find out to what extent the pilot program or your total program:

- Meets its objectives
- Is worthy of implementation
- Was evaluated objectively and selectively
- Should be modified.

The questions to be asked in this step of the cycle have been suggested as follows:

1. Do the results of the new program warrant incorporation into the existing program?
2. Are the results such that another test-run with some modification is warranted?
3. Are the results so bad that the program or goal ought to be dropped?"

Step 9: Implementation

After all of the questions have been answered in the first eight steps, program implementation requires:

- The encouragement, enthusiasm, and participation of all teachers in the new program
- The need for adequate inservice training programs

- An adequate financial commitment for materials, supplies, consultants, etc.
- Continued support and commitment by school administrators.

Some questions to guide you at this stage include:

1. Have you provided teachers with appropriate orientation and in-service opportunities for implementing the curriculum plan?
2. Is the budget for the curriculum plan sufficient for implementing the plan without "cutting corners"?
3. Have opportunities been provided teachers to practice using materials and techniques of the plan?
4. Are in-service sessions planned throughout the first year of the plan for evaluating and identifying problems, strengths, and weaknesses?

Step 10: Continuous Assessment

The instructional program implemented as a result of the evaluation and pilot program and projects needs ongoing evaluation. Thus, you and the faculty should be continually using the following questions as criteria for assessing each program offered in your school.

Criterion 1: Are the program objectives of your school based upon the district's goals and objectives?

Criterion 2: Are the program objectives written in clearly defined, operational terms?

Criterion 3: Are the courses in the program contributing to the achievement of school objectives?

Criterion 4: Are the personal and social needs, interests, talents, skills, and problems of all students being met by the curriculum?

Criterion 5: Does the curriculum reflect the needs of the local community and society at large?

Criterion 6: Does the curriculum provide for the development of student attitudes, values, skills, knowledge, and understanding?

Criterion 7: Are the curriculum materials and resources sufficient to meet teacher and student needs and interests?

Criterion 8: Are the curriculum materials appropriate for the programs offered and the objectives identified?

Criterion 9: Is there articulation of the subject matter and the objectives among grade levels (i.e., K-12 curriculum)?

Criterion 10: Is there an attempt to correlate/integrate skills, objectives, and content among the subjects (i.e., use of content in one subject to reinforce content in another subject; prevention of fragmentation, etc.) in the curriculum?

Littrell and Bailey recommend an eight-step model as a practical strategy for improving the curriculum. The eight steps include: (1) identification of school goals; (2) creation of subject goals; (3) creation of scope and sequence charts; (4) identification of competencies; (5) creation and compilation of curriculum guides; (6) identification of instructional objectives; (7) curriculum evaluation; and (8) curriculum revision.[8]

HOW TO EVALUATE AN EXISTING PROGRAM OR A NEW PROGRAM

Most of the principals and teachers I have worked with in curriculum matters seemed to be faced with two tasks: one is the task of evaluating and improving an existing program, the other is the task of creating new programs. For example, the school board in one district asked the superintendent to have the principal and teachers in a particular school evaluate its reading program. The reason for this was a report in the local newspaper about reading achievement test scores in all schools. This particular school recorded the lowest group mean scores when compared to the other schools in the district. Another school district is considering the implementation of a drug education program and asked one of its schools to develop and try out a program for possible implementation in all of the schools.

These two conditions, evaluating and changing existing programs and/or creating totally new programs, suggest that some pattern may be useful to teachers and principals.

The procedure that follows differs somewhat from the curriculum evaluation and improvement cycle discussed earlier because in this case the focus is on a program within the curriculum or a program that has not been incorporated into the total school curriculum as yet. The following overlay will guide you and the faculty toward program evaluation and improvement:

Step 1: Assess the Present Situation

Existing Program	*New Program*
1. What factors require that you and your teachers examine this program?	1. What factors are influencing the creation of the program?
2. In general, do you and your teachers feel there is a need for changing or revising this program?	2. Do you and your faculty feel there is a need for this program?
3. What evidence is there that this program needs examination?	3. What evidence is available to support the creation of this program?

Assessment

Existing Program		*New Program*

4. Who will do the evaluation?

_____

5. How will you organize the faculty for implementing this evaluation phase?

_____

6. When will the evaluation begin? End?

_____

7. What factors will you and the faculty want to assess?

_____

Existing Program		New Program
__knowledge __skills __other (specify:_____)	a. cognitive factors	__knowledge __skills __other (specify:_____)
__attitudes __opinions __interests __needs __self-concept __self-esteem __values __other	b. affective factors	__attitudes __opinions __interests __needs __self-concept __self-esteem __values __other

__decision making
__communication
__organization
__morale
__policies and
  procedures
__leadership
__teacher effectiveness
__quality of services
  provided teachers
  and learners
__class size
__attendance
__other (specify:_____)
	c. administrative
	  factors
		__decision making
		__communication
		__organization
		__morale
		__policies and
		  procedures
		__leadership
		__teacher effectiveness
		__quality of services
		  provided teachers
		  and learners
		__class size
		__attendance
		__other (specify:_____)

__school culture
__classroom climate
__quality of teacher-
  student relationships
__socioeconomic level
  of students' families
	d. environmental
	  factors
		__school culture
		__classroom climate
		__quality of teacher-
		  student relationships
		__socioeconomic level
		  of students' families

Existing Program

__occupation of
  parents
__kind and quality of
  neighborhood
__violence
__vandalism
__other (specify:___)

New Program

__occupation of
  parents
__kind and quality of
  neighborhood
__violence
__vandalism
__other (specify:___)

8. On the basis of the factors you and your
   faculty checked, who
   will be evaluated?
   Will you use sampling
   techniques?
   How will you deter-
   mine your sample?

9. On the basis of the factors you and your faculty selected and the sample identified, how will
   you assess the sample?
   surveys, polls
   questionnaires
   ability tests
   standardized
   achievement tests
   criterion-referenced
   tests
   anecdotal records
   observation of students
   in and out of class
   attendance, truancy,
   drop-out records
   vandalism records
   records of violence in
   school and community
   self-evaluation
   instruments
   self-concept
   instruments
   school climate scales
   leadership behavior
   scales

Existing Program		*New Program*

Existing Program		New Program
_____	case histories	_____
_____	rating scales	_____
_____	checklists	_____
	records of student	
	awards and per-	
_____	formances	_____
	records of student par-	
	ticipation in school and	
	community programs	
_____	and activities	_____
	motivation assessment	
_____	instruments	_____

10. On the basis of the evidence (data) you and your faculty have collected, what judgments can you make regarding the program?

_____   _____

11. What conclusion can you and your faculty draw from the evidence and judgments?

_____   _____

Step 2: Decide on Objectives

Existing Program	*New Program*

1. Using the results from Step 1, what revisions or modifications are recommended?
2. Have you and your teachers specified objectives based on the answer to the above question?
3. Are the objectives stated in operational, performance terms?
4. Are the objectives stated in a way that will help you when you have to evaluate the extent to which they have been achieved?

1. Using the results from Step 1, what is recommended?
2. Have you and your teachers specified objectives based on what was recommended above?
3. Are the objectives stated in operational, performance terms?
4. Are the objectives stated in a way that will help you when you have to evaluate the extent to which they have been achieved?

Step 3: Decide on Learning Experiences

Existing Program

1. What learning experiences in the existing program can be retained because they will contribute toward the achievement of the objectives?

2. What learning experiences would teachers have to revise? Delete? Add?

3. What subject matter content has to be revised, modified, dropped, added?

4. What classroom situations will give students the chance to express the behaviors implied in the objectives?

5. What classroom situations will give students the chance to express the behaviors implied in the objectives?

6. What out-of-school situations will give students the chance to express the behaviors implied in the objectives?

7. What situations, experiences, and activities will give students the opportunity to use and apply their knowledge, skills, and learnings?

New Program

1. What learning experiences will teachers have to develop that will contribute toward the achievement of the objectives?

2. What subject matter content will teachers have to develop that will contribute to the learning experiences of the students?

3. What skills will teachers have to identify that will contribute to the learning experiences of the students?

4. What classroom experiences will teachers create and implement that will help students express behaviors implied in the objectives?

5. What classroom experiences will teachers create and implement that will help students express behaviors implied in the objectives?

6. What other school experiences will teachers create and implement to give students a chance to express behaviors implied in the objectives?

7. What activities, experiences, and situations will give students the opportunity to use and apply their knowledge, skills, and learnings?

Step 4: Organize Experiences for Teaching and Learning

Although the ideal would be to organize the learning experiences in such a way that they contribute maximally to teaching, learning, and attaining the objectives, there are realities that cannot be ignored. For example, your school operates in an existing organizational plan imposed by the school system itself. The organizational pattern within your school may influence the way teachers have to organize learning experiences for students. A high school may operate on a departmentalized plan with traditional or modular scheduling patterns. Elementary and middle-junior high schools may be organized in a variety of ways: the traditional self-contained classroom, a departmentalized structure, a block-schedule plan, nongraded and/or continuous progress patterns, and open-classroom approaches with a traditional or nontraditional organization scheme.

Therefore, five central questions will help you and your teachers focus on ways to organize the learning experiences in your school.

1. What is the best way to organize the learning experiences?
2. What changes in our existing organization may be required?
3. Are these changes easily implemented? Realistic? Practical?
4. What can be accomplished within each department, each level (primary, etc.), each grade to organize learning experiences in such a way that we account for concerns about scope, sequence, repetition, reinforcement, articulation, etc.?
5. How will organizational changes affect teaching loads, class sizes, and materials and resources?

Maher and Mossip describe a management-oriented system for the evaluation of educational programs for gifted children that may be useful for evaluating other programs as well. The PARS program (Program Analysis and Review System) gathers evaluative information about a program for review by school decision-makers. The authors describe three sequential steps:

1. Program Specification: Gathering specific information about program clients and their needs, program goals, goal attainment indicators, program resources, program assumptions, and evaluation design.
2. Program Documentation: This step compares what is (program operation) to what was (that which was described in Step One). The program evaluator uses process evaluation methods comparing the written document with actual program operation.
3. Program Outcome Determination: This step answers the question, ''To what extent has the program reached its goals and satisfied the clients (met client needs)?'' in a comprehensive written report.[9]

PROGRAM EVALUATION PROFILE

Many principals have expressed concern about newspaper reporting of achievement tests scores, particularly in reading and mathematics. The current emphasis on achievement, literacy tests, minimal competency tests, and competency-based education programs may be contributing to a curriculum that emphasizes cognitive-achievement factors rather than maintaining a balance between these factors and affective-aesthetic factors.

School principals should continually provide their own reports to the public, one that shows the importance and value of all programs in the school curriculum.

School principals have asked for a plan, an "overlay" scheme, a procedure that they can share with their teachers that is applicable to all programs yet enables them to evaluate specific programs.

Two previous examples serve this purpose, but an additional example with emphasis on the content for a public report may be helpful. A profile for evaluating a specific program such as social studies, art, music, reading, or career education is outlined below.

Program Description

The content for this section of the profile includes a description of the school, its students, the community the school serves, the income range and occupations of parents, and other variables or descriptions that you feel would be valuable for readers to know as they read the profile report.

This section would also include the program to be evaluated or already evaluated and the grades in which the evaluation took place (i.e., seventh- and eighth-grade art program, or primary-grade reading programs, or social studies program for high school freshmen).

Program Objectives

The content of this section of the profile would include objectives for knowledge, skills, attitudes, understandings, and appreciations. It would be best that these objectives be stated in operational, student performance terms.

You and your faculty should establish the conditions of attaining the standards established for this program. In other words, attention should be given to the criteria against which the results from program evaluation will be compared. Thus, the faculty would consider the program as meeting the list of objectives if a certain percentage of students reach a certain level of performance or effectively demonstrate a particular skill. For example, a performance statement or standard might be: Seventy percent of the students in American History will have demonstrated some out-of-school political or community service activity. Or: Eighty percent of the students in the seventh- and eighth-grade mathematics programs will have scored above the national norms on achievement tests in both computation and reasoning.

Program Content

This section of the profile would include the content of the subject matter—the concepts, knowledge, etc., that students are to learn or should have learned. For many programs, this will be the table of contents of the texts used; for others, it will be the content described in the curriculum guide. The content to be included would be limited to the specific program and to objectives of the program.

Program Processes

This section would include the processes students learn—the attitudes, interests, skills. Some of the specific processes would include listening, note-taking, questioning, verifying, classifying, summarizing, deciding, solving, constructing, creating, performing, etc. Attitudes might include such factors as tolerance, respect, sensitivity to others, fairness, equality, sense of humor, and so on. The processes to be evaluated would be limited to the objectives of the program.

Program Evaluation

This section of the profile would include only those factors that you and your teachers want to evaluate. You may for one reason or another decide not to evaluate every objective of the program. But once you decide on what objectives will be evaluated, you should decide on how you are going to evaluate these and when the evaluation will take place. There are several evaluation designs you may consider. For example, you may plan an on-going evaluation: that is, certain factors will be evaluated throughout the implementation of the program and the results will be "tested" against the objectives and appropriate changes made. Or, you may wish to create a pre-post test situation (with or without control groups) whereby comparisons will be made (gain-score analysis) between pre-test results and post-test results. Or, you may decide to evaluate at the end of each school year (or every two years) and compare the results to the criteria or standards of performance selected by the faculty.

You and your teachers must then attend to the factors to be evaluated—the "what" of evaluation. Following a decision on what is to be evaluated, consideration must be given to who is to be evaluated. In the examples here, we are talking about student evaluation, but your objectives may call for parent evaluation, teacher evaluation, etc.

Evaluation Package

This section of the profile would include instruments needed to assess those factors that have to be evaluated in order to determine the extent to which the objectives have been accomplished. Included in the package would be a variety of instruments such as standardized achievement tests, objectives-referenced tests, criterion-referenced tests, observation scales, checklists, etc. The outline for this section would include each objective, factors to be evaluated for each objective, and the instruments needed or used for evaluating the factors for each objective.

Data Analysis

This section of the profile reports the data in summary form. But well before this section of the report is prepared, you and your faculty should have examined the data, decided how best to summarize them, and, most important, what it means in terms of student-teacher performance, program emphasis, alternatives, and changes. You and the faculty should discuss such questions as: What did we find? What do the data show us? What does it mean? What conclusions can we draw from the data? What recommendations appear likely? What alternatives should be considered? What additional questions should be asked? What factors should be discussed?

Program Report

This section of the profile deals with the public report. It will include program description, objectives, evaluation, and results. Who will prepare the report, how it will be prepared, and what will be reported are decisions to be made by you and your faculty. Besides a brief description, a statement of objectives, and evaluation procedures, the program report should include a summary of the results and what they mean. Also reported should be constraints and cautions when interpreting the data, and limitations of the evaluation. Included should be concerns of the faculty, future plans, role of parents and community, and alternative programs or changes being considered by you and the faculty.

The report should not be lengthy, and wherever possible data should be presented graphically. However, before the written report is distributed widely throughout the community or in cooperation with the publication of the report, meetings should be arranged with parent-teacher groups, groups of parents (PTA, etc.), and community groups. Discussions of the report and of the alternatives and their impact on personnel, finances, and resources would serve as the agenda for the meetings.

EVALUATING TEXTBOOKS

In most schools, textbooks are the curriculum. Textbooks seem to be the number one teaching tool. The standard among many teachers is to "cover the material" in the textbook. Given the fact that textbooks are the curriculum it is of great importance that tests and texts match, or to put it another way, that what is taught is tested. A study conducted by the Institute for Research on Teaching that focuses on fourth-grade mathematics textbooks and teachers' actual practice in the classroom found great diversity in what was taught and tested. Except for some basic concepts/content such as addition, subtraction, multiplication, division and geometry, texts and tests had little else in common. "There was a great deal of variation in the content matches between individual tests and texts. . . . It means that what fourth-grade mathematics is depends on whose classroom you're in and which textbook you use. It also means that individual standardized achievement tests may be a poor indicator of what students have really learned."[10]

Recently there has been much criticism leveled at the textbooks used in schools, ranging from their readability, to lack of intellectual content, to cost.[11] Whatever the criticism, in most classrooms, instruction includes the teacher, the students, and the textbook. Some teachers use supplemental materials, some do not. In any event, in this age of accountability, with much student testing and the public reporting of school test scores, it is imperative that there be a close match between what is taught, what is used for instruction (textbooks), and what is tested. For these reasons, it might be of interest to survey teachers regarding textbook use.

Although many of the questions in Figure 5-4 are applicable to use

---

Directions: Place a checkmark on the appropriate line. Please feel free to add any other comments on the bottom of this form.

	Yes	No	Not Applicable
1. Has the text contributed to helping you and the students attain the course objectives?	—	—	—
2. Does the content of the text cover all or most of the content of your course?	—	—	—
3. Does the text do the job you expected when you selected it?	—	—	—
4. Is the text a recent (within five years) copyright?	—	—	—
5. Is the text content up-to-date?	—	—	—
6. Does the content accurately portray minority groups?	—	—	—
7. Does the content accurately reflect ethnic cultures and life styles?	—	—	—
8. Is the content free of racist materials and connotations?	—	—	—
9. Is the content free of sexist materials and connotations?	—	—	—
10. Is there satisfactory development of concepts, generalizations, and relationships?	—	—	—
11. Are the concepts, generalizations, and relationships clearly and accurately presented?	—	—	—
12. Are the concepts, generalizations, and relationships developed from the concrete to the abstract when and where appropriate?	—	—	—
13. Do students find the text interesting to read?	—	—	—
14. Do most students find the text easy to read?	—	—	—
15. Does the text highlight new and difficult words in some way?	—	—	—

FIGURE 5-4
Teacher Survey of Textbooks

	Yes	No	*Not Applicable*
16. Are graphs and tables clearly illustrated and easy to read?	—	—	—
17. Are diagrams and scale drawings clearly illustrated and easy to read?	—	—	—
18. Does the text have a table of contents?	—	—	—
19. Does the text have an index?	—	—	—
20. Does each main idea begin each chapter or sub-section?	—	—	—
21. Are there chapter summaries?	—	—	—
22. Are summaries appropriately placed throughout the chapter?	—	—	—
23. Is each chapter summarized?	—	—	—
24. Does each chapter contain a review of the concepts, generalizations, and relationships?	—	—	—
25. Are motivating social or personal situations or issues used to introduce new ideas?	—	—	—
26. Are quotations or other authoritative sources used to highlight the concepts or content?	—	—	—
27. Does the text contain recommended readings for students?	—	—	—
28. Are end-of-the-chapter activities interesting and stimulating?	—	—	—
29. Do end-of-the-chapter activities require students to apply the concepts or content to other situations?	—	—	—
30. Do end-of-the-chapter activities emphasize creative problem solving?	—	—	—
31. Do end-of-the-chapter activities provide for the immediate practice of a skill?	—	—	—
32. Do end-of-the-chapter questions include several forms such as true-false, multiple choice, and essay?	—	—	—
33. Is the text attractive, colorful, and well-designed?	—	—	—
34. Is the type-size easy for students to read?	—	—	—
35. Does the text make use of center heads, side heads, and/or italics to help students in their reading?	—	—	—
36. Is the text binding strong enough to withstand student use over a number of years?	—	—	—
37. If a text contains controversial issues, are these presented objectively and accurately reflecting representative points of view?	—	—	—
38. Does the text provide material or examples of how the concepts or content is correlated with other subjects?	—	—	—
39. Are the directions in the text clear and complete?	—	—	—
40. Is the page-paper of the text of such quality that it will stand up to student use over a number of years?	—	—	—

when selecting a textbook, they are presented here as an example of an instrument that you and your teachers may use for evaluating the texts currently in use.

In addition to the textbooks, teachers should also evaluate the teacher's edition to each textbook series to determine how it helps in their teaching. Some questions worth answering with the teacher's edition in hand are:

1. Does it contain a reprint of the pages of the student's text?
2. Does it provide answers to all questions and problems?
3. Does it provide a bibliography?
4. Does it provide useful reading references for each chapter?
5. Does it include a list of films, filmstrips, tapes, recordings, and games?
6. Does it provide teaching ideas?
7. Does it provide lesson plan outlines and samples?
8. Does it provide an overview of the semester's or year's work?
9. Does it provide discussion questions?
10. Does it provide examples of overhead transparencies that can be made or purchased?
11. Does it provide actual or sample tests?
12. Are suggestions for student activities and projects provided for each chapter?
13. Do the tests in the text match the content to be taught?
14. Is the test format in the text familiar to students?
15. Does the content in the text match with state or district mandated tests and with standardized tests?

These kinds of questions help teachers pay greater attention to instruction—its objectives, content, material, and evaluation.

EVALUATING AVAILABILITY AND CONDITION OF INSTRUCTIONAL MATERIALS

Building principals must insure that teachers have appropriate materials for teaching and learning. The use of an annual checklist regarding the condition of existing supplies and equipment and the availability of these to teachers may be worthy of examination. To help you complete this task, two examples are provided. Figure 5-5 is a checklist to be used for assessing the condition of equipment and supplies. Figure 5-6 shows a sample form that may be used to find out whether teachers feel that the materials they have are adequate or not.

Directions to Teachers: Please evaluate the audio-visual equipment and supplies in the school by placing the appropriate number after the item and checking whether the item should be replaced or repaired. 1—excellent condition; 2—good condition; 3—poor condition; 4—do not have.

Item	*Replace*	*Repair*	*Comments*
1. Overhead projectors			
2. Filmstrip projectors			
3. 16 mm projectors			
4. Masterfax copier			
5. Mimeograph			
6. Tape recorders			
7. Phonographs			
8. Film screens			
9. Television sets			
10. Music equipment			
11. Maps			
12. Charts			
13. Other_____(Specify)			

14. Is there sufficient audio-visual materials in this school?
Yes__ No__ If no, please explain:

15. In what ways could audio-visual materials and equipment be more useful to you?

FIGURE 5-5
Audio-Visual Equipment and Supplies: Condition Form

CLASSROOM USE AND VALUE
OF INSTRUCTIONAL MATERIALS

Students learn from instructional materials just as they learn from teachers. A good book is still one of the most rewarding learning experiences. An effective film can be instructive as well as emotive. A good filmstrip can reinforce new ideas or concepts, or it can be used to introduce students to new learnings. A recording can effectively bring the sounds and voices of people from the past into the classroom. The point is that each classroom should be rich with materials for teaching and learning.

One of the tasks of principals, especially those faced with budgeting restrictions, is to periodically survey the faculty regarding the use and value of the instructional materials in their classrooms. Figure 5-7 shows a survey form that may be useful for this purpose.

After each teacher in your school completes the survey form, a discussion of the results is recommended. Many times, one discovers from

Directions: Please rate the instructional materials available to you and your students using the following scale: 1—adequate; 2—needs improving; 3—not adequate; 4—does not apply.

Comments

1. Library resources
2. Reference books (encyclopedias, etc.)
3. Textbooks in science
4. Textbooks in arithmetic
5. Textbooks in reading
6. Textbooks in social studies
7. Textbooks in_____(Specify)
8. Tradebooks
9. Paperbacks
10. Supplementary material (newspapers, magazines, etc.)
11. Programmed learning material
12. Science equipment and/or kits
13. Classroom supplies
14. Professional literature
15. Films
16. Filmstrips
17. Overhead transparencies
18. Records
19. Slides
20. Tape recordings
21. Pictures
22. Maps, charts
23. Dioramas, models, etc.
24. Other (Specify:_____)

FIGURE 5-6
Teacher Evaluation Form—Instructional Materials

the results of the survey that a sharing of materials prevents duplication and creates opportunities for purchasing needed or additional supplies and equipment. This procedure helps you practice the principle that those who use the material should have a voice in the selection of the materials.

STUDENT EVALUATION OF INSTRUCTIONAL MATERIALS

Are textbooks, workbooks, films, and the like used, selected, and purchased for the benefit of the teacher or the learner? In other words, are the textbooks that your teachers select purchased for them to teach from, or are they selected and purchased as a learner resource? You may say that

School:_____ Grade or subject:_____
Date:_____

Directions: We would like your opinion of the use and value of instructional materials provided by this school for this year only. Please check the appropriate space after careful thought.

Material	*Frequency of Use*					*Value*		
	Often	*Very Often*	*Some-times*	*Seldom*	*Never*	*Absolutely Necessary*	*Useful, Not Necessary*	*Could Do Without It*
1. Textbooks	___	___	___	___	___	___	___	___
2. Workbooks	___	___	___	___	___	___	___	___
3. Supplementary books	___	___	___	___	___	___	___	___
4. Reference books, encyclopedias	___	___	___	___	___	___	___	___
5. Duplicated materials	___	___	___	___	___	___	___	___
6. Newspapers and magazines	___	___	___	___	___	___	___	___
7. Models and mockups	___	___	___	___	___	___	___	___
8. Chalkboard materials	___	___	___	___	___	___	___	___
9. Drawing and construction materials	___	___	___	___	___	___	___	___
10. Television programs	___	___	___	___	___	___	___	___
11. Radio programs	___	___	___	___	___	___	___	___
12. Motion picture films (16mm)	___	___	___	___	___	___	___	___
13. 8mm film loops (single concept)	___	___	___	___	___	___	___	___
14. Overhead transparencies	___	___	___	___	___	___	___	___
15. Videotapes	___	___	___	___	___	___	___	___
16. Recordings	___	___	___	___	___	___	___	___
17. Programmed materials (self-instruction)	___	___	___	___	___	___	___	___
18. Picture, drawings, and paintings	___	___	___	___	___	___	___	___
19. Slides	___	___	___	___	___	___	___	___
20. Filmstrips	___	___	___	___	___	___	___	___
21. Maps, charts, graphs	___	___	___	___	___	___	___	___
22. Posters, cartoons	___	___	___	___	___	___	___	___
23. Others (Specify)	___	___	___	___	___	___	___	___

FIGURE 5-7
Survey of Use and Value of Instructional Materials

a textbook series in your school is purchased for the benefit of both the teacher and learner. Then answer this question: Do students in your school or district serve on selection committees, or, at the very least, have the opportunity to evaluate the instructional material they use? The point is that students' perceptions of the value or lack thereof of the materials used in class are worthy of examination regardless of what salespeople say about their product.

A teacher may find a textbook, film, or record to be very interesting and challenging from the teacher-training point of view, but if students in the class do not share this perception, then one could easily question the value of the instructional resource to the learner. There may be few opportunities to find this out beforehand. So, if it seems appropriate for students to be involved in the selection process, then their judgments of the material used in class should be sought. There are several reasons for both approaches. First, learners need to develop skills in discerning what kinds of resources will help solve specific kinds of problems. Second, practice in evaluating instructional materials will help students develop critical reading, viewing, and listening skills. Third, when learners have an opportunity to select and evaluate learning resources, they may take seriously the value of using instructional materials for independent learning of knowledge and skills. Fourth, the involvement of students in selecting and evaluating instructional materials may help teachers help students to read and study more effectively.

What instruments would help you and your teachers involve students in the evaluation of instructional materials? The first example is a checklist that teachers may use for student evaluation of a film, filmstrip, recording, or a television or radio program. The teacher would suggest that students write in the instructional resource being evaluated on the line above the list of questions and that each question should be answered with a "yes" or "no." The teacher should also recommend that students add any qualifying comments they wish after each question.

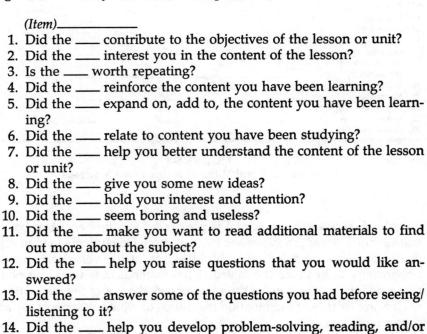

*(Item)*_____

1. Did the ___ contribute to the objectives of the lesson or unit?
2. Did the ___ interest you in the content of the lesson?
3. Is the ___ worth repeating?
4. Did the ___ reinforce the content you have been learning?
5. Did the ___ expand on, add to, the content you have been learning?
6. Did the ___ relate to content you have been studying?
7. Did the ___ help you better understand the content of the lesson or unit?
8. Did the ___ give you some new ideas?
9. Did the ___ hold your interest and attention?
10. Did the ___ seem boring and useless?
11. Did the ___ make you want to read additional materials to find out more about the subject?
12. Did the ___ help you raise questions that you would like answered?
13. Did the ___ answer some of the questions you had before seeing/listening to it?
14. Did the ___ help you develop problem-solving, reading, and/or study skills?
15. Did the ___ give you some ideas of projects you would like to work on?

A second example suggests two ways teachers can obtain students' perceptions of textbooks, workbooks, study sheets, and the like. Some questions teachers might ask:

1. What do you like about this textbook?
2. What do you dislike about this textbook?
3. What changes would you like made in this textbook?
4. Is this textbook too easy or too difficult for you to read?
5. Do you like to read the textbook? If not, why not?

Using these and other questions or a series of statements requiring the students' reactions should be of value to teachers. In the example that follows, students would be asked to indicate whether they strongly agree, agree, are neutral, disagree, or strongly disagree to the following statements.

1. In my opinion, this textbook is not worth using in class.
2. This textbook helps me learn.
3. This textbook encourages me to use other resources.
4. This textbook doesn't interest me at all.
5. This textbook stimulates me to explore other aspects of the subject.
6. This textbook helps answer some questions I had about the subject.
7. This textbook is one of the best I ever used in school.
8. This textbook is colorful, attractive, and has a variety of print and pictures.
9. This textbook has interesting things to do at the end of each chapter.
10. This textbook is one I would recommend to my friends.

A third example asks the students to check those words that tell how they feel about any instructional resource from worksheets to transparencies. One writes the item to be evaluated on the line and then checks the words that apply.

(Item) _____

____challenging	____too difficult
____stimulating	____terrible
____colorful	____successful
____thought-provoking	____boring
____too easy	____clear
____worthless	____readable
____important	____well organized
____demanding	____valuable
____interesting	____exciting
____asks good questions	____dull
	____profitable

These suggestions are recommended as ways of involving students in the evaluation of instructional materials. In the words of one social studies teacher, and as a summary of the major point of this section, "We spent thousands of dollars two years ago for textbooks that are too difficult for students to read, for films that are less than interesting, and for workbooks that even I wouldn't want to do. Obviously, something is wrong with the way we do things around here."

STUDENT PROGRESS AND
CURRICULUM PLANNING

One of the effective school indicators is the frequent monitoring of student progress. Student progress has been defined by many practitioners and most legislators as academic achievement—how well students do on state, district, or commercial standardized achievement tests.

Earlier in this chapter we discussed evaluating the curriculum to determine whether or not it helps focus on the needs of students. One of those needs, the "need for proficiency in basic skills," seems to be a priority need if newspaper reports on how well students are doing in school are accurate. There are nineteen other needs in the list (see Figure 5-2) and most might be of major importance (creative and critical thinking skills, multicultural understandings, civic and environmental knowledge, to name a few).

The point is that the current view of student progress, their ability to score well on achievement tests through the "proud" reporting of SAT scores is much too narrow an approach for curriculum planners and supervisors. The needs list in Figure 5-2 suggests that assessment of student progress be much broader. Academic achievement is influenced by variables that are on this list (satisfaction, interests, abilities) and factors that include student attitudes, behavior, home environment, school assessment, school support services and the like.

Planners must design the curriculum and the instructional program that "drives" the content, processes, and skills with a variety of individual, school, home and community factors in mind. They must continually remind parents, the public, and the press that academic achievement (students' scores on tests) does not occur in a vacuum. They must help school-site principals and teachers implement the school-district's curriculum guided by these questions:

1. What information is needed to monitor student progress with regard to the existing curriculum?
2. What assessment instruments are needed to get this information?
3. Once the information has been collected, how will it be used?
4. Based on the information, what curriculum changes need to be made?

5. Based on the information, what changes are required in the instructional program?
6. Based on the information, what changes are required in assessing and reporting student progress?

The current answer to this last question by many school districts is merely to report student test scores. But, as indicated earlier, this is too narrow a view because, as you well know, there is more to school life and learning than achievement test results. As I write this, there is a bill before the California legislature that would require school site administrators to let both the parents and the public know what is going on in their schools in addition to the students' test results. That is, every two years, at every school site, the report would tell parents and the public the conditions for learning, including class size, teaching loads, teachers assigned outside their areas of expertise, the quantity and quality of textbooks, counseling services for students, and teachers' assessment of the quality of school leadership. To see student progress in light of these and other factors—I would add number of latch-key pupils, pupils from single-parent families, socio-economic level of attendance area, number of children/families on welfare, assessment of home support for learning, etc.—would provide the public a portrait of the school, its school clientele, and their progress.

But even that is not enough. Just as one could present a school portrait, one could also create a student portfolio, which might include student test scores, samples of the student's work, self-assessment material, anecdotal notes from the teacher, homework assignment samples, absentee and tardy rate, pleasure reading checklist, and anything else teachers feel would give a parent a better sense of what and how well a student is progressing in his/her school life. To do this, teachers must have assessment skills that include designing teacher-made tests, interpreting standardized tests, developing mastery skills checklists, developing criterion-referenced tests, refining classroom observational skills, assessing student attitudes and beliefs, and developing individual student portfolios of progress.

In summary, curriculum planners and supervisors should use portraits of the school and each of its students to plan an effective curriculum, to improve the instructional program, to improve student performance, to provide for the special needs of students within resource limits, and to educate parents and the public that student test scores are only one criterion upon which to evaluate a school and a student.

A FINAL COMMENT

The research literature on effective schools emphasizes the need for a coordinated-articulated curriculum. To recap what was highlighted in this chapter regarding the need for a tightly coordinated curriculum, you are reminded that an effective curriculum is one that has:

- Clearly defined goals and objectives.
- Content, skills, attitudes that are clearly delineated.
- Subject matter that encompasses the above content and processes.
- Instructional materials that are matched to the goals, objectives, content, and skills.
- Instructional practices that "deliver" the above.
- Assessment instruments that "match" the curriculum.

Neither textbooks nor standardized tests should "drive" the curriculum. Yet, the reality of it is that in most school districts textbooks are the curriculum, covering material is the standard, and having students score well on tests is the goal. There should be more to a student's education than this.

NOTES

1. Ernest L. Boyer, *High School: A Report on Secondary Education in America* (New York: Harper & Row, 1983), p. 95.
2. "Network Schools Define What Students Need to Know," *ASCD Update* 25 (October, 1983).
3. Vincent A. Rodgers, "Curriculum Research and Evaluation," in *Fundamental Curriculum Decisions*, Fenwick W. English, ed., (Alexandria, VA: Association for Supervision and Curriculum Development, 1983), p. 146.
4. *Model Curriculum Standards: Grades Nine Through Twelve* (Sacramento, CA: State Department of Education, 1985).
5. *Performance Report for California Schools* (Sacramento, CA: State Department of Education, 1984).
6. Sharon K. and Weldon F. Zenger, "Straightening Out the Curriculum Tangle," *Principal* 63 (March 1984): 9–12.
7. William J. Gephart, "Who Will Engage in Curriculum Evaluation?" *Educational Leadership* 35 (January 1978): 256.
8. J. Harvey Littrell and Gerald L. Bailey, "Eight-Step Model Helps Systematic Curriculum Development," *Bulletin of the National Association of Secondary School Principals* 67 (September 1983): 2–9.
9. Charles A. Maher and Caroline E. Mossip, "An Evaluation System for Development and Improvement of Educational Programs for Gifted Children in the Public Schools," *Educational Technology* 24 (May 1984): 39–44.
10. "Do Tests and Textbooks Match?" *Communications Quarterly*, (East Lansing, MI: Michigan State University, The Institute for Research on Teaching) 7 (Spring 1985).
11. See *ASCD Update* 27 (September 1985) for a discussion of eight indictments of textbooks.

REFERENCES

Baum, Elizabeth, and Brady, Kirk P. "A Working Model for the External Audit of Instructional Programs." *Educational Leadership* 43 (February 1986): 80–81.
English, Fenwick, ed. *Fundamental Curriculum Decisions*. Alexandria, VA: Association for Supervision and Curriculum Development, 1983.

Felt, Marilyn. *Improving Our Schools: Thirty-Nine Studies That Inform Local Action.* Newton, MA: Educational Development Center, Inc., 1985.

Grisham, H. A. "Program Articulation." *The Effective School Report* 3 (October 1985): 5.

Guba, Egon. *Toward A Methodology of Naturalistic Inquiry in Educational Evaluation.* Los Angeles: UCLA, Center for the Study of Evaluation, 1978.

Horsley, Susan L., and Hergert, Leslie F. *An Action Guide To School Improvement.* Alexandria, VA: Association for Supervision and Curriculum Development, 1985.

Kimpston, Richard D.; Barber, Diane J.; and Rogers, Karen B. "The Program Audit." *Educational Leadership* 41 (May 1984): 50–58.

Molnar, Alex, ed. *Current Thought on Curriculum.* Alexandria, VA: Association for Supervision and Curriculum Development, 1985.

CHAPTER 6

Evaluating the Effectiveness
of the Student Activities Program

> At the core of every true talent there is an awareness of the difficulties inherent in any achievement, and the confidence that by persistence and patience something worthwhile will be realized.
>
> *Eric Hoffer*

A recent survey illustrates the value of the school's student activities program and its potential for fostering students' self-confidence and sense of citizenship.

In 1985, the National Federation of State High School Associations[1] polled 144 principals and nearly 7,000 students regarding extracurricular activities. Some findings from school principals showed that:

- 99 percent agreed that participation in such activities as sports, debate, drama, cheerleading, and music promotes good citizenship among students.
- 95 percent agreed that participation teaches lessons to students that cannot be learned in the regular classrooms.
- 72 percent said the extent of support for the school activities programs from parents in the community was strong.
- 51 percent said that low faculty interest in sponsoring school activities was a problem.
- 52 percent of the principals called for greater financial support.
- 92 percent said that less than 10% of the students were excluded from participation in activities because of expenses.
- 86 percent felt that the school activities programs helped enhance community support for the school.

- 95 percent believed that the activities program contributed to the development of "school spirit among students."
- 90 percent approved school policies that forbade students with low grades from participating in the activities program.

High school students surveyed revealed that:

- 69 percent believed that the activities program contributed to status and acceptance among the students.
- 53 percent disagreed with eliminating the practice of excluding students because of low grades.
- 59 percent indicated satisfaction with the variety of activities offered by their schools.

This survey was about the student activities program at the high school level. However, elementary and middle schools can and should have student activities programs as part of the total school program, including such activities as student government, athletics, clubs, bands, choruses, to name a few. For this and other reasons, the term *student activities programs* will include both levels of education unless otherwise indicated specifically or by the content of certain sections of this chapter.

The discussion in this chapter will focus on ways for school principals to evaluate existing programs with guidelines presented for organizing and administering such programs.

EVALUATING SCHOOL ACTIVITIES: SOME IDEAS

Elementary and secondary principals have responsibilities regarding the evaluation of the student activities program in their school. The student activities program is an important part of the total educational program of a school and as such deserves periodic evaluation based on the criteria of effectiveness. Effectiveness, in this sense, means that you as the school principal and your faculty evaluate in terms of:

- The goals of the student activities program
- The objectives of each activity within the program
- The academic requirements for student participation
- The opportunities offered to every student
- The kinds of learning experiences provided in each activity

- The number of participating students
- The attitude of students, teachers, and parents toward the program
- The budgetary considerations
- The limiting factors such as participation, space, interest, and supervision
- The per pupil expenditures, income, debts; expenditures of each activity
- The extent to which school personnel and the community work together to meet program goals.

Some questions you and others might ask concerning the student activities program in your school include:

1. Is the student activities program achieving its goals and objectives?
2. What are the rules for participation? Does your school have academic requirements for participation in each activity such as cheerleading, drama, sports?
3. Does the school have academic standards for student participation in service organizations, school publications, and intramural sports?
4. What are the opinions and attitudes of students and parents toward current activities in the program?
5. What are the opinions and attitudes of teachers and moderators toward the school activities programs?
6. What is the cost of operating the student activities program? The cost for each activity?
7. Is the money and time spent in student activities worth the results?
8. What activity is having problems, needs revision, or needs attention of the principal and faculty?

These and other questions can form part of an evaluation plan that may be implemented by an advisory council, or an in-school committee of teachers, students, and administrators, or by the principal.

Assessing Moderator and Student Views

Examples of questionnaires designed to obtain information from students and moderators are shown in Figures 6-1 and 6-2. While questionnaires of this type will provide information of value, one should be reminded of the equal value of observing each activity and making an analysis; of holding conferences with students in each activity; and of consulting with moderators individually and as a group to determine progress, strengths, weaknesses, needs, etc.

School:_____   Date:_____

Directions: Please answer each question in order to help us evaluate the effectiveness of the particular activity identified.

1. Name of organization:_____
2. Are you an ____officer ____member ____representative ____nonmember?
3. Purpose of organization as you know it:

4. Do you feel the organization ____achieves, ____partially achieves,
   ____does not achieve, its purpose or objectives?
5. If you are not a member, please indicate why:

6. If you are a member, do you attend ____all, ____most, ____some,
   ____none of the meetings?
7. Do you feel most members of the organization are ____very interested,
   ____very active, ____somewhat active, ____indifferent?
8. Do you feel the moderator of the organization is ____very interested,
   ____somewhat interested, ____indifferent to its success?
9. Do you feel that the organization's moderator and officers cooperate to serve the needs
   and interests of its members? ____Definitely ____Somewhat ____Not at all
10. What suggestions do you have for improving this organization?

FIGURE 6-1
Student Evaluation: School Activities

As many principals know, not all advisers/moderators want this responsibility, particularly after they have been teaching for several years. Nothing can detract from the effectiveness and value of an activity than to have an adviser who lacks the motivation and interest to guide and supervise students in the activity. Therefore, self-evaluation by an adviser would contribute to ways to improve the student activities program. Figure 6-3 shows a device that can be used for adviser self-evaluation.

EVALUATING SPECIFIC ACTIVITIES

The examples that follow illustrate ways you may use to evaluate specific activities such as the student council, school assemblies, school fairs, and school publications. It is not intended that each example be used alone;

Name:_____ Date:_____
Moderator of (organization):_____

1. Organization's Objectives:

2. Requirements for Membership:

3. Procedures for Selection of Officers:

4. Frequency of Meetings:_____
5. Number of Members:_____ Number of Active Members:_____
6. List the specific activities the organization has engaged in this year:
   a.

   b.

   c.

7. Do you feel the organization is achieving its objectives? Explain:

8. Identify difficulties you find moderating this organization.

9. How is the organization financed?

10. How is the money used?

11. Who keeps the financial records?

12. What suggestions can you offer for improving the organization?

FIGURE 6-2
Moderator Evaluation: School Activities

1. Am I interested in my activities assignment?_____
2. Do I attempt to inspire student interest in activities?_____
3. Do I believe that activities participation can be of great value?_____
4. Do I yield my "teacher" role to become a partner in the activity?_____
5. Do I provide ideas and leadership subtly?_____
6. Do I attend meetings regularly and arrive promptly?_____
7. Do I earn and keep the respect and confidence of the group?_____
8. Am I following administrative policy and decisions, and at the same time aiding students in understanding and respecting these decisions?_____
9. Do I maintain an adequate personality at neither extreme?_____
10. Do I keep a sense of humor and good nature at all times?_____
11. Do I exercise a good sense of relative values; stress only those things really important and valuable?_____
12. Do I give adequate preparation, time, and thought to my group's activities; keep aware of their progress and needs?_____
13. Do I try to expand my effectiveness in activities?_____
14. Do I try not to become discouraged easily, even if students do?_____
15. Do I ever consider when I might be wrong and admit it?_____
16. Do I have the courage to try something new?_____
17. Do I try to understand and observe regulations and procedures related to activities?_____
18. Do I evaluate activities constantly with a view toward change where the need is indicated?_____

FIGURE 6-3
Evaluation Sheet for Activity Adviser
James R. Marks, Emery Stoops, and Joyce King-Stoops, *Handbook of Educational Supervision: A Guide for the Practitioner* (Boston: Allyn and Bacon, 1971), pp. 493–494.

that is, evaluating each activity requires several methods (observation, checklists, conferences, etc.) and a plan to analyze the information, discuss results, and implement changes when necessary.

Student Council

The earlier we get children and young people involved in the government of the school, the quicker they will learn their rights and more importantly their responsibilities. They may even come to appreciate the problems and processes of decision making in a democracy and the role of principals and teachers in operating a school.

The degree of student involvement will vary according to the level of the school (elementary or secondary) and the age, skills, and talents of the student body. The process should begin in the lower elementary grades where children become involved in the governance of their classroom—cleanup work, attendance, distribution and collection of supplies and materials, classroom management, class officers (elected each month), hall monitors, etc. In upper elementary grades students can serve, via the election process, on the principal's advisory council, where they can be encouraged to make recommendations about policies, procedures, rules, regulations, assemblies, programs, projects, etc.

At the secondary level the process becomes more sophisticated but nevertheless as valuable in developing student leadership, student first-hand knowledge and experiences in representative democracy, as well as other goals resulting from student council participation. Again the council serves as a recommending body to the administration, electing its officers via democratic procedures, and planning and implementing programs, activities, and services.

Three groups should be involved in a periodic evaluation of the student council; again, the degree and extent of the evaluation will depend on the level of the school in which the council operates. The three groups include the student council itself, who should engage in a self-evaluation; the student body, the recipients and beneficiaries of the council's work; and the administration and faculty.

To assist each of these three groups in the evaluation process, the following rating scale is provided (Figure 6-4). The items have been categorized into two broad areas, student council organization and student council activities and services. One of the reasons for this is that although a student council may be well organized, they may not, for one reason or another, be delivering the services and activities expected by the student body and others. Other items can be added to meet the situations of a particular school.

This example and other evaluation methods should be used to answer such questions as: Are there ways to improve the student council? Does the student body understand and accept the purpose and function of the student council? Is the student council attaining the objectives established for it?

Assembly-Type Activities

School assemblies, once a popular activity, have declined for several reasons, particularly in large schools. Principals discovered that the behavior of students detracted from the value of assembly programs. Many schools did not have auditoriums that could house the entire student body. However, in small- and medium-sized high schools and in many elementary and middle schools assembly-type activities are still considered a worthwhile activity.

There is much to be said for assembly-type activities that bring the entire student body together or significant portions thereof. Many schools have assemblies for subgroups within the student body, such as all fresh-

Directions: Circle the number that best describes your feelings.

Student Council Organization

		Adequate/ Satisfactory		Inadequate/ Unsatisfactory	
1.	Student council objectives are compatible with the goals of the school's student activities program.	1	2	3	4	5
2.	Student council objectives are published in several school publications.	1	2	3	4	5
3.	Student council has a constitution and by-laws.	1	2	3	4	5
4.	Student council conducts its own elections and meetings.	1	2	3	4	5
5.	Student council uses democratic election procedures.	1	2	3	4	5
6.	Student council and moderator are left to decide procedures for electing officers.	1	2	3	4	5
7.	Student council understands its "limits" of responsibility as delegated by the principal.	1	2	3	4	5
8.	Student council moderator guides and supervises activities, meetings, services.	1	2	3	4	5
9.	Student council provides all students the opportunity to be elected.	1	2	3	4	5
10.	Student council members are elected by the entire student body.	1	2	3	4	5

Student Council Services/Activities

11.	Student council uses the committee structure to carry out its services and activities.	1	2	3	4	5
12.	Student council seeks and receives faculty and administrative support for its activities and services.	1	2	3	4	5
13.	Student council seeks and receives student body support for its activities and services.	1	2	3	4	5
14.	Student council has procedures for soliciting and solving real student problems.	1	2	3	4	5
15.	Student council involves itself with academic as well as nonacademic problems.	1	2	3	4	5
16.	Student council attends to problems of student behavior in school and at school functions.	1	2	3	4	5
17.	Student council attends to matters relating to school publications.	1	2	3	4	5
18.	Student council involves itself with nonacademic awards and honors.	1	2	3	4	5

FIGURE 6-4
Evaluation of Student Council

men, students in tenth and eleventh grade social studies, intermediate grades students, and the like.

Principals and teachers recognize the value of assembly-type activities as an expansion of knowledge and content of the regular curriculum, an opportunity to interest and motivate students, a chance to promote large audience behavior habits, and a method of promoting school spirit.

Several recommendations should be considered when organizing assembly-type activities:

1. Establish a student assembly committee; this can be a subcommittee of the student council but it should include both teachers and students.
2. Establish procedures that insure that assembly-type activities are properly planned, organized, directed, and evaluated.
3. Establish procedures that insure that teachers prepare students for the type of program to be presented.
4. Establish procedures that insure that most, if not all, assembly-type activities are planned well in advance and are listed in the school's activity calendar.
5. Establish procedures (and publish them in student handbooks) for student behavior in assemblies.

There are a variety of assembly-type activities worth considering:

1. Subject matter departments, particularly in high schools, should suggest programs to the assembly committee such as science programs, musical programs, and so on.
2. Films, motion pictures
3. Lectures, discussions by locally or nationally famous people
4. Demonstrations and exhibits
5. Debates, panel discussions, forums on a variety of problems and issues
6. Formal ceremonies—patriotic, awards, graduation
7. Student demonstrations, exhibits, and council activities
8. Rallies, "pep" assemblies
9. Dramatizations and musical groups and programs.

School assemblies provide an opportunity for the entire student body or large groups of students to come together for educational and recreational purposes. Thus, the evaluation of assembly activities is important and should be assigned to the Assembly Committee if you create one or by some other group, including yourself, if you don't use the Assembly Committee recommendation.

The checklist shown in Figure 6-5 can be used for assessing the organization and administration of assembly-type activities.

We Do	We Don't	We Should	
____	____	____	have an assembly committee.
____	____	____	have school assembly policies and procedures.
____	____	____	have an assembly calendar.
____	____	____	have students involved in assembly planning.
____	____	____	publicize the program before and after the assembly.
____	____	____	have a welcoming committee to greet guests.
____	____	____	have criteria for evaluating assembly programs.
____	____	____	have teachers discuss with students behavior rules for assembly programs.
____	____	____	keep records of each assembly program.
____	____	____	make an effort to start and finish the assembly program on time.
____	____	____	assign blocks of seats to each class.
____	____	____	have the program presided over by students.
____	____	____	have a fire drill exercise while the students are in the assembly program.
____	____	____	have a policy about student attendance at assemblies.

FIGURE 6-5
School Assemblies: A Checklist

School Fairs

One of the activities that can enrich the curriculum and encourage students to apply what they are learning in various subject matter areas is school fairs. Whether the activity is a total school activity, a departmental activity, or an activity confined to one or more classrooms, the objectives are the same:

- To develop a greater interest in the subject matter
- To balance subject matter learning with an opportunity for creative expression
- To develop a student's problem-solving skills through experimentation with various materials
- To promote community interest in the content students are learning at school by exhibiting the work of all students.

Fairs, then, should be evaluated in light of these four objectives. The questions in Figure 6-6 can serve as a checklist for evaluating fairs in your school.

Directions: Place a checkmark on the appropriate line.

	Outstanding	A Great Deal	Moderately	Very Little	Not at All
1. Did the project show that students understand principles of the subject matter?	—	—	—	—	—
2. Did the work with projects result in a clarification of classroom instruction?	—	—	—	—	—
3. Did students' interest in fair projects stimulate inquiry?	—	—	—	—	—
4. Did student-initiated learning result from the projects?	—	—	—	—	—
5. To what extent were students involved in the discovery process?	—	—	—	—	—
6. Were better students challenged?	—	—	—	—	—
7. Because of the fair did the teacher(s) discover unsuspected talent?	—	—	—	—	—
8. Did the exhibits give evidence of:					
a. mastery of skills?	—	—	—	—	—
b. neatness?	—	—	—	—	—
c. accuracy?	—	—	—	—	—
d. creativity?	—	—	—	—	—
9. Were the students able to explain their own projects satisfactorily?	—	—	—	—	—
10. Did students use instructional tools (scientific equipment, art materials, etc.) in a knowledgeable manner?	—	—	—	—	—
11. Did the projects reveal originality and creative thinking?	—	—	—	—	—
12. To what extent did students draw conclusions from their own observations?	—	—	—	—	—
13. To what degree did interest in the projects stimulate self-evaluation in the students?	—	—	—	—	—
14. How did parents respond in terms of attendance at the fair?	—	—	—	—	—
15. Did the fair create community interest beyond families who had students in the fair?	—	—	—	—	—
16. To what extent were the comments of visitors favorable?	—	—	—	—	—
17. Has the fair stimulated interest in other areas of school involvement?	—	—	—	—	—
18. Has it encouraged better parent-teacher cooperation?	—	—	—	—	—
19. Has the fair resulted in improving school-community relations?	—	—	—	—	—
20. What suggestions do you have for future school fairs?					

FIGURE 6-6
Checklist for Evaluating School Fairs

School Publications

Most schools, particularly those at the secondary level, provide opportunities for students to publish their own newspapers, yearbooks, and magazines. Student publications have been seen historically as methods for students to apply skills learned in the curriculum, as an opportunity to develop self-expression and creative writing abilities, and as a learning experience that benefits the individual student, the student body, and the school. These publications receive financial support from the school budget, student activities fees, advertising revenue, and/or community sponsorship.

The discussion in this section will be limited to the evaluation of school newspapers, not from a content point of view but from the principal's viewpoint—how his or her policies and procedures affect newspaper content and publication. A school newspaper is a valuable asset to both elementary and secondary schools. It provides a valuable learning experience for students, be they interested in editorializing, reporting, printing, or handling the business aspects of the newspaper. In addition, a school newspaper can serve as a focus for student ideas, opinions, and concerns; it can be the vehicle for reporting school events, announcements, and activities; it can entertain; it can interpret happenings; and it can promote and improve school-community relations. It can also damage school-community relations and be a major headache for the principal and faculty.

The turbulent sixties brought a new emphasis to the content of school newspapers. Rather than reflecting the content prescribed by administrators and teachers, student editors and reporters began reporting, editorializing, criticizing everything and everybody, and using words that were less than complimentary and often "profane" to say the least. From reporting student attitudes, opinions, and activities regarding sex and drugs to criticizing school personnel and programs, newspaper staffs across the country "discovered" the freedom of the press. And in most cases where the students have been challenged in the courts, the courts have responded to the dangers of censorship by ruling in favor of the students.

With these circumstances in mind, it would be to your benefit, as principal, to examine your procedures regarding the student newspaper. In addition, an evaluation of the publication every other year would be of value to you, the adviser, and the newspaper staff.

The following questions serve as a means of self-evaluating how you currently administer the student newspaper. Each question is a guideline that requires your attention.[2]

1. Has your school board adopted policies that define what school publications are?
2. Has your school board adopted policies that do not violate the First Amendment?
3. Do you have publication guidelines and procedures that reflect the policies of the school board?
4. Do your guidelines detail the rights and responsibilities of student editors and reporters?
5. Do students receive a copy of these rights and responsibilities before being assigned to a publication?

6. Do your journalism teachers, publication advisers, and students know the tenets and ethics of good journalism?
7. Do your guidelines state explicitly what the school expects from its publications?
8. Do you, the advisers, and students know the exceptions to the First Amendment protecting students' rights to publish material? (Example: libel, privacy, etc.)
9. Have you established a publications advisory committee?
10. Does this committee include students, advisers, teachers, parents, and others? (Example: local newspaper personnel, lawyer, etc.)
11. Are the responsibilities of the advisory committee described, in writing, for members and others?
12. Do the responsibilities include:
    a. recommending policies and procedures?
    b. mediating censorship disputes?
    c. reviewing articles and editorials before publications?
    d. evaluating and improving the newspapers?

Directions: Please help us publish a better school newspaper by giving us your views of the present newspaper. Place a check on the space that tells how you rate the item. Also take a few minutes to answer the questions. Your name is not necessary.

How would you rate the school
newspaper regarding:

	Excellent	*Good*	*Fair*	*Poor*
1. Overall	___	___	___	___
2. Style, format	___	___	___	___
3. Print	___	___	___	___
4. News coverage	___	___	___	___
5. Sports coverage	___	___	___	___
6. Coverage of social activities	___	___	___	___
7. Coverage of club, organization activities	___	___	___	___
8. Advertising used	___	___	___	___
9. Reviews	___	___	___	___
10. Editorials	___	___	___	___
11. Student columns	___	___	___	___
12. Other (specify)_____	___	___	___	___

13. What do you like best about our school newspaper?

14. What do you like least about our school newspaper?

15. What suggestions do you have for improving our school newspaper?

FIGURE 6-7
Student Newspaper Rating Scale

13. Are the qualifications for selecting students to serve on the newspaper explained in writing? (Example: minimum grade point average, years in school, interests, etc.)
14. Are the budgetary procedures recommended in chapter four applied to this activity?
15. Does the newspaper staff receive the necessary supplies and equipment to do their job effectively?
16. Are students able to work on preparing the newspaper during school hours?

It is obvious that these questions are applicable to other student publications besides the school newspaper. The student press should be, under your guidance, a compliment to the school curriculum and an enrichment to student learning, not a vehicle that creates complaints and controversy.

Should you, the faculty adviser, or student staff be interested in obtaining student views and perceptions of the school newspaper, two suggestions may be helpful. One procedure is to have the editors run a small blocked column asking "How Are We Doing?" Students respond to this question using a coupon under the question that requires a written response. A second way is to send out a questionnaire to students, teachers, parents, and others who receive the publication, soliciting their views, perceptions, and recommendations. Figure 6-7 shows a sample questionnaire.

EVALUATING THE ATHLETIC PROGRAM

There are two kinds of athletic programs offered in today's secondary schools: intramural and interschool sports. At the elementary level, the program is usually restricted (and properly so) to intramural sports. The quality of both programs is related to program objectives, program organization and administration, program activities, and program finances and facilities. The purpose in this section is to provide school principals with a framework for evaluating both the intramural and interschool athletic programs and the personnel responsible for each program.[3]

Many of the suggestions for evaluating the student activities program discussed in the previous sections of this chapter are applicable to the evaluation of the athletic program. For example, the role of the principal (supporting, supervising, organizing, staffing, scheduling, financing, and evaluating) remains critical to program effectiveness as does the principal's use of self-evaluation suggestions. Yet, both programs are highlighted for three reasons. One, participation in both is usually greater than in other activities and is increasing as girls are provided greater athletic opportunities. Two, there is a dramatic increase in adult interest and appreciation of physical activity (running, jogging, swimming) and dual sports (tennis, racquetball) which permeates the school's athletic program. Three, interschool sports remain the most costly yet publically supported extra-class activity. It contributes to school publicity, to school and community spirit, and to the needs, interests, and skills of its participants. Thus, the programs deserve the rigors and benefits occurring from periodic evaluation. The evaluation should be made in terms of its objectives, focuses, degree of student participation, school-community factors, and instruction-coaching. Its organizational factors include scheduling, health, and safety standards.

Objectives

The importance of establishing and evaluating a program in terms of its objectives cannot be over-emphasized. Therefore, the following questions about the objectives of the athletic program are worthy of your consideration and that of the personnel conducting the athletic program.

1. Is there a statement of objectives for the intramural and interschool athletic programs?
2. If so, is it in writing and does it "flow" from the school district's statements on goals and objectives? If not, why doesn't your school have a written set of objectives for the athletic program? Do you plan to do anything about this?
3. Are the objectives used by personnel to plan the program, the activities?
4. Are the objectives updated periodically to reflect changes in individuals and community needs and interests?
5. Are the objectives used by personnel to evaluate the program and activities?

There are many objectives proposed by a variety of individuals and associations. For principals who administer schools without athletic program objectives, or for those with objectives who would like to compare objectives, the following set of objectives are offered.

The objectives of the athletic program are to help *all* students:

- Learn skills that may contribute to wiser use of their leisure time
- Learn rules and regulations governing a variety of sports
- Learn sportsmanship and self-control
- Learn the pleasures and disappointments of competing against oneself or an opponent
- Learn the techniques and finesse required for exemplary performance in a particular sport
- Develop, to the best of their abilities, skills and talents in one or more sports

- Try activities that are not normally included in interschool competition or in physical education classes
- Develop positive attitudes toward recreational and competition sports
- Develop attitudes and interests toward physical and mental well-being
- Develop a positive attitude about themselves
- Develop a positive attitude toward school.

This list is not inclusive, but the point is that outcomes should reflect the knowledges, skills, and attitudes you and your staff wish to offer students in the athletic program. The emphasis is on all students, including the atypical students. The emphasis reflects an ideal since there are a variety of factors that will prevent all students from participating.

One suggestion for summarizing the degree to which the objectives have been attained is to prepare a scale that will enable you to compare results over a three-year period based upon evidence collected regarding each objective (Figure 6-8). Comparing third year assessments of each objective with the first year's evidence you can place a checkmark on the extent to which the objectives have been attained.

Two requirements are essential. First, you and the advisers/coaches should have, after examining the evidence collected during the first year, established criteria/standards/specific parameters for each objective. For example, you and your group may decide that efforts will be made during the next three years to increase student participation in intramural sports by 70 percent or by a specific number of students. Then you can translate the degree of attainment, based on the evidence collected, into "great" if you reached the objective, "moderate" if you came close, or "little" if the

	Intramurals			Interschool		
	Great	Moderate	Little	Great	Moderate	Little
Objective 1: Increased student participation	—	—	—	—	—	—
Objective 2: Worthy use of leisure time	—	—	—	—	—	—
Objective 3: Variety of activities	—	—	—	—	—	—
Objective 4: Sportmanship and self-control	—	—	—	—	—	—
Objective 5: Knowledge of rules and regulations	—	—	—	—	—	—
Objective 6: Competition	—	—	—	—	—	—
Objective 7: Application of learning	—	—	—	—	—	—
Objective 8: Attitude towards physical activity/sports	—	—	—	—	—	—
Objective 9: Well-being	—	—	—	—	—	—
Objective 10: Self-concept	—	—	—	—	—	—
Objective 11: Attitude towards school	—	—	—	—	—	—

FIGURE 6-8
Measurement Scale for Goal Attainment

Intramural Program

	Yes	No
1. The program is operated according to school board policies.	___	___
2. The program is governed by written policies.	___	___
3. The school board finances the program completely.	___	___
4. The program is governed by written rules and regulations.	___	___
5. All concerned parties have copies of or access to the written policies, rules, and regulations.	___	___
6. The program is governed by an advisory council of students, parents, and teachers.	___	___
7. The program is evaluated regularly in terms of its objectives.	___	___
8. Activities are selected according to the age, grade level, interests, and needs of students.	___	___
9. Activities are offered within financial and personnel limitations.	___	___
10. The administration and faculty recognize and appreciate the value of intramurals as part of the total school program.	___	___
11. Complete records are required for all activities, inspections, schedules, etc.	___	___
12. Activities are scheduled to make maximum use of facilities.	___	___
13. Activities are scheduled to accommodate as many students as possible.	___	___
14. Activities are supervised by competent personnel.	___	___
15. The health and safety of participants is a major concern.	___	___
16. Competent, trained officials are used to officiate intramural competition.	___	___
17. Every student who wishes to participate is able to do so.	___	___
18. Every student who does participate must complete a physical examination.	___	___
19. Athletic equipment and apparatus are inspected regularly.	___	___
20. Athletic facilities (showers, bleachers, etc.) are inspected regularly.	___	___
21. The program does not discriminate in its offerings or participation between boys and girls.	___	___
22. There is effective communication between the principal and intramural personnel.	___	___
23. An annual report is required of each activity adviser and/or director of the program.	___	___
24. The principal has scheduled regular supervisory visits to the activities.	___	___
25. Each activity adviser and/or director is provided a job description and salary statement.	___	___

(cont.)

FIGURE 6-9
Intramural/Interschool Checklist

Interschool Program

	Yes	No
1. All coaches and assistants are qualified to coach the assigned sport.	___	___
2. Coaches are required to be in attendance to supervise all practices and contests.	___	___
3. The program is evaluated regularly by coaches, athletic director, and principal.	___	___
4. On-call medical services are available at all contests/games.	___	___
5. Medical services are available at all contests/games.	___	___
6. Written parental permission is required for all participating students.	___	___
7. Girls' sports are provided the same resources, proportionately, as boys' sports.	___	___
8. Requirements for participation in a sport are in writing and available for those interested.	___	___
9. Practice and game schedules do not interfere with the regular school program.	___	___
10. Participants are not exempt from physical education classes.	___	___
11. No student—spectator or participant—is excluded from interschool contests/games because of financial reasons.	___	___
12. Official association contracts are used for scheduling contests/games.	___	___
13. Qualified officials are provided contracts for officiating games/contests.	___	___
14. Efforts are made to insure crowd control and sportsmanlike conduct at contests/games.	___	___
15. Association standards are used to evaluate programs and personnel.	___	___
16. Monies collected from this program are returned to the general school fund.	___	___
17. Coaches/directors are expected to file periodic reports regarding receipts and expenditures.	___	___
18. Internal audits are conducted annually.	___	___
19. Students participating in all sports are provided with proper equipment.	___	___
20. All participants are required to be properly insured.	___	___
21. State eligibility requirements are implemented for each sport.	___	___

FIGURE 6-9 (*cont.*)

participation increase was minimal. Second, as suggested, you need to use a variety of methods and instruments for obtaining the evidence.

Organization and Administration

As principal, you obviously delegate most of the organizational and administrative responsibilities to competent personnel such as the recreation director, athletic director, director of intramural activities, and/or activity advisers. Yet the delegation of these responsibilities is limited since, by the nature of your position, you must make decisions regarding the schedule, the finances, the facilities, and the supervision and evaluation of programs and personnel. How well you accomplish these responsibilities has a direct effect on whether the athletic program and its personnel will meet its objectives. Therefore, the evaluation checklist (Figure 6-9) is designed to help you assess the extent to which you meet the implied standards. Note that the standards in the checklist are examples and are not intended to be an exhaustive list of standards that include every detail for organizing and administering the athletic program. However, you can evaluate your athletic program using these standards. The list does not include many statements about evaluation of personnel because this topic will be discussed in the section that follows. Also, many of the intramural statements are applicable to the interschool athletic program and are not restated therein.

EVALUATING ATHLETIC PROGRAM PERSONNEL

Coaches, assistant coaches, intramural activities advisers, and other personnel responsible for carrying out the school's athletic program should be supervised and evaluated regularly. This can be done by the principal, the coaching staff, the school's athletic council, the athletic director, and/or the assistant principal. The use of self-evaluation and supervisor evaluation techniques (observation, etc.) and instruments should be utilized.

Criteria by which coaches and advisers could be evaluated would include such factors as organizational ability, administrative ability, on-field/court supervision and behavior, selecting and encouraging student participation, relationships with players and other students, relationships with administration and faculty, performance standards during practices and competitions, attitudes and support of other school programs, and relationships with professional associations, parents, and the public.

The literature presents many traits of successful coaches that are applicable to intramural advisers as well and that may be used as a basis for the evaluation. Included among these traits are:

- A knowledge of the sport—the basics, the changes, the innovations
- The ability to analyze and evaluate game situations and make appropriate decisions
- Demonstrated respect for his or her own and opponents' players and coaches
- A dedication to assignment and responsibilities
- Demonstrated honesty, integrity, sincerity
- An eagerness and enthusiasm for the sport(s) he or she coaches
- An enjoyment of and commitment to his or her work

- The ability to place winning and losing in the proper perspective
- The valuing of team and individual effort and discipline.[4]

These traits and some of the recommendations made for the evaluation of teachers and other personnel in the previous chapters may be useful for the evaluation of coaches and intramural advisers. Many schools use a combination of self-evaluation and supervision-evaluation techniques. Both techniques are recommended and illustrated here, but no technique should be used without pre- and post-conferences. Many districts require a pre-conference between the coach/adviser and the principal/designee to review the previous year's work and performance and to establish some objectives for the up-coming year. The use of checklists for self-evaluation and supervisor-evaluation remains the most popular method of evaluation. A self-evaluation instrument for use by coaches is shown in Figure 6-10. A self-evaluation instrument for use by intramural activity advisers is in-

---

Name:_____ Date:_____ School:_____

Directions: Circle the number that best describes how you rate your performance on the criteria listed. "1" is poor performance, "3" is average performance, and "5" is outstanding performance.

Part I

I rate my performance regarding _____ as:

1.	records and reports	1	2	3	4	5
2.	relationship with coaching staff	1	2	3	4	5
3.	relationship with players	1	2	3	4	5
4.	relationship with other players and coaches	1	2	3	4	5
5.	relationship with administration	1	2	3	4	5
6.	relationship with faculty/staff	1	2	3	4	5
7.	relationship with parents and public	1	2	3	4	5
8.	ability to coach the sport	1	2	3	4	5
9.	ability to be a leader	1	2	3	4	5
10.	cooperation/consideration	1	2	3	4	5
11.	acceptance of suggestions/criticisms	1	2	3	4	5
12.	effectiveness of practice sessions	1	2	3	4	5
13.	preparation of players for the game	1	2	3	4	5
14.	behavior at games	1	2	3	4	5
15.	sportsmanship	1	2	3	4	5
16.	financial responsibilities	1	2	3	4	5
17.	supervisory responsibilities	1	2	3	4	5
18.	motivational and teaching responsibilities	1	2	3	4	5
19.	other (specify)	1	2	3	4	5

FIGURE 6-10
Self-Evaluation Form for Coaches

Part II

Directions: Complete each of the following incomplete sentences.

1. In general, I think I am . . .

2. From my perceptions of my coaching staff, I think they would . . .

3. The community seems to . . .

4. It appears to me that the administration of this school . . .

5. The problem(s) with the athletic program at this school . . .

6. Some of my strengths are . . .

7. Some of my weaknesses are . . .

8. If I were to plan self-improvement objectives, I would include . . .

FIGURE 6-10 (*cont.*)

cluded in Figure 6-11. Frequency of use and the sharing of results of these instruments should be determined during the pre-conference.

Information from these instruments and observational methods can be useful in post-conferences with coaches and intramural advisers. Many school districts have coaches' evaluation forms; a composite of several is shown in Figure 6-12. With some modifications, the form can also be used to help you evaluate intramural advisers.

The evaluation form (Figure 6-12) enables the principal to develop a profile of her or his evaluation of a coach. This profile can be retained and then lines of a different color can be drawn at the next evaluation to help the principal and coach note changes. Additional items can be added under each category.

In addition to paper and pencil checklists, the use of audiotape and/ or videotape recordings of coaches' behaviors at practice and in game situations would be informative. If the purpose of coaches' evaluation is to change behavior, or to improve it if necessary, then it seems that they require the same scrutiny as classroom teachers. The use of audiotape and videotape recordings was suggested for classroom teachers and is rec-

Activity Advisor for:_____ Date:_____
Name:_____ School:_____

Directions: Please answer the following questions by making a check.

	Yes	No
1. Do you have a job description for this activity?	___	___
2. Are you paid extra for this activity?	___	___
3. If no, are you compensated in some other way?	___	___
4. Is this activity part of your regular teaching load?	___	___
5. Would you supervise this activity if you had a choice?	___	___
6. What self-improvements do you feel are necessary?		

7. How would you rate yourself on the following?

	Excellent	Good	Fair	Poor
a. Knowledge of the activity	___	___	___	___
b. Supervision of students	___	___	___	___
c. Performance in carrying out tasks in job description	___	___	___	___
d. Self-confidence	___	___	___	___
e. Training and experience	___	___	___	___
f. Willingness to spend the extra hours required	___	___	___	___
g. Interest and enthusiasm	___	___	___	___
h. Communication with administrative and athletic personnel	___	___	___	___
i. Relationship with students in your activity	___	___	___	___
j. Methods of stimulating student interest	___	___	___	___
k. Planning and scheduling activities	___	___	___	___
l. Other (specify)_____	___	___	___	___
m. Overall rating	___	___	___	___

FIGURE 6-11
Athletic Activity Adviser Self-Evaluation Form

ommended here. An analysis of the written checklists and of the tapes will provide excellent content for discussion, for planning behavior change, during post-conferences.

EVALUATING ACTIVITY ADVISERS

Every activity adviser in your school should have a job description. The purpose of a job description is that it lets each adviser know what is expected of each person. The job description serves as the basis for the eval-

| Coach's Name:_____ | Principal/Supervisor:_____ |
| Date:_____ | Activity/Sport:_____ |

Personal Qualities

		Poor		Average		Excellent
1. Character	0	25	50	75	100
2. Personal habits	0	25	50	75	100
3. Cooperative relationships	0	25	50	75	100
4. Appearance	0	25	50	75	100
5. Health	0	25	50	75	100
6. Enthusiasm	0	25	50	75	100
7. Communication	0	25	50	75	100

Professional Qualities

		Poor		Average		Excellent
8. Interest in coaching	0	25	50	75	100
9. Dedication to job	0	25	50	75	100
10. Willingness to work	0	25	50	75	100
11. Knowledge of sport she or he is coaching	0	25	50	75	100
12. Sets an example for students and others	0	25	50	75	100
13. Knowledge of physical training/conditioning	0	25	50	75	100
14. Attitude toward self-improvement	0	25	50	75	100
15. Attends association and clinic meetings	0	25	50	75	100
16. Motivates players	0	25	50	75	100
17. Takes the initiative to get things done	0	25	50	75	100
18. Administrative duties	0	25	50	75	100
19. Supervisory duties	0	25	50	75	100
20. Conduct during practice sessions	0	25	50	75	100
21. Conduct during games	0	25	50	75	100
22. Discipline—firm, fair, consistent	0	25	50	75	100
23. Concern for health and safety of players	0	25	50	75	100
24. Organization of staff	0	25	50	75	100
25. Instructional techniques, methods	0	25	50	75	100
26. Promotes teamwork, spirit	0	25	50	75	100
27. Delegates tasks to assistants	0	25	50	75	100
28. Sportsmanship	0	25	50	75	100
29. Care and responsibility for supplies and equipment	0	25	50	75	100
30. Scheduling of practices, games	0	25	50	75	100

Comments:

| Principal's/Supervisor's Signature:_____ | Date:_____ |
| Coach's Signature:_____ | Date:_____ |

FIGURE 6-12
Coaches' Evaluation Form

uation. It makes clear to both you and the adviser what expectations, tasks, and responsibilities will serve as the basis for the evaluation. The result should lead to less misunderstanding, fewer disagreements about what should and what should not be evaluated, and a greater potential for improvement of performance. The job description you provide each adviser should include, at minimum, the following information:

- The title of the position
- The person to whom the adviser reports
- A "mission" statement or the school district's goals for including the activity in its program
- The objectives for the activity in your school's program
- Your school's policies and procedures regarding the organization and administration of the activity
- A specific list of the adviser's task and responsibilities which may include: (1) financial, (2) supervision, (3) organization, (4) reports and records, (5) active membership lists, (6) handbook preparation, and (7) publicity
- Criteria for the evaluation—agreed upon by you and the adviser
- Evaluation procedures including checklists, observations, and conferences
- Annual report about the activity, its evaluation, and recommendations.

Rather than provide you with another evaluation form, the list of sample items that follow can be used as part of an evaluation checklist you and the adviser design. Items should be selected on the basis of the kind of activity and the job description you develop.

1. ____ This adviser demonstrates respect for students, teachers, and others involved in the activity.
2. ____ This adviser assumes responsibility for his or her own conduct.
3. ____ This adviser assumes responsibility for using democratic procedures in the organization and administration of the activity.
4. ____ This adviser demonstrates a respect for excellence in organizing and administering the activity.
5. ____ This adviser adequately interprets the activity to others when the occasion demands.
6. ____ This adviser accepts constructive criticism and willingly attempts to make changes.
7. ____ This adviser accepts recognition graciously and shares it with the students in the activity.
8. ____ This adviser has a minimum number of absences because of illness.

9. ____ This adviser is calm and mature in reacting to situations concerning the activity.

10. ____ This adviser actively participates in professional in-service and other programs to improve knowledge and skills in this activity.

11. ____ This adviser effectively leads students in the governance of activity business.

12. ____ This adviser devotes the time necessary to administer this activity.

13. ____ This adviser stimulates student interest in the activity.

14. ____ This adviser is rated highly by students in the activity.

15. ____ This adviser supervises students in all aspects of the activity.

16. ____ This adviser cooperates with the administration and faculty in administering this activity.

17. ____ This adviser demonstrates interest and enthusiasm in the activity.

18. ____ This adviser communicates effectively with students in the activity.

19. ____ This adviser has a positive attitude toward self-improvement.

20. ____ This adviser demonstrates confidence in students' abilities to carry out responsibilities in this activity.

21. ____ This adviser has positive, personal characteristics (sense of humor, respectful, patience, good natured, etc.)

22. ____ This adviser effectively implements administrative policies and decisions.

23. ____ This adviser demonstrates an awareness of needs and interests of students in this activity.

24. ____ This adviser evaluates activity progress, plans, and procedures regularly.

25. ____ This adviser shares evaluation results with students, faculty, and administration.

26. ____ This adviser is not easily discouraged.

27. ____ This adviser requires students to meet high standards of work in this activity.

28. ____ This adviser engages in effective short- and long-range planning.

29. ____ This adviser effectively updates the activity handbook.

30. ____ This adviser willingly tries out new ideas for the activity.

31. ____ This adviser listens to the opinions and suggestions of others.

32. ____ This adviser has made this activity a valuable part of the students' total school program.

33. ____ This adviser demonstrates that students know and understand their rights, responsibilities, and limitations.

34. ____ This adviser respects the rights and confidences of students in the activity.

35. ____ This adviser attends all activity meetings regularly and promptly.

36. ____ This adviser demonstrates ability to lead students toward attaining activity objectives.

37. ____ This adviser evaluates with the intent to improve.

38. ____ This adviser has been a major factor for increasing student participation in the activity.
39. ____ This adviser demonstrates skill in developing the talents of students.
40. ____ This adviser meets administrative deadlines promptly.
41. ____ This adviser files a complete and comprehensive annual report.

A FINAL COMMENT

An effective and comprehensive student activities program should contribute to the accomplishment of some of the school's objectives. In addition, it should help enhance the academic program and contribute to school spirit and morale. There are few out-of-the classroom activities that provide students with leadership opportunities, chances to practice citizenship and sportsmanship skills, ways to develop self-discipline and team-play, and opportunities to develop life-long sport and leisure time activities as does the student activities program.

Having said this, one must recognize the current dilemma principals face because of the state and/or district mandated academic standards (usually a minimum grade point average of "C") established as a condition for student participation in selected activities. In most cases, the minimum standard is applicable only to participation in interscholastic sports. In some cases, this standard has been applied to cheerleading and student government. But in any case, the principal must apply the standards and urge faculty and parents to assist students who have difficulty meeting the standards but who have the desire and talent to participate in these activities.

The school principal should continuously examine the student activities program in relation to the school's objectives. He should look for leaders (coaches, advisers) of each activity who are well trained, competent, willing to do the work and spend the time required, and who are interested and enthusiastic about the activity. Program quality will be directly related to the quality of instruction and supervision provided by student activity personnel.

The leadership in each school must help faculty, students, and parents maintain a proper perspective between the student activities program and the instructional program, between interschool (where a few participate) and intramural (where many participate), and between the cost of each event and its worth to students.

NOTES

1. Information of this survey can be obtained by writing Boise Durbin, National Federation of State High School Association, 11724 Plaza Circle, P.O. Box 20626, Kansas City, MO 64195.

2. The first eight questions are based on two articles by M. Chester Nolte, "School Board vs. The Student Press," *American School Board Journal* 165 (February 1978): 23–25; and "The Student Press and the Ways You Can Control It," *American School Board Journal* 165 (March 1978): 35–36.

3. To compare your student activities program to a recommended model, see James A. Vornberg et al., "A Model for Organizing Your School's Activities Program," *Bulletin of the National Association of Secondary School Principals* 67 (October 1983): 86–90.

4. Matthew C. Resnick and Carl E. Erickson, *Intercollegiate And Interscholastic Athletics for Men and Women* (Reading, MA: Addison-Wesley, 1975), pp. 243–244.

REFERENCES

Firth, G. H., and Clark, R. "Extracurricular Activities: Academic Incentives on Nonessential Functions?" *Clearinghouse* 57 (March 1984) 325–327.

Hoover, Kenneth H. *A Sourcebook of Student Activities: Techniques for Improving Instruction.* Boston: Allyn and Bacon, 1981.

Sybouts, Ward, and Krepel, Wayne J. *Student Activities in the Secondary School: A Handbook and Guide.* Wesport, CT: Greenwood Press, 1984.

CHAPTER 7

Evaluating the Effectiveness of Pupil Personnel Services and Personnel

> What is crucial is that we agree on the need to respect and enhance the uniqueness of each of our charges, to reinforce his often fragile sense of worth, and to strengthen his ability to function in his own best interests, as well as in the best interests of society.
>
> *Bruno Bettelheim*

There is little research to support this statement, but common sense suggests that effective schools (defined here to mean more than just student achievement) provide effective and efficient counseling and guidance services, social and psychological services, and health services to students. A principal's roles and responsibilities for organizing, administering, and supervising pupil personnel services and staff will vary in direct proportion to the number of students and teachers, the kinds and extent of existing services, and the availability of administrative assistance (i.e., a director of pupil personnel services). But size does not detract from the principal's responsibility to see to it that the program is one of quality and that personnel effectively provide services approved by the school board.

ORGANIZING FOR EVALUATION

In Chapter 1, a plan for organizing personnel for evaluating programs, projects, etc., was described. Two specific procedures for organizing the personnel in your school for determining the needs, effectiveness, and resources of the pupil personnel programs and services are outlined here.

Charles Maher[1] suggests a "Program Evaluation Team" of five members: (1) the director of special services, (2) a special education teacher, (3) a regular teacher, (4) a support specialist, and (5) a school administrator. The team uses a five-phase plan approach for assessing services: (1) identifying evaluation information needs, (2) designing program evaluation services, (3) implementing the services, (4) disseminating evaluation information, and (5) evaluating the team's operating procedures.

A second strategy suggests that you appoint a PPS (Pupil Personnel Services) Committee. Committee membership should include teachers, parents, students (if a high school), and pupil personnel staff. The number of members of the committee depends upon the number of faculty and personnel staff and the school's student enrollment. Nine committee members should be the limit, however. Subcommittees can be appointed if the work load appears burdensome. The charge of the committee should be to assess the pupil personnel program and services using the following framework:

Program Goals/Objectives.   Specific statements, in measurable terms if possible, should be identified as an indication of what the program intends to accomplish. In other words, each program within the school's total pupil personnel offerings should have clearly defined statements of goals and objectives. The committee's task, should these not exist, is to work on obtaining program goals and objectives from pupil personnel staff.

Program and Personnel Evaluation.   There are several guidelines that the committee should consider when developing plans for the evaluation of pupil personnel programs and its personnel:

1. The evaluation should be made in terms of the stated goals and objectives.
2. The evaluation instruments selected should be valid and reliable.
3. The evaluative procedures should involve those who are working with the program on a daily basis and who have a firsthand knowledge of how the program operates.
4. The evaluation should be planned, ongoing, and provide an annual review of progress and problems.
5. The evaluation plan may include one or more of the following methods:
   a. Discrepancy methods. Once standards, goals, and/or objectives are established for the entire program or each service within the program, standards are used to assess actual performance in terms of design, installation, personnel, programs, and cost. In other words, the committee sets out to find out how well the program and personnel are doing what they set out to do—the application of the standards to actual performance.

b. Before and after methods. Once the goals and objectives are identified, the committee may wish to find out how effective a certain program is (such as work-study program) in relation to its objectives—the reasons for establishing such a program. Assuming that the work-study program did not previously exist, the committee can measure certain factors before and after the program (end of the first year), such as the number of participants, the attitudes of participants toward the program, the attitudes of employers toward the program, the skills students learned, and other factors relating to the objectives of the program. During the second year of the program, evaluation data can be compared to the data collected before the program began and to data collected at the end of the first year with the intent toward program improvement.

c. Comparison methods. Once the goals and objectives are identified, the committee may wish to compare one group of students in a program with another group of students not in the program; or they can make comparisons against some existing norms; or they may wish to compare programs and services in their school to schools of similar size, locations, etc.

Feedback and Follow-Through. The committee must use the evaluative data. To collect data and not use it for program and personnel improvement is a waste of time and energy. Personnel involved in pupil personnel programs should be given the data and the results to help them in decision making, program planning and development, and continuous evaluation planning. To paraphrase a famous quotation, "evaluative data keeps no better than fish." It must be used to provide feedback to those who are responsible for program development and implementation.

A CHECKLIST FOR THE EVALUATION
OF SERVICES

As you and others examine and evaluate the pupil personnel services offered in your school, it may be helpful to assess all services in relation to specific questions. In the checklist that follows (Figure 7-1), questions are provided to assess counseling and guidance serices, social and psychological services, and health and welfare services. This checklist may be given to the committee or to members providing each service to be used as a self-evaluation instrument. Specific questions should be added by your pupil personnel staff under each major category to reflect indicators peculiar to the school's programs and services.

Directions: Circle the number that represents your feelings. The scale ranges from 5 (yes, definitely) to 0 (no, not at all).

A. Are Services Comprehensive?

   1. Do the programs include counseling and guidance services, social and psychological services, health and welfare services? 5 4 3 2 1 0
   2. Are the objectives for each service stated in writing? 5 4 3 2 1 0
   3. Is the budget adequate to support each service? 5 4 3 2 1 0
   4. Do the services attempt to help teachers work with students of differing abilities, talents, needs, and problems? 5 4 3 2 1 0
   5. Do the services include opportunities for individual, small-group, and large-group counseling? 5 4 3 2 1 0
   6. Do the services provide students and others with educational, vocational, and other appropriate information? 5 4 3 2 1 0
   7. Do the services provide studies (descriptive, experimental, longitudinal, short-term) of school clientele? 5 4 3 2 1 0

B. Are Services Accessible?

   1. Are services available to all students in the school? 5 4 3 2 1 0
   2. Are services offered by appointment only? 5 4 3 2 1 0
   3. Are services available without an appointment? 5 4 3 2 1 0
   4. Can students, parents, and teachers review records and reports with a minimum of "red-tape"? 5 4 3 2 1 0
   5. Do physical facilities promote the accessibility and use of the services? 5 4 3 2 1 0
   6. Are services available to parents and teachers at times convenient to them? 5 4 3 2 1 0
   7. Can students visit service centers/areas unannounced and use information or seek consultation? 5 4 3 2 1 0
   8. Are students informed about their assessment/evaluative data and encouraged to ask questions and discuss results? 5 4 3 2 1 0

C. Are Services Coordinated?

   1. Do personnel in each service meet regularly to coordinate activities? 5 4 3 2 1 0
   2. Is the organization and administration of the services such that they contribute to program effectiveness and efficiency? 5 4 3 2 1 0
   3. Are classroom teachers provided opportunities to become actively involved in services provided students? 5 4 3 2 1 0
   4. Are written policies concerning procedures, responsibilities, referrals, etc., available for each service? 5 4 3 2 1 0
   5. Are student records comprehensive, reliable, and coordinated among the services? 5 4 3 2 1 0
   6. Are duplicative and repetitive data, record collection, and storage minimized? 5 4 3 2 1 0
   7. Do all services insure confidentiality of student records and reports? 5 4 3 2 1 0

FIGURE 7-1
Evaluation of Services

D. Are Services Continuous?

1. Is the budget adequate to support each service each year?   5 4 3 2 1 0
2. Are there sufficient supplies and equipment for continuous delivery of each service?   5 4 3 2 1 0
3. Do service personnel meet with teachers and administrators regularly to inform them of students with special needs, problems, etc.?   5 4 3 2 1 0
4. Are records and reports maintained in a way that is easily retrievable and accessible?   5 4 3 2 1 0
5. Are student records and reports regularly reviewed for planning assistance to students?   5 4 3 2 1 0

E. Are Services Evaluated?

1. Are committees formed to evaluate each service?   5 4 3 2 1 0
2. Are services evaluated annually?   5 4 3 2 1 0
3. Are service personnel evaluated annually?   5 4 3 2 1 0
4. Is each service required to file an annual report?   5 4 3 2 1 0
5. Are evaluative data used by each service area to plan improvements?   5 4 3 2 1 0
6. Are evaluation plans developed from the objectives of each program?   5 4 3 2 1 0

F. Are Services Personnel Qualified?

1. Is leadership provided by personnel in each service?   5 4 3 2 1 0
2. Are personnel in each service certified to carry out their tasks?   5 4 3 2 1 0
3. Do personnel engage in activities to update their skills?   5 4 3 2 1 0
4. Is there evidence of staff activity in continuing their education?   5 4 3 2 1 0
5. Do personnel demonstrate skill and talent in carrying out their tasks?   5 4 3 2 1 0

A DISCREPANCY EVALUATION PLAN

As the school's principal you might find it valuable to have the PPS Committee use the discrepancy methods suggested earlier as one additional way to evaluate pupil personnel services. One interesting model was designed by a task force for the Illinois State Board of Education. It is outlined here for your and the committee's review. The task force began by defining an exemplary pupil personnel services program:

An examplary pupil personnel services (PPS) program is an integral comprehensive component of a total education program delivered through the effective teaming efforts of school guidance counselors, school nurses, school social workers, and school psychologists. The program assists all students to achieve their maximum potential through services aimed at their physical, emotional, personal, social, educational, and career goals. This assistance is accomplished directly through services to students and indirectly by helping staff, parents, and other persons in the community provide optimal teaching and learning conditions for students.[2]

Using this definition as the guide, the task force then went on to describe these criteria for exemplary programs:

Accessibility: The program is accessible to all students, parents, staff, and community members.

Board Commitment: School Board commitment is evidenced by board policies, the organizational structure, and fiscal allocations.

Communication: Communication is planned and enlists public support for pupil personnel services programs.

Community Outreach: Coordination of services with community agencies is demonstrated.

Dissemination: The district personnel are willing to share program ideas with others.

Establishment: The pupil personnel services program has a historical foundation upon which it is based.

Evaluation: Evaluation is a continuous process throughout the planning, structuring, and implementation of the program.

Four Disciplines: School nurses, school psychologists, school social workers, and school guidance counselors are key participants in the program delivery system.

Goals, Objectives, Activities: The pupil personnel services program has written goals, objectives, and activities which are revised, at a minimum, on an annual basis.

Needs Assessment: Pupil personnel services are determined from a comprehensive needs assessment process.

Ratios: Sufficient staff are available (due to their student/professional staff ratios) to provide and insure a full continuum of pupil personnel services.

State-Certification: School nurses, school psychologists, school social workers, and school guidance counselors are state-certified.

Student Needs: The pupil personnel services program assists students to achieve their career, social, physical, emotional and educational goals.

Teaming: The school nurse, school psychologist, school social worker, and school guidance counselor meet on a regular basis to analyze the problems of students.

Training: The pupil personnel services program provides staff development activities for pupil personnel services professionals and allows pupil personnel services professionals to provide staff development for others and share their resources with others.[3]

EVALUATING SCHOOL COUNSELORS

A national survey of 112 of the largest public school districts in this country seeking information about career guidance and counseling services in urban schools revealed that they: (1) are not properly funded, (2) lack resources, (3) need to develop models to improve services, (4) are pressured to add more duties despite staff shortages, (6) need inservice training and skill development, and (7) need to improve communication skills with faculty and the community.[4]

The results of this survey clearly suggest that any evaluation of counseling personnel needs to occur within the parameters of expectations, responsibilities, and resources. At the district level, this is the responsibility of the school board, the superintendent, and the director of special services or guidance services. At the school site level, the responsibility is yours in cooperation with the guidance and counseling personnel working at the school.

A counselor evaluation program should focus on performance, services, and relationship. It might be organized as follows:

- Performance objectives are established for the school year.
- Criteria for evaluating these objectives are described in writing; for example, it may be decided that multiple methods will be used including observation, self-evaluation, student evaluation, and teacher evaluation.
- Counselor and principal decide what evaluation instruments are to be used.
- An evaluation schedule is planned.
- Conferences are scheduled including pre-evaluation conferences, post-evaluation conferences; the purposes of each conference should be delineated in advance.
- Conference results are in writing with both parties agreeing to the content and if not, so indicating.

One example is that recommended by the Alaska State Department of Education. It includes a program assessment instrument designed to evaluate guidance and counseling programs. The instrument is presented as a useful tool for validating exemplary programs, conducting self-appraisals, developing long-range goals, planning inservice training and dissemination efforts. The instrument's criteria rating items assesses philosophy, leadership, program, personnel, resources, education. The evaluation section of the "district profile sheet" includes needs assessment, operational process, written criteria, teacher-student-community involvement, evaluation results and record keeping.[5]

Evaluating Counselor Services and Relationships

Evaluating the performance of school counselors should, as mentioned earlier, focus on services and relationships. Figure 7-2 suggests one way for evaluating counselor services. Figure 7-3 suggests a method for evaluating counselor relationships.

The ten items in Figure 7-2 are examples only. Specific items should be based on the performance objectives discussed earlier. It should be noted that there are some disagreements regarding the roles and responsibilities

---

Counselor's Name _____   Evaluator's Name _____

Date _____

Expectations	*Is This Your Expectation?*	*Rate Counselor's Performance on This Item*
1. Helps student(s) with course selection	yes – no – not sure	Excellent – Good – Needs Improving
2. Helps student(s) selection of an occupation or further education	yes – no – not sure	Excellent – Good – Needs Improving
3. Administrates and interprets student(s) test results	yes – no – not sure	Excellent – Good – Needs Improving
4. Provides student(s) with personal counseling services	yes – no – not sure	Excellent – Good – Needs Improving
5. Assists in student(s) achievement evaluation	yes – no – not sure	Excellent – Good – Needs Improving
6. Provides student(s) study skills counseling	yes – no – not sure	Excellent – Good – Needs Improving
7. Provides *group* guidance and counseling opportunities	yes – no – not sure	Excellent – Good – Needs Improving
8. Handles disciplinary cases	yes – no – not sure	Excellent – Good – Needs Improving
9. Conducts home visits	yes – no – not sure	Excellent – Good – Needs Improving
10. Does follow-up studies on students leaving or graduating from school	yes – no – not sure	Excellent – Good – Needs Improving

---

FIGURE 7-2
Evaluating Counselor Services

Counselor's Name:_____ Evaluator's Name:_____ Date:_____

Relationships	Self-Evaluation			Principal/Supervisor Evaluation		
	Poor	Average	Exceptional	Poor	Average	Exceptional
1. Work with individual student	___	___	___	___	___	___
2. Work with groups of students	___	___	___	___	___	___
3. Work with parents	___	___	___	___	___	___
4. Work with teachers	___	___	___	___	___	___
5. Work with principal	___	___	___	___	___	___
6. Work with school personnel	___	___	___	___	___	___
7. Work with colleagues in guidance department	___	___	___	___	___	___
8. Work with community personnel	___	___	___	___	___	___
9. Work with guidance personnel in other schools	___	___	___	___	___	___
10. Work with other administrators	___	___	___	___	___	___

Items rated as poor:

Items rated as exceptional:

Recommendations for improvement:

Commendations:

_____   _____
Signature of Counselor   Signature of Principal/Supervisor

FIGURE 7-3
Evaluating Counselor Relationships

of school counselors. In the survey cited above, counselors recommended that their roles be modified to include these additions: *group* guidance and counseling, career guidance periods in the classroom, organizing pupil personnel teams, staff development opportunities, human relations training, greater leadership by counseling staff, and coordinating work with faculty and parents. The counselors also recommended dropping clerical and administrative functions, student class scheduling, recordkeeping, hall monitoring, and administration of discipline.[6]

Evaluating the work of school counselors must focus upon the quality of their relationships with others as well as their effectiveness in performing tasks.

Figure 7-3 is one example of a scale that combines both self-evaluation and principal/supervisor evaluation of relationships with others. The scale should be completed by the counselor and principal/supervisor separately. Either party can summarize the results and use the comparative data for discussion during the conference.

One may wish to specify tasks under each of the relationships listed, thus providing more detailed information for use in conferences. For example, the scale could be rewritten to specify items under each category:

- Motivates students to seek counseling
- Is sensitive to students' needs
- Has good rapport with all groups of students
- Encourages groups of students to use available resources.

A variety of instruments may be designed to evaluate the effectiveness of a counselor's performance relative to specific responsibilities. Counselors and the principal/supervisor could develop their own set of performance objectives and then develop a scale that would rate each counselor's performance on a particular responsibility or objective.

EVALUATING HEALTH SERVICES

School health services are an important adjunct to the school's health education program. Health services implement many of the concepts and content of the health curriculum. Health education and health services have as their major objectives the concept of *wellness*; that is, a way of living designed to help one achieve potential for well being including four dimensions—nutrition, physical awareness, stress reduction, and self-responsibility.[7]

Programs and services that promote positive health attitudes and knowledge with an emphasis on care and prevention may contribute to the decrease or elimination of unhealthy practices such as poor nutritional practices, failure to exercise, and the use of alcohol, tobacco, and drugs. However, many school districts, reacting to budget limitations, have sought other ways of providing health services rather than decreasing existing services. Greater reliance on community health services, the local health department, paramedical personnel, and visiting nurses, are but a few examples. Some districts have developed health teams, many have decided to assign the school nurse, psychologist, dental hygienist (or other members of the team if one exists) to several schools on a rotating schedule. Regardless of the means used to deliver the necessary health services, it is imperative that a goal-directed (with measurable objectives) school health program and accompanying services be designed so that appropriate measuring instruments can be used to determine the effectiveness of these programs and services. The school principal's roles and responsibilities for leadership in this area is crucial to its success. The same is true for the school nurse who, working closely with the school principal, faculty, and other school members, functions to advise, evaluate, organize, and integrate.

Two examples for evaluating the health services offered in your school will be described. In each of these examples, it is best that the evaluation be done by a committee representing faculty, health personnel, and administrators. Another procedure would be to have the faculty, the administration, and the health service staff evaluate health services separately, and then compare the results.

Regardless of how you decide to organize for evaluating health services, the intent should be to improve these services within the parameters created by budget limitations, the number of personnel, community resources, and the like.

The first example requires an analysis of current practices as well as determining what could be done, which in essence, provides ideas for the improvement of health services. Four questions should be answered for each of the ten factors listed. The four questions are:

1. Where are we currently?
2. How well are we doing currently?
3. How well could we be doing it?
4. Where would we like to be?

		Yes	No
1.	The school health services are based upon specific measurable objectives.	___	___
2.	The objectives are understood by faculty and administrators.	___	___
3.	The objectives are understood by students and parents.	___	___
4.	School health personnel are provided written descriptions of their job and expectations.	___	___
5.	School health personnel are supervised and evaluated periodically throughout the school year.	___	___
6.	School health personnel are accessible to faculty, students, and administrators.	___	___
7.	The services offered meet the health needs of students.	___	___
8.	Health services are evaluated periodically with the results used for planning improvements.	___	___
9.	Faculty and community view the services as a valuable adjunct to the total school program.	___	___
10.	Health service offerings make use of community resources.	___	___
11.	School health services are organized in such a way that the potential for achieving objectives are great.	___	___
12.	School health services are administered in such a way that the potential for achieving objectives are great.	___	___
13.	Plans for the continuous evaluation of school health services have been developed.	___	___
14.	Achievements, failures, and school health service activities are identified in an annual report.	___	___
15.	Achievements, failures, and activities of health services are reported to parents and public.	___	___

FIGURE 7-4
School Health Services Checklist

The ten factors that each of these questions could be applied to include health service:

- Objectives
- Offerings
- Organization
- Administration
- Budget
- Personnel
- Facilities
- Resources
- Needs
- Improvements.

Another way to evaluate school health services is to use a checklist similar to that shown in Figure 7-4.

EVALUATING SOCIAL AND PSYCHOLOGICAL SERVICES

In most school districts the school social worker and the school psychologist work out of the central office and visit individual schools on a scheduled basis and are on call in case of special needs or emergencies. Personnel who divide their time among several schools find it difficult to develop the human and professional attachments that one finds among faculty and staff assigned to a specific school. In addition, the sharing of professional services among several schools can easily lead to misunderstandings by principals and teachers about roles and responsibilities.

It is apparent that the building principal must take the lead in developing an attitude of acceptance of the social worker and school psychologist. To do this requires that you, as the building principal, know the roles and responsibilities of the school social worker and school psychologist. Once you understand their roles and responsibilities, it is important that you develop policies and procedures that govern their work and clearly define, in writing (for them as well as the faculty and staff), the job they are expected to perform in your school with students, teachers, and parents.

Principal and Faculty Self-Evaluation

In order for you and your faculty to better understand and appreciate roles and responsibilities, and utilize services provided by the school social worker and the school psychologist, ten questions are presented for self-evaluation and discussion at faculty meetings. Each question includes some information that may be utilized to guide the discussion:

Question 1: How would you (principal-teacher) rate your knowledge of the role and responsibilities of the school social worker?
The responsibilities include:

1. Working with students who have social and emotional difficulties or other school adjustment problems
2. Working with the parents of students who have been referred for help
3. Conducting home visitations and reporting conditions and cirumstances to principal and specific teachers
4. Constructing family histories and making other psychosocial assessments
5. Serving as a liaison between the school and community social service agencies
6. Interpreting services provided by him or her to teachers, parents, and the community.

Question 2: How would you (principal-teacher) rate your knowledge of the role and responsibilities of the school psychologist?
The responsibilities include:

1. Helping students with emotional problems and educational maladjustments
2. Performing diagnostic (testing) services
3. Helping teachers understand the meaning of group test results
4. Working as an effective member of the diagnostic/prescription team
5. Working with teachers for improving the classroom climate and procedures to maximize student academic and personal growth
6. Working with teachers to develop curriculum and programs for maximizing student learning
7. Demonstrating concern for the mental health of teachers and students
8. Serving as a liaison between the school and community
9. Preparing appropriate case studies with diagnostic write-ups, data analysis, counseling activities, and plans of action
10. Interpreting case study to personnel at staff conferences
11. Conducting continuous evaluations of student programs and, where appropriate, revising suggested remediation.[8]

Question 3: Do you (principal) have a written sample that teachers receive describing students who may be eligible for social work or psychological services?

As principal, you should help the social worker and school psychologist provide teachers with descriptions of the kinds of student problems, behaviors, and maladjustments that they are qualified to work with. This process contributes to the discussion and helps teachers become more aware of who does what and why.

Question 4: Do you (principal) have written procedures that describe exactly how students are to be referred to either the social worker or the school psychologist?

Clear, step-by-step procedures cooperatively developed by you and the school social worker and psychologist can contribute to teacher understanding and use of each specialized service. It can also promote a positive attitude toward personnel and the services performed because it lists procedures that are precise and contribute to a team effort rather than an individual responsibility.

Question 5: Do you (principal) use a team approach to study specific referrals?

In many school districts the concept of a multidisciplinary team has made significant contributions for helping specific students and their parents understand and cope with their particular needs. The "M-team" may include teachers, school social worker, school psychologist, principal, school nurse, and others selected for their specialities.

Question 6: Do you (principal) insure that adequate records and reports are developed and maintained?

It is important that school policies regarding student records and reports be created, properly administered, and periodically evaluated as suggested in an earlier chapter.

Question 7: Do you (principal) and your faculty evaluate, annually, the social work and psychological services provided students, teachers, and parents in your school?

Like other services provided school personnel, you and the faculty should evaluate services rendered by the school social worker and the school psychologist. Some information can be gleaned from the evaluation of their performance. An example of an evaluation scale is shown in Figure 7-5.

As you know, faculty and staff perceptions can differ. For example, Abel and Burke developed a School Psychological Services Questionnaire to find out how staff in an elementary school district perceived their school psychologists. Perceptions differed regarding how school psychologists spend their time and how this time should be spent. Perceptions of psy-

	Out- standing	Satis- factory	Needs Improving*	Unsatis- factory*
1. How would you rate the social services this school receives? *Explain:	___	___	___	___
2. How would you rate the psychological services this school receives? *Explain:	___	___	___	___
3. How would you rate our procedures for referring students to either of these two services? *Explain:	___	___	___	___
4. How would you rate the effectiveness of our M-team (multidisciplinary) approach? *Explain:	___	___	___	___
5. How would you rate the contributions/suggestions of the school social worker to the M-team? *Explain:	___	___	___	___
6. How would you rate the contributions/suggestions of the school psychologist to the M-team? *Explain:	___	___	___	___
7. How would you rate the services provided by the social worker in helping individual teachers? *Explain:	___	___	___	___
___Check here if you have been a recipient of this service.				
8. How would you rate the services provided by the school psychologist in helping individual teachers? *Explain:	___	___	___	___
___Check here if you have been a recipient of this service.				
9. How would you rate the services provided by the social worker in helping individual students? *Explain:	___	___	___	___
10. How would you rate the services provided by the school psychologist in helping individual students? *Explain:	___	___	___	___

11. Explain any questions you have answered "Needs Improving" or "Unsatisfactory."

FIGURE 7-5
Evaluating Services: A Form for Principals and Teachers

chologists' knowledge was generally favorable and their helpfulness related positively to frequency of contact. The respondents recommended service provisions in three specific courses: special education activities, interpersonal or school-climate activities, and administrative responsibilities.[9]

Brady took a different approach, using a case study method, for assessing teacher satisfaction with school psychology services. She found that teachers' evaluation of these services may be more accurate when reporting on recent and specific cases than when reporting on psychological services in general.[10]

EVALUATING SOCIAL, PSYCHOLOGICAL, AND HEALTH SERVICE PERSONNEL

Personnel in each of these three services must be evaluated regarding the performance of their tasks stated in their job descriptions and in any other documents detailing expectations. There are tasks specific to the school nurse that are not applicable to the school psychologist nor the school social worker. Therefore, it is important, in any evaluation scheme, to include the tasks that are unique to the position being evaluated.

The evaluation instrument in Figure 7-6 may be used as a self-evaluation instrument, an administrator evaluation instrument, and a teacher evaluation instrument. Teacher evaluation of social, psychological, and health service personnel is important because teachers are a valuable source of information about the effectiveness of these personnel and the quality of services provided them and their students. The instrument provides you and the person being evaluated the opportunity to write in specific performance tasks to be evaluated (five examples are provided for a school psychologist). The principal should meet individually with the school nurse, school psychologist, and school social worker to develop a list of specific performance statements related to the job description. At the same time, other items suggested in Part II of Figure 7-6 can also be examined. Part II was designed to examine factors common to all three positions.

Many school districts have specific kinds of rating scales and checklists instruments for evaluating social, psychological, and health service personnel. Whether one uses the instrument in Figure 7-6, a locally constructed instrument, or a commercially prepared instrument (including instruments suggested in the literature), it is appropriate to recall the discussion about the purpose and procedures for supervising and evaluating personnel. The importance of pre-evaluation and post-evaluation conferences should not be overlooked by the school principal. In other words, pupil service personnel should be afforded the same courtesies and opportunities in performance evaluation as those provided teachers.

Name:_____ Title:_____ Date:_____
Evaluator's Name:_____ School:_____
Date of Evaluation:_____   _____   _____

Directions: Place a check in the box after each statement which expresses your assessment/judgment of that statement.

Part I: Performance	*Commendable*	*Satisfactory*	*Needs Improving*	*Poor/ Unsatisfactory*
1. Assists teachers in interpreting group and individual test data	——	——	——	——
2. Assists teachers in planning, developing, and evaluating special education needs of certain children	——	——	——	——
3. Confers with parents regarding special needs of their child and how to provide these needs	——	——	——	——
4. Serves as a liaison between the school, parents, and community resource personnel	——	——	——	——
5. Engages in effective individual and group counseling services with students	——	——	——	——
6. Other	——	——	——	——

Part II: Personnel/Professional Qualities	*Commendable*	*Satisfactory*	*Needs Improving*	*Poor/ Unsatisfactory*
1. Calm in emergency situations	——	——	——	——
2. Efficient in carrying out tasks	——	——	——	——
3. Effective in carrying out tasks	——	——	——	——
4. Resourceful	——	——	——	——
5. Cooperative	——	——	——	——
6. Accessible to teachers	——	——	——	——
7. Accessible to parents	——	——	——	——
8. Job knowledge	——	——	——	——
9. Professional development	——	——	——	——
10. Dependable	——	——	——	——
11. Leadership	——	——	——	——
12. Promotes team spirit	——	——	——	——
13. Effectiveness with students	——	——	——	——
14. Effectiveness with teachers	——	——	——	——
15. Counseling/communication ability	——	——	——	——

Areas of Strength:

Areas of Weakness:

Specific Improvements To Be Tried:

_____   _____
       (Signature of supervisor)   (Signature of person being evaluated)

_____   _____
 (Date)   (Date)

FIGURE 7-6
Sample Form for Evaluating a School Nurse, Psychologist, or Social Worker

A FINAL COMMENT

In this day and age, when children and teenagers need, more than ever, the benefits provided by counseling and guidance, social work, psychological, and health services, the principal's task of administering, coordinating, delivering, and evaluating these services takes on added importance. The task is complicated by the fact that most pupil personnel services are located in a department in the central office or in a central service agency. This situation leads to a staff that is part-time in a particular school both in practice and people's perceptions. Dividing their time among many schools, pupil personnel staff are often misunderstood regarding their roles, their work, and their contributions. This situation adds to the responsibilities faced by school principals with regard to the organization, administration, and supervision of pupil personnel services.

NOTES

1. Charles A. Maher, "Evaluating Special Services Using a Program Evaluation Team," *Psychology in the Schools* 20 (October 1983): 456–458.
2. *Exemplary Pupil Personnel Services Program in Illinois.* (Springfield: Division of Specialized Education Services, Illinois State Board of Education, 1983), p. 1.
3. *Ibid.,* pp. 2–3. Reprinted with permission of the Board.
4. Keith D. Barnes, *The State of Urban School Guidance and Counseling in the Major School Districts of America* (Columbus: Ohio State University, National Center for Research in Vocational Education, 1980).
5. *Promising Practices: Criteria for Excellence in Guidance and Counseling* (Juneau: Alaska State Department of Education, 1981).
6. *Op. cit.,* p. 124
7. See, for example, Halbert L. Dunn, "What High Level Wellness Means," *Health Values: Achieving High-Level Wellness* 1 (January/February 1977): 9–16; John Travis, *Wellness Workbook(s) for Health Professionals* (Mill Valley, CA: The Wellness Resource Center, 1977); and Lydia Ratcliff, *Health Hazard Appraisal: Clues for a Healthier Lifestyle* (New York: Public Affairs Committee, 1978).
8. Emery Stoops; Max Rafferty; and Russell E. Johnson, *Handbook of Educational Administration: A Guide for the Practitioner* (Boston: Allyn and Bacon, 1975), p. 569; and Richard A. Gorton, *School Administration: Challenge and Opportunity for Leadership* (Dubuque, IA: W. C. Brown Co., 1976), p. 307.
9. R. Robert Abel and Joy Patricia Burke, "Perceptions of School Psychological Services From a Staff Perspective," *Journal of School Psychology* 23 (Summer 1985): 121–131.
10. Helen Vogel Brady, "A Case Study Method of Assessing Consumer Satisfaction With School Psychology Services," *School Psychology Review* 14 (1985): 215–221.

REFERENCES

Batsche, George, and McCoy, George. School Psychology: *Recommended Practices and Procedures Manual.* Springfield: Illinois State Board of Education, 1983.
Crabbs, Michael A. "Reduction in Force and Accountability: Stemming the Tide." *Elementary School Guidance and Counseling* 18 (February 1984): 167–175.
Ensen, Harold B., and Noeth, Richard J. "Assessing Quality in Career Guidance Programs: One State's Approach." *The Vocational Guidance Quarterly* 32 (December 1983): 80–88.
Fairchild, Thomas N. "STEPPS: A Model for the Evaluation of School Psychological Services." *School Psychology Review* 9 (Summer 1980): 252–258.

Kraetzer, Ann V. *School Social Work Services Evaluability Assessment.* ED 221 798, March 1982, 40 pages.

Maher, Charles A. "Evaluation of Special Service Delivery Systems: An Organizational Domain-Referenced Approach." *Psychology in the Schools* 17 (January 1980): 60–68.

Meares, Paula Allen, and Yeck, Dorothy. *School Social Work: Recommended Practices and Procedures Manual.* Springfield: Illinois State Board of Education, 1983.

Peterson, Gary W., and Burck, Harman D. "A Competency Approach to Accountability in Human Service Programs." *Personnel and Guidance Journal* 60 (April 1982): 491–495.

Report of the Task Force on School Counseling and Guidance in Alberta: Planning and Research. Edmonton, Alberta, Canada: Alberta Department of Education, 1981.

Wentling, Tim L., and Piland, William E. *Assessing Student Services: Local Leader Guide V.* Springfield: Illinois State Board of Education, 1982.

CHAPTER 8

Evaluating the Effectiveness of School-Community Relations

The key unit for educational change is in the individual school, with its principal, teachers, students, parents, and community setting.

John Goodlad

The principal has the major responsibility for organizing and implementing a plan for an effective school-community relations program. The ten responsibilities that follow can be used as the basis for the organizational plan:

1. The principal should know the public and parents in her or his school's attendance area.
2. The principal should know the school district and the community in which the school is a part.
3. The principal should establish leadership practices involving faculty and staff that promote effective school-community relationships.
4. The principal should promote a team effort for improving school-community relations by creating a representative advisory council.
5. The principal should use the advisory council and its subcommittees for implementing an effective, well-planned school-community relations program.
6. The principal should provide in-service education opportunities for faculty, staff, advisory council members, and others involved in the program.
7. The principal and advisory council should use a variety of communication resources in its program.

8. The principal and advisory council should create opportunities and use methods that insure parent-public feedback.
9. The principal and advisory council should periodically evaluate the school-community relations program.
10. The principal and advisory council should use the evaluative data to improve the school-community relations program.

These responsibilities and plans will be discussed in the pages that follow. The discussion will include suggestions for evaluating your current program, your knowledge of the community, how to poll parents and the public, assessing your communication efforts, how to use the news media, how to conduct follow-up studies, and how to evaluate adopt-a-school programs.

PRINCIPAL'S SELF-EVALUATION
OF CURRENT PROGRAM

School-community relations begin in two specific places: the principal's office and the teacher's classroom. Two suggestions for examining your school-community relations program follow. You may wish to involve faculty and staff in this self-evaluation.

The first suggestion requires that you answer the question: How effective is your school-community relations program? To do this, consider:

1. Objectives. State the purposes of your school-community relations program.
2. Activities. Indicate how you have achieved these purposes to date. What have you actually done?
3. Evaluation. State how well your program or activities have achieved stated purposes. What evidence do you have?
4. Planning. What do you need to do as a result of the evaluation?

The second suggestion requires answers to fifteen questions. Each question can serve as a guideline for developing an effective program.

1. Are you aware of the needs and attitudes of parents and public in your school's attendance area?
2. Are the faculty, staff, and students making maximum use of community resources?
3. Do you have a school-community relations program plan?
4. Do you and your faculty and staff make adequate use of the media available to you?
5. Do you and your faculty and staff create situations that actively involve the parents and public in school programs and activities?

6. Do you know the percentage of parent-public participation in school affairs this past year?
7. Do you know what impact this participation has had on the school's programs and activities?
8. Are you and your faculty and staff doing everything you should to let your public know how "good" your school is?
9. Do you take annual or biannual public polls to find out the public's perceptions of your school?
10. Are the personnel in your school aware of the need and value of an effective school-community relations program?
11. Do you know what percentage of your faculty and staff participate in community affairs and organizations?
12. Does your public know the problems, needs, and issues regarding your school's programs and personnel?
13. Do you use strategies that seek feedback from parents and public regarding their perceptions of the programs, activities, personnel and other matters in your school?
14. Do you develop a yearly school-community relations activities calendar?
15. Do you use methods to examine the effectiveness of materials (newsletters, bulletins, etc.) your school sends to parents?

These questions and suggestions reinforce the ten responsibilities/plans listed in the previous section. These questions imply that there is a need for an organized school-community relations plan; that your public be queried regarding the types of programs and activities their school should be offering; that an effort be made to find out how parents and public perceive the strengths and weaknesses of your school; that parents and public react to the quality and quantity of information they receive from the school; and that periodic evaluation of the program be made to insure its improvement.

PRINCIPAL'S EVALUATION OF KNOWLEDGE OF THE COMMUNITY

Almost every textbook with chapters on school-community relations and/ or public relations recommends that the principal know his or her community. This charge was also identified as one of the major responsibilities of the school principal in the previous sections of this chapter. The reasons for this are well described in the purposes and needs underlying an effective school-community relations program. You have to know your community if you expect to effectively utilize its resources. You must know the pressure groups, special interest groups, opinion makers, and the power structure if you expect to ally forces for school financial, program, and activity support. Two suggestions for evaluating your knowledge of your community follow. One is the use of a checklist, the other is a rating scale.

Know Your Community Checklist

The following checklist may be used to assess your knowledge of the community in your school's attendance area or the town or city in which your school is located. You should place an "A" in the space provided if you rate your knowledge as "adequate"; use "NI" if you feel you need more information than you currently have about a particular item; and use "I" if you have little or no knowledge about an item.

How would you rate your knowledge of the community's:

1. ___ attitudes
2. ___ incomes
3. ___ occupations
4. ___ ethnic backgrounds
5. ___ racial composition
6. ___ educational level
7. ___ prejudices, biases
8. ___ conflicts
9. ___ problems, issues
10. ___ aspirations/goals
11. ___ elected officials
12. ___ appointed officials
13. ___ opinion makers
14. ___ media sources
15. ___ power structure
16. ___ organizational leaders/officers
17. ___ growth patterns
18. ___ graduates of your school or other schools
19. ___ mobility of the population
20. ___ health factors/problems/issues
21. ___ safety factors/problems/issues
22. ___ private and public schools
23. ___ other educational institutions
24. ___ religious institutions
25. ___ service agencies
26. ___ recreational and youth programs
27. ___ adult programs
28. ___ minority groups
29. ___ special interest groups
30. ___ housing patterns
31. ___ industrial areas
32. ___ redevelopment plans
33. ___ financial and tax structure

Directions: Use the following scale to determine your activity in school-community relations.
Scale: I do this: (1) often; (2) sometimes; (3) seldom; (4) never.

	Activities	*Rating*

1. Serve as a member of a civic organization. ____
2. Initiate communication between the school and existing civic organizations. ____
3. Initiate communication between the school and other school personnel. ____
4. Plan informational meetings to acquaint the staff with the existing civic organizations. ____
5. Invite community agencies to participate in staff in-service training programs and/or parent education programs. ____
6. Study the changes taking place in the family patterns of the community. ____
7. Study the changes taking place in the educational facilities of the community. ____
8. Study the changes taking place in the cultural facilities of the community. ____
9. Study the racial and nationality make-up of residents in school attendance areas. ____
10. Study community agencies to learn about their functions and services. ____
11. Make use of the services offered by the community agencies. ____
12. Help facilitate work in the community agencies involved in the field of organized recreation and in youth activities. ____
13. Cooperate with community civic organizations in promoting better schools. ____
14. Cooperate with community civic organizations in establishing laws for protection, welfare, and education of youth. ____
15. Cooperate with community civic organizations by making school building meeting hall facilities and/or recreational facilities available to the community when need is demonstrated. ____
16. Cooperate with community civic organizations in planning new programs for community development. ____
17. Develop monthly school-community relations functions. ____
18. Use parents and others to help with the school's community relations functions. ____
19. Foster staff cooperation in encouraging students to use local cultural facilities (e.g., museums, art galleries, etc.). ____
20. Campaign with civic groups for improved health and recreational facilities. ____
21. Utilize public news media for bringing about an awareness of school programs and activities. ____
22. Utilize the public services organizations or other community agencies to enrich the school curriculum and promote school projects. ____
23. Provide school personnel with information about how to improve and promote school-community relations. ____
24. Make significant contributions to service organizations through a process of evaluation of services. ____

FIGURE 8-1
Principal's Community Activity Scale

Community Activity Scale

Principals have been encouraged and many times cajoled to be active members of the community. To help you evaluate this aspect of administration, a self-evaluation rating scale has been developed (Figure 8-1).

One of the major points to these self-evaluation suggestions is to highlight the fact that school principals can be powerful and positive influences in community affairs provided they willingly demonstrate leadership, know their community, and use its resources.

POLLING PARENTS AND PUBLIC

If you have heard it once you have heard it a thousand times—communication is a two-way process. The parents and the public in your school's attendance area need ways of communicating with the school that are informal, psychologically and socially safe, and not particularly time-consuming. As principal you are the one that has to create the methods by which the school's public can communicate with the school.

People evaluate their school everyday whether the administration or teacher likes it or not. They talk about their satisfactions and dissatisfactions about a school practice, a procedure, a teacher's behavior, an administrative decision. Their discussions occur at work, at parties, on the telephone, in meetings, and over the back fence. Your job is to channel the public's ideas, questions, criticisms, and concerns into some semblance of order so that you can plan appropriately.

That plan calls for you and your faculty to develop procedures for soliciting information from parents and other citizens and then to use the information for improving school programs, activities, policies, procedures, etc.

Feedback will help you and your faculty and staff gather and summarize information that will focus attention on specific problems, help dispel rumors and misunderstandings, stimulate discussion, contribute to bringing parents and school personnel together to solve their problems, allow school personnel to organize efforts to correct or change things, and keep school personnel abreast of organized "attacks" on their school.

You and your faculty and staff have to know the community your school serves if effective communication and feedback is to be realized. Some suggestions for studying the community were presented in a preceding section of this chapter. To highlight the number and varied audiences you have in your school's attendance area, the following example by R. Olds (with a space for your analysis) follows:

Setting: 2,000-student school (high school); area of medium population density. Inventory:

Example		*Your School*
160	Staff	_____
3,000	Parents	_____
25,000	Citizens in attendance area	_____
250	Community agencies, groups, churches	_____
100	University and other post-high school institutions	_____
200	Local employers	_____
2,000	Students	_____
5,000	Alumni	_____
4,000	Students in feeder schools	_____

Olds suggests that a count of 35,000 to 45,000 persons is present in many school attendance areas and that these audiences have "diverse, even conflicting, interests in the school."[1] Although the size and total audience may be smaller for your school, the diversity will probably be there and the need to communicate with and receive feedback from these people is not diminished.

SOME IDEAS FOR CONDUCTING A POLL

There are several ways you can obtain feedback from parents and others regarding their ideas, concerns, questions, and perceptions about what goes on at school.

School Publications.   Place in all school publications, such as the school newsletter, special activity announcements, and the like, a feedback section titled "How Are We Doing?" Leave space for parents and others to respond. If you wish, you can add two additional open-ended questions: "What are we doing right?" and "What are we doing that bothers you?"

Telephone Surveys.   This is a procedure that requires the use of sampling procedures. A random sample of persons in the school attendance area could be selected. Specific questions should be listed for the callers to use. In secondary schools, this would be a good project for a sociology class; at other levels, parent volunteers could be used.

Door-to-Door.   Again, a selection procedure is necessary. Students or volunteers would go to the homes with a checklist of items that would take ten to fifteen minutes to complete. They can simply ask each respondent the question and check or write in the reply on the form.

Telephone Hot-Line.   Advertise a "hot-line" number throughout the school's attendance area. People can call to get answers to their questions, to share their concerns, to "sound-off," to check on rumors, etc.

Local Newspaper. A letter to the editor by the principal or advisory council soliciting comments regarding specific concerns (homework, discipline, drug use, etc.) may be helpful. In addition, the principal may arrange with the editor to publish a questionnaire soliciting parent-public reaction to school programs, activities, policies, and procedures.

Meetings, Forums, Groups. Feedback from parents and the public can also be elicited through contacts at meetings, by talking to groups, and by arranging forums on particular issues. The parent-teacher association remains one of the best vehicles for information about public attitudes toward the school. Forums designed to attract people to respond to specific issues is also informative. Inviting representatives to lunch or breakfast (or in an informal setting) is also effective. These methods not only provide feedback to school personnel but they also enable school personnel to react, to inform, and to influence.

Survey. The formal or informal survey through the use of questionnaires, opinionnaires, checklists, and scales remains one of the most popular, easy, and effective ways of eliciting information from the school's public. Two examples are provided.

Figure 8-2 shows a questionnaire designed to have parents rate the various programs offered by the school.

Figure 8-3 suggests a way that parent-public attitudes about the school

---

Years in school district:_____
Children attending J.D.H.S.:_____
Children graduated from J.D.H.S._____

John Doe High School: Parent Questionnaire

Purpose: This questionnaire is designed to gather information for the teachers and administrators. The data collected will be useful in providing the best possible education to your children.

Directions: Please answer each question by circling the appropriate letter. Comment whenever you wish to do so. Return this questionnaire in the self-addressed, stamped envelope provided or give it to your child to bring to his or her teacher. Scale: E—Excellent; G—Good; F—Fair; P—Poor, DK—Don't Know

  1. In general, how would you rate your son's/daughter's
     education at J.D.H.S.?   E G F P DK
     Comment:

FIGURE 8-2
Parent Evaluation of School Programs

2. How would you rate the basic academic program your
   son/daughter receives?　　　　　　　　　　　　　　E　G　F　P　DK
   Comment:

3. What do you think of the elective program?　　　　　E　G　F　P　DK
   Comment:

4. What do you think of the guidance program?　　　　　E　G　F　P　DK
   Comment:

5. What do you think of the athletic program?　　　　　E　G　F　P　DK
   Comment:

6. How would you evaluate discipline at this school?　　　E　G　F　P　DK
   Comment:

7. How would you rate the student activity program?　　　E　G　F　P　DK
   Comment:

8. How do you feel about the communication between school
   and your home?　　　　　　　　　　　　　　　　　E　G　F　P　DK
   Comment:

9. How well do you feel the parent-teacher group fulfills its
   obligation of improving cooperation between home and
   school?　　　　　　　　　　　　　　　　　　　　E　G　F　P　DK
   Comment:

10. How would you rate the teaching in the
    a. English Dept.　　　　　　　　　　　　　　　　E　G　F　P　DK
    b. Mathematics Dept.　　　　　　　　　　　　　　E　G　F　P　DK
    c. Science Dept.　　　　　　　　　　　　　　　　E　G　F　P　DK
    d. Foreign Language Dept.　　　　　　　　　　　　E　G　F　P　DK
    e. Social Studies Dept.　　　　　　　　　　　　　E　G　F　P　DK
    f. Physical Education Dept.　　　　　　　　　　　E　G　F　P　DK
    Comment:

11. What program needs our immediate attention? Why?

12. What program seems to be our strongest? Why?

Purpose: This questionnaire is designed to determine your attitudes toward our school. Our study will be incomplete without your opinions.

Directions: Please answer each question as frankly and accurately as possible. Your name is not necessary. The questionnaire will only take a few minutes of your time. Please complete and return in the enclosed stamped envelope.

Section I

1. In general, what is your opinion regarding the quality of education provided by this school?
   ____excellent ____good ____fair ____poor
   Comment:

2. Do you feel that the cost of education in this community could be reduced?
   ____absolutely ____I think so ____probably not

3. Do you feel that the costs could be reduced by cutting out some unnecessary courses?
   ____absolutely ____I think so ____probably not
   What courses?

4. Are you generally satisfied with the education children/youth receive in this school?
   ____yes ____no ____needs improving
   Comment:

5. Do you feel that the schools are trying out too many new methods, new ways of teaching, etc.?
   ____not at all ____they could do more ____too much
   Comment:

Section II

Please rate this school on each of the following items. Scale: 1—Excellent; 2—Good; 3—Fair; 4—Poor; 5—Don't Know.

Administration	1	2	3	4	5
Teachers	1	2	3	4	5
Student body	1	2	3	4	5
Conduct of students	1	2	3	4	5
School discipline	1	2	3	4	5
Textbooks	1	2	3	4	5

FIGURE 8-3
Community Attitude Scale

Instructional supplies	1	2	3	4	5
Academic program	1	2	3	4	5
Community use of school facilities	1	2	3	4	5
Athletic program	1	2	3	4	5
Extracurricular activities	1	2	3	4	5
School plant	1	2	3	4	5
School site and area	1	2	3	4	5
Communication with parents	1	2	3	4	5
Communication with the community	1	2	3	4	5
General attitudes of public toward the school	1	2	3	4	5

Section III

1. Age of person completing this questionnaire:
   a. ( ) 18–20   d. ( ) 31–45
   b. ( ) 21–25   e. ( ) 46–60
   c. ( ) 26–30   f. ( ) over 60
2. Sex of person completing this questionnaire:
   a. ( ) Male   b. ( ) Female
3. This questionnaire has been answered by:
   a. ( ) An unmarried man, woman, widow, or widower without children.
   b. ( ) A married (or widow or widower) couple, all of whose children are below school age.
   c. ( ) A married couple (or widow or widower), some or all of whose children are of school age.
   d. ( ) A married couple (or widow or widower), all of whose children are over school age.
   e. ( ) Single person living with parents.
   f. ( ) Single person living alone.
4. Are you the major financial supporter of the family?
   a. ( ) Yes   b. ( ) No
5. If you answered "No" to question 4, are you
   a. ( ) housewife
   b. ( ) employed (working) wife
   c. ( ) single and employed
   d. ( ) unemployed male
   e. ( ) a student
   f. ( ) other, please specify_____
6. How many children in your family?
   a. ( ) None   d. ( ) Three   g. ( ) Six
   b. ( ) One   e. ( ) Four   h. ( ) Seven
   c. ( ) Two   f. ( ) Five   i. ( ) Eight
7. How many children attend the public schools?
   a. ( ) None   d. ( ) Three   g. ( ) Six
   b. ( ) One   e. ( ) Four   h. ( ) Seven
   c. ( ) Two   f. ( ) Five   i. ( ) Eight
8. Do you believe your family would make its decisions concerning public education in the same way you have in answering this questionnaire?
   a. ( ) Yes   b. ( ) No

(cont.)

9. Your income (combined if both husband and wife are working):
   a. ( ) Less than $5,000
   b. ( ) $5,001 to $7,500
   c. ( ) $7,501 to $10,000
   d. ( ) $10,001 to $15,000
   e. ( ) over $15,000
10. Your education (highest grade completed, either husband or wife):
   a. ( ) Elementary school only
   b. ( ) Some high school
   c. ( ) High school graduate
   d. ( ) Some college
   e. ( ) College graduate
11. Your occupation (occupation of principal wage earner):
   a. ( ) Professional (doctor, lawyer, banker, etc.)
   b. ( ) Manager, owner, government official
   c. ( ) Salesman or clerical worker
   d. ( ) Craftsman (skilled worker)
   e. ( ) Factory or mill worker (unskilled)

FIGURE 8-3
(cont.)

can be elicited. The intent of the demographic data (Section III) is to provide an overview of the respondents—to provide data about the people the school serves.

The methods described here should not be viewed as something the principal does to *appear* to be concerned and interested in community beliefs and attitudes. The methods are designed to elicit information that can be used as both a prelude for change and as a way of communicating with the community.

POLLING PARENTS AND CITIZENS
ABOUT SPECIAL EDUCATION SERVICES

One of the principal's responsibilities is to address the need for planning and implementing an evaluation of special education programs and services. To help school principals and parents assess the extent to which the program is in compliance with one of the mandates of Public Law 94-142, specifically, providing a written educational program for each child to meet his or her unique educational needs, the National Committee for Citizens in Education has designed a survey instrument for this purpose. The questionnaire is reprinted in Figure 8-4 with permission from NCCE.

Improving Services for Children in Special Education Public Law 94-142 (The Education for All Handicapped Children Act of 1975) is a federal law which provides for a free and appropriate public education for all handicapped children regardless of the degree or type of handicap. This law also requires that a written educational program (IEP) be developed for each child to meet his/her unique educational needs.

This questionnaire is designed to find out about the parents' views concerning one aspect of this law—the Individual Educational Plan (IEP). We value the amount of time and help you are about to give. Keep in mind that your help could improve services for children throughout the country. As one example, we plan to produce a handbook for parents on how to participate more successfully in the IEP process.

School Building:_____

School System:_____

Parent's Name:_____

Address:_____
    Street   City   State   Zip

Child's Age:_____ Sex: M_____ F_____

What is your child's primary handicapping condition?

_____

Is your child in a public school?   Yes_____   No_____

If NO, what type of school? i.e., parochial, private, state_____

Your phone number (would be held confidential) could be helpful to us if we want to follow up._____
    Area Code   Number

Please answer the following questions after you have attended the meeting at which your child's IEP was developed for the coming school year.

Parts and Procedures of the Individual Educational Plan

Please circle your answer

1. The IEP meeting was held within 30 days following evaluation of my child. If NO, please check when the IEP meeting was held following the evaluation: Yes   No

   _____   _____   _____
   2 mos. later   3 mos. later   4 mos. later

   _____   _____   _____
   5 mos. later   6 mos. later   never

2. The information from my child's evaluation before the IEP was fair and useful for planning a program for my child.   Yes   No

3. The following were present at the IEP meeting:
   a. my child   Yes   No
   b. child's teacher   Yes   No
   c. school representative (other than child's teacher)   Yes   No
   d. parent or Guardian   Yes   No
   e. other_____

                                                                         (cont.)

FIGURE 8-4
A Parent/Citizen Survey

4. The IEP for my child contained the following items:
   a. annual goals   Yes   No
   b. short-term objectives   Yes   No
   c. specific service(s) to be provided   Yes   No
   d. present level of performance   Yes   No
   e. date services were to begin   Yes   No
   f. ways to check my child's progress   Yes   No
   g. special materials, equipment or media   Yes   No
   h. percentage (%) of time in regular class placement   Yes   No
   i. place for me to indicate my approval   Yes   No
   j. educators informed me of how the IEP was to be developed and
      what would be in it   Yes   No
5. The description of my child's present educational performance in the
   IEP included information in all four of these areas:
   a. self-help skills (personal maintenance)   Yes   No
   b. academic skills (reading, math, etc.)   Yes   No
   c. social behavior (how s/he gets along with others, etc.) Yes   No
   d. physical skills (coordination, running, etc.)   Yes   No
6. There were major areas of educational needs for my child which were
   ignored during the IEP meeting.   Yes   No
7. The short-term objectives are written as specific steps my child will
   achieve in the next three months or more.   Yes   No
8. The short-term objectives did seem closely related to the annual
   goal(s).   Yes   No
9. The annual goal(s) in the IEP did not fully meet the educational
   needs of my child.   Yes   No
10. The IEP clearly stated what specific service(s) my child would be
    receiving.   Yes   No
11. The dates for the beginning of services for my child were quite
    clear.   Yes   No
12. I know when the IEP services will end for my child.   Yes   No
13. The service(s) for my child in the IEP was determined by what was
    available rather than what was needed (for example: if a certain service
    was known to be needed but the final decision was made based on
    what the school district currently had).   Yes   No
14. A specific date was set for reviewing my child's progress under this
    IEP.   Yes   No
15. The method of checking my child's progress in the IEP included:
    a. how it would be checked   Yes   No
    b. when it would be checked   Yes   No
    c. who would be responsible for making sure it's done   Yes   No
16. Some regular class placements for my child were considered during the
    IEP meeting.   Yes   No
17. Every attempt was made by educators to provide services for as much
    time as possible in a regular classroom.   Yes   No
18. A completed copy of the IEP was:
    a. made available to me to look at   Yes   No
    b. made available to me to keep   Yes   No
19. The IEP for my child was completed before the meeting with me.   Yes   No

What Were Your Feelings About the Following:

20. Educators presented information during the IEP meeting in understandable language.   Yes   No
21. I was given the opportunity to ask questions about points I didn't understand regarding the IEP.   Yes   No
22. I was encouraged to contribute significant information to my child's IEP.   Yes   No
23. The IEP that was developed seemed to fit my child's needs.   Yes   No
24. Educators provided information that helped me understand the IEP process.   Yes   No
25. I felt like a fully participating member with the educators during the planning of the IEP.   Yes   No
26. The school which my child attends has a program for preparing parents to participate in the IEP process.   Yes   No
27. I refused to consent to the IEP.   Yes   No
28. I was given specific information on how to appeal the program assignment decisions in the IEP.   Yes   No
29. I was asked to assume costs connected to services in my child's IEP.   Yes   No
30. I am hopeful that the IEP for my child will improve next year.   Yes   No

FIGURE 8-4
(*cont.*)

COMMUNICATION: MESSAGE AND MEDIUM

The principles and practices, as well as the self-examination recommendations, highlighted three important administrative tasks:

1. You and the faculty should know the parents and public in your school's attendance area.
2. Opportunities should be provided for parents and public to share their ideas, concerns, and questions (feedback) with school personnel.
3. An organized school-community relations program should be developed in your school.

With the help of the advisory council, one of the components of a school-community relations program worth assessing is the current communication practices used by you in your school. How effective is your school-community relations program? Does the school's public get the message? Additional questions on this point may be helpful:

1. Do you send home most communication materials with students?
2. Do you have evidence that the information sent home via students gets to their parents?

3. Do you have methods of informing the public (other than parents) about the school?
4. How do you inform the public about school events, activities, etc.?

Many principals testify to the fact that sending communication home with the students is not one of the better ways of insuring that parents get the message. Many prefer a direct mailing. There are two advantages to mailing communication to a home. First, the message gets there. Second, it goes to homes of nonparents as well. With bulk mailing rates and computer mailing lists (labels), a principal can mail material that is of interest to all people in the school attendance area at a minimum cost. Obviously, you have to be selective. There is little need to mail all residents in your area a parent handbook, but there may be a valuable service rendered by sending the public a school calendar of events.

Examining Past Practices

Once the advisory council determines whether the message is received or not, it may be worth the time and effort to examine past practices in how the message was presented. The checklist in Figure 8-5 may be helpful.

The analysis leaves the central question unanswered; namely, to what extent is the written communication sent to homes from the school judged effective by you, the council, the faculty and the staff, the parents and public? Three examples to help you answer this question follow.

Examining the Medium

Example 1. The advisory council selects five items that were sent to parents and/or public during the past school year and asks a random sample

Medium	*How Distributed*	*No. of Issues*	*Purpose*
1. Bulletins	————	————	————
2. Newsletters	————	————	————
3. School newspaper	————	————	————
4. Class newspaper	————	————	————
5. Flyers/brochures	————	————	————
6. Special announcements	————	————	————
7. Handbooks	————	————	————
8. Calendars	————	————	————
9. Memos	————	————	————
10. Other (specify)	————	————	————

FIGURE 8-5
Communication Effectiveness Checklist

(see Chapter 1 for sampling methods) of people to react to them. It should be noted that this procedure could also be done with teachers, students, and council members with minor changes in the form that follows.

After five items have been selected (newsletter, bulletin, school newspaper, a letter, and calendar, for example) a packet is prepared for the sample of parents to be polled. A letter explaining the purpose of the study and directions for completing and returning the questionnaire would also be included. Among the questions the council should ask include those shown in Figure 8-6.

Examining the Message: Two Examples

The idea here is to obtain feedback from the consumers of school information. Rather than use last year's materials, the council could do the assessment during the middle of the school year and use material that was sent out during the first few months of school.

Example 1. In this example a questionnaire is sent to parents and public (or a sample of) for their reactions and perceptions of the material sent to them during the year. Each principal would have to provide a statement

---

1. Did you receive these materials last year?
   __Yes   __No   __Not sure
2. Did you, as far as you remember, read these materials?
   __Yes   __No   __Not sure
3. As you read the materials now, does the content of all five interest your?
   __Most of it does   __Some of it does
   __Little of it does   __None of it does
   Why?

4. Which two of the five do you like best?
   __Newsletter   __Bulletin   __School Newspaper
   __Letter   __Calendar
5. Which of the two do you like least?
   __Newsletter   __Bulletin   __School Newspaper
   __Letter   __Calendar
6. Which two of the five should the school continue to send you on a regular basis?
   __Newsletter   __Bulletin   __School Newspaper
   __Letter   __Calendar
7. Which two of the five has information that is of greatest interest to you?
   __Newsletter   __Bulletin   __School Newspaper
   __Letter   __Calendar

FIGURE 8-6
School Information Follow-Up Form

of directions for completing and returning the questionnaire, but, in general, the questionnaire (Figure 8-7) is designed to get parent/public reaction to the material the school sent to them during the school year.

There are several questions on this sample form that are worthy of exploration. Those questions deal with the opportunity of your school's public to provide you with information about what they would like to see and hear about the school. The emphasis in previous discussions has been on two-way communication. Some suggestions have already been provided to solicit parent-public feedback. What we want to examine here is a way of finding out what parents and public want to hear about. To do this, it is suggested that once every two to three years you or your advisory council poll parents and public about the content of the materials being sent to them, as well as solicit information about what they would like to read about. Some of the items based upon an examination of the literature suggest that the content include curriculum matters, discipline, teacher qualifications, grades and achievement, current teaching methods, school

---

1. Are you generally satisfied with the printed information you received from the school during this year?
   __Very satisfied   __Somewhat satisfied   __Not satisfied
2. Do you feel that this school only sends you material when it needs your support?
   __I generally feel this way.   __I sometimes feel this way.
   __I seldom feel this way.   __I never feel this way.
3. Do you feel that the information this school sends you is self-promoting, part of a public relations campaign?
   __I generally feel this way.   __I sometimes feel this way.
   __I seldom feel this way.   __I never feel this way.
4. Does the information this school sends you tell you things you really want to know about?
   __Most of it is.   __Some of it is.
   __Little of it is.   __None of it is.
5. What do you like best about the material this school sends you?

6. What do you like least about the material this school sends you?

7. What suggestions do you have to help us improve the content of the material we send you?

8. Do the materials we send you give you an opportunity to inform us about your ideas, opinions, questions, concerns?
   __Most of it does   __Some of it does   __None of it does
9. What materials cause you to communicate with this school?

10. Do you have ideas, questions, or concerns you would like to share with us at this time?
    __Definitely   __Not now, but later   __None at this time

---

FIGURE 8-7
Parent-Public Evaluation of School's Communication Material

rules and regulations, school administration and organization, career and guidance information, athletic and other school events, problems and solutions, student abilities, talents, achievements, and the like. An examination of the content of the material you send to parents and public in view of this list may be interesting and informative.

Example 2. This example suggests that you or the advisory council survey parents regarding a specific piece of information sent to parents. During the first day of school, many school principals give each student an information packet for their parents. For this example, the information packet is a five-page mimeographed sheet on a variety of topics regarding school rules, regulations, programs, and activities that parents should know about. (We'll call it the Parent Information Packet—PIP). The sample form in Figure 8-8 is an attempt to attain the objective.

Directions: Place a check mark on the line that indicates your answer/preference to the question/statement.

1. Person completing questionnaire:
   __mother   __father   __ward/guardian
2. Grade of son/daughter:
   __freshman   __sophomore   __junior   __senior
3. Did you receive the information packet given to your son/daughter the first day of school?
   __yes   __no
4. If "yes," was the information of value to you?
   __all of it was   __some of it was   __none of it was
5. Was the packet
   a. attractive?   __yes   __no
   b. readable?   __yes   __no
   c. well-organized?   __yes   __no
6. Did you understand the information regarding
   a. student fees?   __definitely   __somewhat   __no
   b. student activities?   __definitely   __somewhat   __no
   c. school board?   __definitely   __somewhat   __no
   d. school rules?   __definitely   __somewhat   __no
   e. school calendar?   __definitely   __somewhat   __no
   f. school/class schedule?   __definitely   __somewhat   __no
7. Please rate the effectiveness of this packet.
   __excellent   __good   __fair   __poor
8. What information was not in the packet that may have been helpful to you?

FIGURE 8-8
Parent Evaluation of Information Packet

It is important to note that it may be useful to periodically evaluate specific pieces of information sent to parents to find out if the parents reviewed them and whether or not the content was of value to them.

EVALUATING USE OF THE NEWS MEDIA

One of the best ways to get your message to the public is to use the news media. The local newspaper, in particular, is a most effective medium for you because not only will it help you communicate with the public, but many times it is a factor in molding public opinion—hopefully in your favor. There is nothing wrong with publicity; you should seek it for your school, not for yourself. Many principals are not aggressive enough in seeking out the news media as a vehicle of public communication.

The following questions will help you or the advisory council assess your use of the news media. Each question implies a worthwhile practice.

1. How often have you sent information to your local newspaper about school programs, activities, and personnel?
2. How much of the material you send might be classified as "PR material," self-promoting material? How much of it is newsworthy and human-interest oriented?
3. Of the items you sent your local newspaper, how much of it was published?
4. Of the items that were not published, did you find out why they weren't published?
5. How often have you sent information to your local radio stations?
6. How often have you sent information to your local television stations?
7. Have you ever invited the news media to the school to cover a story, event, activity, etc.?
8. Do you know the names and telephone numbers of the editor and reporters at your local newspaper?
9. Do you know the names and telephone numbers of the community relation directors and reporters of the local radio and television stations?
10. Have you sent the news media copies of materials you send the public in you school's attendance area (and some of the material you send parents)?

CONDUCTING FOLLOW-UP STUDIES

A study of students who leave your school either to continue their education, to enter the job market, or to join the armed services serves two purposes. First, follow-up studies help you keep in contact with your graduates. Second, studies of this kind serve as another way of evaluating the school, another way of determining the extent to which the objectives have been accomplished (product evaluation).

Two kinds of follow-up studies will be described. One is a within the school district follow-up study; that is, a study of students as they progress from school to school. The other is the typical study of graduates (the alumni of the senior high school).

The purposes of follow-up studies is the same for both kinds of study. First, it will help school personnel determine the perceptions of graduates concerning their academic preparation and their attitudes, interests, and activities. Second, it will enable school personnel to trace the mobility and career choices of the student population. Third, it will provide data for decision making about curricula and personnel needs (i.e., vocational education, additional counselors). Fourth, it will provide additional information for student and parent counseling. Fifth, it will provide data for the continuous evaluation of programs and personnel. Last, it will enable the high school principal to create an active alumni association.

SCHOOL TO SCHOOL FOLLOW-UP STUDIES

Principals at the elementary, middle, and/or junior high school levels might ask the question: "Is our school doing a good job of preparing students for their next level of education?" To answer this question there appear to be three sources to investigate—teachers at the next level, parents, and students.

Figure 8-9 is an example of a scale that could be used to assess teacher opinions regarding how your school prepared its students. The intent here is not to lay blame, but rather to find out if your school is perceived to be doing an adequate job of preparation by teachers who are the recipients of the students your school educates. The scale is in three parts. Part one is an attempt to find out how teachers perceive your students' attitudes, skills, and interests; part two attempts to assess perceptions regarding subject matter preparation; and part three examines teacher comments to specific questions.

An example of a parent questionnaire appears in Figure 8-10. This questionnaire can be given to all parents of the last class in your school one or more years after that class has left the school. Again, one must be cautious about the interpretation of data received from an example such as this. Nevertheless, the information can be added to the pool of information collected to evaluate and improve school programs and personnel.

The student questionnaire can follow the format suggested for the parent questionnaire with certain modifications in directions and the wording of some of the questions. In addition to assessing students' attitudes, interests, and perceptions of their preparation and the like, each principal who decides to conduct such a study should visit the school the graduates

Directions: The faculty and administrators at _____ School are interested in your opinion regarding the students who leave our school and attend your school. We ask that you take a few minutes to complete this questionnaire. Your name is not necessary. Scale: HAS—High Ability-Achieving Students; MAS—Middle-Average Ability-Achieving Students; LAS—Low Ability-Achieving Students

Part I: Behavior/Attitudes/Skills

	HAS				MAS				LAS			
	Most	Some	Few	None	Most	Some	Few	None	Most	Some	Few	None
1. Courteous	—	—	—	—	—	—	—	—	—	—	—	—
2. Respectful	—	—	—	—	—	—	—	—	—	—	—	—
3. Polite	—	—	—	—	—	—	—	—	—	—	—	—
4. Positive	—	—	—	—	—	—	—	—	—	—	—	—
5. Attentive	—	—	—	—	—	—	—	—	—	—	—	—
6. Concerned	—	—	—	—	—	—	—	—	—	—	—	—
7. Independent	—	—	—	—	—	—	—	—	—	—	—	—
8. Cooperative	—	—	—	—	—	—	—	—	—	—	—	—
9. Helpful	—	—	—	—	—	—	—	—	—	—	—	—
10. Participatory	—	—	—	—	—	—	—	—	—	—	—	—
11. Creative	—	—	—	—	—	—	—	—	—	—	—	—
12. Responsible	—	—	—	—	—	—	—	—	—	—	—	—
13. Social skills/etiquette	—	—	—	—	—	—	—	—	—	—	—	—
14. Work-study skills	—	—	—	—	—	—	—	—	—	—	—	—
15. Social interests	—	—	—	—	—	—	—	—	—	—	—	—
16. Problem-solving skills	—	—	—	—	—	—	—	—	—	—	—	—
17. Discussion skills	—	—	—	—	—	—	—	—	—	—	—	—
18. Speaking skills	—	—	—	—	—	—	—	—	—	—	—	—
19. Writing skills	—	—	—	—	—	—	—	—	—	—	—	—
20. Listening skills	—	—	—	—	—	—	—	—	—	—	—	—
21. Reading skills	—	—	—	—	—	—	—	—	—	—	—	—
22. Study skills	—	—	—	—	—	—	—	—	—	—	—	—
23. Self-concept	—	—	—	—	—	—	—	—	—	—	—	—

Part II: Interests

	HAS				MAS				LAS			
	Most	Some	Few	None	Most	Some	Few	None	Most	Some	Few	None
1. In learning	—	—	—	—	—	—	—	—	—	—	—	—
2. In school	—	—	—	—	—	—	—	—	—	—	—	—
3. In social activities	—	—	—	—	—	—	—	—	—	—	—	—
4. In student activities	—	—	—	—	—	—	—	—	—	—	—	—
5. In student government	—	—	—	—	—	—	—	—	—	—	—	—
6. In sports	—	—	—	—	—	—	—	—	—	—	—	—
7. In dances, dancing	—	—	—	—	—	—	—	—	—	—	—	—
8. In assemblies, rallies	—	—	—	—	—	—	—	—	—	—	—	—
9. In drama, plays, musicals	—	—	—	—	—	—	—	—	—	—	—	—
10. In debate, forensics	—	—	—	—	—	—	—	—	—	—	—	—
11. In films	—	—	—	—	—	—	—	—	—	—	—	—
12. In radio/TV	—	—	—	—	—	—	—	—	—	—	—	—
13. In class activities	—	—	—	—	—	—	—	—	—	—	—	—

FIGURE 8-9
Student Follow-Up: Teacher Scale

14. In school spirit ___ ___ ___ ___   ___ ___ ___ ___   ___ ___ ___ ___
15. In physical
    activities ___ ___ ___ ___   ___ ___ ___ ___   ___ ___ ___ ___
16. In clubs, orga-
    nizations ___ ___ ___ ___   ___ ___ ___ ___   ___ ___ ___ ___
17. In student
    publications ___ ___ ___ ___   ___ ___ ___ ___   ___ ___ ___ ___
18. In musical
    activities ___ ___ ___ ___   ___ ___ ___ ___   ___ ___ ___ ___
19. In school/
    service
    committees ___ ___ ___ ___   ___ ___ ___ ___   ___ ___ ___ ___
20. In community
    service activities ___ ___ ___ ___   ___ ___ ___ ___   ___ ___ ___ ___
21. In volunteer
    activities ___ ___ ___ ___   ___ ___ ___ ___   ___ ___ ___ ___
22. In local, state,
    national politics ___ ___ ___ ___   ___ ___ ___ ___   ___ ___ ___ ___
23. In themselves ___ ___ ___ ___   ___ ___ ___ ___   ___ ___ ___ ___
24. In forming
    cliques ___ ___ ___ ___   ___ ___ ___ ___   ___ ___ ___ ___
25. Other (specify)
    _____ ___ ___ ___ ___   ___ ___ ___ ___   ___ ___ ___ ___

Part III: Academic Preparation

	HAS				MAS				LAS			
	Most	Some	Few	None	Most	Some	Few	None	Most	Some	Few	None
1. Reading	___	___	___	___	___	___	___	___	___	___	___	___
2. Science	___	___	___	___	___	___	___	___	___	___	___	___
3. Social Studies	___	___	___	___	___	___	___	___	___	___	___	___
4. English	___	___	___	___	___	___	___	___	___	___	___	___
5. Mathematics	___	___	___	___	___	___	___	___	___	___	___	___
6. Music	___	___	___	___	___	___	___	___	___	___	___	___
7. Art	___	___	___	___	___	___	___	___	___	___	___	___
8. Physical Education	___	___	___	___	___	___	___	___	___	___	___	___
9. Health	___	___	___	___	___	___	___	___	___	___	___	___
10. Other (specify)	___	___	___	___	___	___	___	___	___	___	___	___

Part IV: Questions

1. Are you generally satisfied with the students from_____School regarding their academic preparation?

2. Are you generally satisfied with the students from_____School regarding their attitudes toward school?

3. Are you generally satisfied with the students from_____School regarding their social/personal behavior?

4. Are you generally satisfied with the students from_____School regarding their interest and attitudes toward learning?

5. Are you generally satisfied with the students from_____School regarding their learning skills?

6. What specific recommendations do you have to help us better prepare students for your program?

7. What appear to be our greatest strengths?

8. What appear to be our greatest weaknesses?

9. How would you rate the degree of personnel communication between our two schools?

10. How would you rate the degree of program articulation between our two schools?

<hr>

FIGURE 8-9
(cont.)

go to and collect information regarding the following for each class every year or at least every two years:

- Average daily attendance
- Tardiness rate
- Detention rate
- Discipline notices
- Honors, recognitions
- Grades in school subjects; number and percent of A's, B's, C's, D's, F's
- Number and percent of class who participate in student activities
- Drop-out rate
- Out-of-school activities
- Other data that may help quantify student behavior, achievement, activities, and interests.

Graduate-Alumni Studies

Many high school guidance departments conduct follow-up studies of their graduates. Several high schools have active alumni associations. Both activities can be of value as a means of improving school-community communications, of utilizing community resources, and for evaluation purposes.

Five-Step Follow-Up Plan

A five-step plan is recommended for high school principals who want to or are currently conducting graduate follow-up studies.

Step 1: Purposes and Plans. The following questions will be helpful in beginning a follow-up study:

1. What are your purposes? Objectives? Why do you want to conduct or why have you been conducting follow-up studies of the school's graduates?

Directions: The faculty and administrators at_____School are interested in your opinion regarding how well we prepared your child for his or her continuing education at_____School. We ask that you take a few minutes to complete this questionnaire. Your name is not necessary. Please return in the self-addressed, stamped envelope.

Part I: General

1. Number of years your child attended_____School:_____
2. Sex of your child: F____   M____
3. General ability of your child:
   High____   High Average____   Average____   Low Average____   Low____
4. General achievement of your child while he or she attended_____School:
   Excellent____   Very Good____   Good____   Fair____   Poor____

Part II: School Effects

What effect do you feel that _____School, its faculty/staff/principal and programs had on your child's:

	Great	Moderate	Little	None	Positive	Negative
			Effect			
1. attitude toward school	____	____	____	____	____	____
2. attitude toward learning	____	____	____	____	____	____
3. attitude toward teachers	____	____	____	____	____	____
4. attitude toward authority	____	____	____	____	____	____
5. attitude toward himself or herself	____	____	____	____	____	____
6. interest in school	____	____	____	____	____	____
7. interest in continuing his or her education	____	____	____	____	____	____
8. interest in reading	____	____	____	____	____	____
9. interest in student activities (council, clubs, publications, etc.)	____	____	____	____	____	____
10. interest in sports	____	____	____	____	____	____
11. interest in plays, musicals	____	____	____	____	____	____
12. interest in music, concerts	____	____	____	____	____	____
13. interest in community affairs	____	____	____	____	____	____
14. skills in doing school work	____	____	____	____	____	____
15. reading skills	____	____	____	____	____	____
16. math skills	____	____	____	____	____	____
17. ability to do school work	____	____	____	____	____	____
18. study-work skills	____	____	____	____	____	____
19. emotional skills	____	____	____	____	____	____
20. social skills	____	____	____	____	____	____
21. personality	____	____	____	____	____	____
22. skills to do homework	____	____	____	____	____	____
23. possible career choice	____	____	____	____	____	____
24. success in school	____	____	____	____	____	____
25. lack of success in school	____	____	____	____	____	____

Part III: Questions

1. What did you like best about the way we prepared your child for his continuing education at _____School?

2. What did you like least about the way we prepared your child for his continuing education at _____School?

3. What could we have done that you feel we didn't do to prepare your child?

4. What recommendations do you want to offer to help us do a better job?

5. What questions do you have about our progress or personnel that you feel we should answer?

FIGURE 8-10
Student Follow-Up: Parent Scale

2. What are your plans for conducting the study?
3. What is your study cycle? Every year? Every two years?
4. What methods will or do you use? Interviewing? Questionnaire?
5. Who will be responsible for tabulating the data? For summarizing the data? For interpreting the data?
6. What sampling procedures will you use? Entire population? Random sample?
7. What will it cost to do the study? Where will the money come from?

Step 2: Scope and Schedule.   The following questions will help focus your attention on additional plans and procedures:

1. What geographic area will you study?
2. What class or group will be studied?
3. How will the information be solicited?
4. Who will design the questionnaire?
5. What factors will be included in the questionnaire?
6. If interviews are planned, who will do the interviewing? What questions will be asked? Who will prepare the question?
7. When will the study be made?
8. When will the study be completed?
9. Will follow-up letters be sent to graduates who do not reply?

Step 3: Collection and Tabulation.   The following questions will help you in collecting the data:

1. What attention will be given to collecting the data to avoid population or sample bias?
2. Will cross-tabulations be necessary to meet the purposes of the study?
3. Who will be responsible for tabulating the data?
4. Will the data be hand- or computer-tabulated?
5. Will the data be separated into two major response categories; one for graduates who enter college, the other for students who enter the vocational, commercial, or other occupational fields?

Step 4: Interpretation and Reporting.   The following questions will help you make decisions regarding the interpretation and reporting of the tabulated data:

1. Who will interpret the data?
2. How will the data be interpreted?

3. How will the data be reported?
4. Will there be several small reports or one large report?
5. What graphic materials will be provided?
6. Who will be reading the report?
7. Who will receive copies of the report?
8. What will it cost to prepare the report?

Step 5: Recommendations and Action. This final step suggests, through the questions asked, that action be taken on the information collected and interpreted:

1. What specific recommendations result from the study?
2. What specific actions are necessary?
3. Who will impelement the actions or recommendations?
4. What actions or recommendations will take priority?
5. What will be involved in terms of cost, personnel, and programs if all or some of the recommendations and actions are implemented?
6. In terms of the time, energy, and cost, was the follow-up study worth it?

An example of a high school follow-up questionnaire is shown in Figure 8-11.

Name:_____ Maiden Name:_____

Present address:_____ Phone:_____ Date:_____

Year graduated:____ Male____ Female____ Married____

Single____ Divorced____

1. Present occupation category:
   Professional____ Service____ Clerical____ Technical____
   Agricultural____ Sales____ Armed Forces____
   Management____ Skilled____ Semi-Skilled____
   Unskilled____ Unemployed____

2. Income:
   Below $5,000____
   Over $5,000 but less than $10,000____
   Over $10,000 but less than $20,000____
   Over $20,000 but less than $40,000____
   Over $40,000____

(cont.)

FIGURE 8-11
A Sample High School Follow-Up Study Form

3. Employment since graduation (list):

Firm Name	*Type of Work*	*Time in Position*
a. _____	_____	_____
b. _____	_____	_____
c. _____	_____	_____

4. Armed Services since graduation:

Branch_____   Type of work_____

Rank_____   Length of service_____

Not Applicable_____

5. Education since graduation:

School/College	*Course/Major*	*Degree or Years Attended*	*Did You Graduate?*	
_____	_____	_____	yes____	no____
_____	_____	_____	yes____	no____
_____	_____	_____	yes____	no____

6. Is your present job one that you thought you would be doing when you graduated from high school?

Definitely; exactly what I planned____   Close to what I planned____

Not even close to what I planned____   I made no plans in high school____

7. What are you currently doing? Is this a part-time or full-time job?

8. Please rate your degree of satisfaction with each of the following:

	Very Satisfied	*Satisfied*	*Not Satisfied*
a. Your high school teachers	____	____	____
b. Guidance counselors	____	____	____
c. Administrators	____	____	____
d. Coaches	____	____	____
e. Activity advisors	____	____	____
f. Academic program	____	____	____
g. Extracurricular programs	____	____	____
h. Social activities/programs	____	____	____

9. How much help did you receive from the following high school personnel in choosing and planning an occupation or school/college?

	None	*Very Little*	*Some*	*Much*	*Very Much*
a. Counselors	____	____	____	____	____
b. Teachers	____	____	____	____	____
c. Administrators	____	____	____	____	____
d. Others (specify)____	____	____	____	____	____

(cont.)

10. How would you rate your high school education in your present job?
No help at all___   Very helpful___   Gave me some background___

11. How did your high school education help you most?

Least?

12. What problems did you have going from high school to a job or to college?

13. What major advice would you give a high school student today?

14. What should this high school be doing to help students prepare for college or work when they graduate?

15. Please rate the value of high school courses as you look back on your preparation:

	Very Valuable	Valuable	Little Value	Worthless	Didn't Take
a. English	___	___	___	___	___
b. Social Studies	___	___	___	___	___
c. Science	___	___	___	___	___
d. Mathematics	___	___	___	___	___
e. Foreign Languages	___	___	___	___	___
f. Industrial Arts	___	___	___	___	___
g. Music	___	___	___	___	___
h. Art	___	___	___	___	___
i. Physical Education	___	___	___	___	___
j. Home Economics	___	___	___	___	___
k. Speech	___	___	___	___	___
l. Other (specify_____)	___	___	___	___	___

16. What subjects were not offered that you now feel would be of great value to you?

17. How would you rate yourself during your years in high school

	Top Quarter	Third Highest Quarter	Second Lowest Quarter	Lowest Quarter
a. Academically	___	___	___	___
b. Athletically	___	___	___	___
c. Socially	___	___	___	___
d. Reading achievement	___	___	___	___
e. Math achievement	___	___	___	___
f. Music or Art achievement	___	___	___	___
g. Confidence	___	___	___	___
h. Relationship with others	___	___	___	___

(cont.)

18. Honors and Awards:
    a. In high school:

    b. Since graduation:

19. Activities/Sports:
    a. Extracurricular activities you participated in during your high school years:

    b. Sports and other activities in which you currently participate:

20. Community activities in which you currently participate:

Activities	*Offices Hold or Have Held*
a. Civic clubs/organizations _____	_____
b. Social clubs/organizations_____	_____
c. Religious organizations _____	_____
d. Other (specify_____) _____	_____

21. Are you interested in forming an alumni association?   Yes__   No__
22. Are you willing to help form an alumni association?   Yes__   No__
23. Are you interested in participating in a class reunion?   Yes__   No__
24. Are you interested in helping develop plans for a class reunion? Yes__   No__

FIGURE 8-11 *(cont.)*

PARTNERSHIP PROGRAMS

President Reagan proclaimed 1983–1984 the historical year of Partnerships in Education. In his proclamation he said:

> Recently, many schools have developed private sector partnerships in an effort to broaden valuable resources and reach out to their communities for support. The private sector has much to offer the growing national movement to improve our education system. Some of the most effective methods include helping education identify the learning needs of our society; encouraging professional exchanges between teachers, educators, and businesses; contributing expertise, financial resources, and equipment; and providing technical assistance in school administration and curriculum development.

Throughout the country, the one school-community program that has captured the essence of this proclamation is the ''Adopt-A-School'' program.[2] The purpose of this program is well described in the Proclamation.

There are several key factors that are involved in evaluating an adopt-a-school plan or assessing the benefits of a program that is in place. We will examine four of these factors—planning, implementation, continuity, and evaluation. Let us assume that your board of education has a policy regarding such programs and the school district office has an adopt-a-school coordinator. Let us further assume, at least at the planning stage, that your school does not have a program. For the other three stages, we'll assume that an adopt-a-school program is operating at your school site.

Planning. The evaluative questions you and your faculty would ask about being "adopted" by a business are these:

1. What are our needs?
2. Would an adopt-a-school program help us meet these needs?
3. If so, what would be the purposes of the program?
4. If not, in what other ways can these needs be met?

At this stage, you and the faculty should meet with the district adopt-a-school coordinator to discuss whether or not the needs can be met by such a program and to discuss board policy regarding the program. If you do not have a district coordinator, then you, as principal, must be the source for discussion and direction. It may be of value at this stage to find out what other schools and districts do regarding such programs. But before going out seeking business support, develop a school profile (a fact sheet telling about your school) and a list of needs. This information will be very helpful to potential partners.

Implementing. The evaluation strategies that follow are designed for schools that currently are involved in an adopt-a-school program. The evaluation questions are these:

1. Are your purposes clear? For example, in 1981 the Monsanto Company adopted five elementary schools in St. Louis. The results of several meetings focus on three straightforward objectives: "(1) To improve the performance of pupils; (2) To increase the satisfaction and productivity of teachers; (3) To enhance pupil/community understanding of the schools."[3]
2. Is the fact sheet precise and concise?
3. Do you have a list of local contacts that may help you find the appropriate business? For example, are you using your community contacts and those of your faculty? Does the district coordinator have a list of interested businesses? Have you contacted the local Chamber of Commerce?
4. Have you given thought to the following factors before contacting your partnership choice?

- Where is the business located?
- How far is it from the school?
- How many employees does it have?
- Is it a branch or a home office? In other words, where are the decisions made?
- Does it have a community involvement record?
- Is it a product or service business?
- Have you decided how you will make the initial contact and to whom?
- Have you decided your approach in the first meeting and those that may follow? Do you have a plan of action?

5. Are your teachers ready to use the community service brought to them by this plan?
6. Have you and the faculty designed specific strategies for meeting your needs and for using the personnel and other resources that will be provided by your partnership choice?
7. Have you and your faculty scheduled orientation meetings for the adopting business or service club?
8. Have you established a place and a date for a formal adoption ceremony?

Continuity. One of the problems with many innovations is that there is a great deal of enthusiasm at the beginning and then this wanes after the program is implemented. This should not be the case with the adopt-a-school program because of the benefits it brings to the teachers, students, and parents of the school and for the sense of community involvement it provides for business and industry. Therefore, such a program in your school must be given priority, continually being attended to by you or your delegate, and under constant supervision and review.

Here is a checklist of strategies that you should review to insure continuity in your adopt-a-school program.

- Keep this topic on the agenda at each faculty meeting.
- Hold bimonthly meetings with the business or service agency volunteers.
- Meet regularly with district coordinator.
- Report progress to parents and the district office.
- Inform the community, through the media, about the progress of the program.
- Invite the volunteers to school functions.
- Involve the business or service agency in planning and induction sessions.
- Display student work and photographs of volunteers working with teachers and students in the business itself.

• Create a monitoring committee of teachers, administrators, and business personnel.

These and other activities will help insure continuity, publicity, and interest. Of course, interest and enthusiasm will be maintained if the relationships between teachers, students, and volunteers are positive and rewarding ones.

Evaluating.   In the above strategy, a monitoring committee was recommended. It is apparent that any new program should be evaluated periodically to determine if the objectives and activities are being effectively and efficiently accomplished. Here is an evaluation scheme your adopt-a-school committee can use, modifying the plan according to school and community factors.

EVALUATING OBJECTIVES

The committee should refer to the statement of objectives and in doing so answer the following questions:

1. At the end of the first year, have the objectives been attained?
2. If not, what factors prevented attainment?
3. If so, what factors contributed towards attainment?

EVALUATING ACTIVITIES

The committee should review all of the activities that took place over the year as well as the evaluation information gathered while the program was operating. These questions can serve as guidelines for assessing the adopt-a-school activities.

1. Were the activities consistent with the objectives?
2. Did the activities interfere with instructional time?
3. Did the activities enhance the teaching and learning in each classroom and the culture and climate of the school?
4. Were the activities of value in broadening the interest and meeting the needs of the students?
5. Did the recipients respond positively to the activities?
6. What activities seem to work best? Why?
7. Were the activities evaluated by the participants? If so, what does the evidence show about each activity?

These questions provide information the committee needs to examine. For example, if one of the objectives was to raise the reading interest level of students and the major activities were to read to students and to provide tutors from the business community, then these questions should be applied to that objective and the two major activities.

EVALUATING PARTICIPANTS

The committee should also review the performance of each of the participants in the program. Recommended is a plan involving self-evaluation coupled with a committee evaluation. The purpose of evaluating participants is to gather information to improve elements of the program in the next year and to look at participant behavior as a clue for making the program more effective and efficient. To accomplish this evaluative task, the committee should recommend that:

- Each participant list his/her responsibilities in the adopt-a-school program
- Each participant determine the extent to which these responsibilities were effectively and efficiently accomplished
- Each participant make a judgment of the performance of others in the program—district coordinator, principal, teachers, students, volunteers, others.

After this information has been collected and discussed by the committee, its members should interview all or a sample of the participants to verify the self-evaluation information and to gather additional data that will enable the committee to prepare a final report of the program's successes and/or failures.

After the written report has been disseminated to all participants, a meeting should be held so all can discuss its content and collaboratively recommend ways for improving the program. The committee should then write the new objectives for the next year and develop an operation plan that attends to the strengths and weaknesses found in the evaluative process.

SUMMARY

Milly Webb, Director of Education and Training for the Grossmont District Hospital (San Diego) has recommended the procedures for a successful adopt-a-school program in the following "Recipe for Success."

Collaboration: Designate a Steering Committee with representatives from the education and business sectors to develop a yearly plan.

Input: Sponsor activities at each location in order to brainstorm Adopt-A-School ideas.

Agreement: Establish an Administrative Agreement, which has been shared with staff members of both parties and delineates activities on a monthly basis.

Celebrate: Have a special get-together to become acquainted with each other and the students of the adopted school.

Share Responsibility: Rotate people in charge of each activity so that a contribution is made by all departments.

Team Concept: Establish a team concept in which everyone assists each other with the projects.

Public Relations: Communicate your activities, disseminating information to the community and the press, reporting your Adopt-A-School activities.

Critique: Evaluate each activity, outlining recommendations for future projects.[4]

A FINAL COMMENT

This chapter provided ideas and suggestions for evaluating and improving home-school-community relationships. It took a broad-brush approach. Yet there is a bottom line and it is this. The involvement of parents, community leaders, community volunteers, businesses, service agencies—any community resource—will help you and the faculty develop a program for improving the effectiveness of your school.

The opportunities for involvement should be both short-term and long-term. They should involve traditional resources (PTAs, room-parents, etc.) and new resources (Adopt-A-School program). The greater the commitment, the more probable the impact on student achievement, on student attitudes toward school and community, and on student behavior. There are no guarantees but there are a number of examples of schools that have effective home-community programs that are worth investigating and evaluating.

NOTES

1. Robert Olds, "The Principal's PR Role," *Bulletin of the National Association of Secondary School Principals* 58 (January 1974): 18–19.

2. For information about one of the oldest and best programs write to the Adopt-A-School Coordinator, San Diego Unified School District, 4100 Normal Street, San Diego, CA 92103; and Coordinator, San Diego County Office of Education, 6401 Linda Vista Road, San Diego, CA 92111-7399.

3. Marcie Wolfrum, "The Monsanto Effective Schools Project," *The Effective School Report* 3 (January 1985): 1–2.
4. Reprinted by permission from the author.

REFERENCES

Dandy, Evelyn B. "Parent Initiated Involvement: What Can We Do?" *The Effective School Report* 3 (September 1985).

Fink, Arlene, and Kosecoff, Jacqueline, eds. "How To Do Your Own Demographic Analysis." *How To Evaluate Education Programs*. Arlinston, VA: Capital Publications, Inc., March 1984.

Here's How: Ideas for Principals. National Association of Elementary School Principals. "You and Your Newsletter" (September 1984); "How To Go On Television" (October 1984); "Parent Involvement Program" (December 1984).

Long, Claudia. "How to Get Community Support." *Principal* 64 (May 1985): 28–30.

Parents Can Make A Difference. San Diego, CA: San Diego County Office of Education, n.d.

Rich, Dorothy. *The Forgotten Factor in School Success: The Family*. Washington, D.C.: The Home and School Institute, 1985.

CHAPTER 9

Evaluating the Effectiveness of Office, Food, and Transportation Services

We think in generalities, but we live in details.

Alfred North Whitehead

A school principal is many things to many people. The varying perceptions people have about the role and expectations of the school principal is testimony to this point. The job, however perceived, requires melding the manager-administrative tasks with the instructional-leadership tasks. One of the major problems the school principal copes with each day is how to maintain a balance between these two roles. Most principals appreciate the time and energy required to manage the school plant and its operations as well as the several noninstructional services provided students. Many principals feel guilty when they find that they are not giving enough of their time to the instructional-leadership role. However, it is impossible for today's school principal to abandon either role. Both roles are essential to first-rate quality education at the building level; both require time and energy; and both require periodic review and renewal.

In this chapter, the focus will be centered on three services requiring managerial skill and leadership: school office services, food services, and transportation services. Volumes have been written on each of these three school services. For this reason, this one chapter will not delve into the details for organizing and administering these services.

SCHOOL OFFICE SERVICES

There is general agreement among school principals that the school office is the school's service center and that the principal is the person responsible for operating it efficiently and effectively.

In order for the varied school services to be managed and delivered when needed, there are certain tasks that each principal must do to insure that the school office is an effective service center. As service center personnel, the staff should understand that they are part of the total educational program, that their performance influences the school culture and climate, and that they are there to deliver services to the administration, to teachers, to students, to staff, and to parents.

Some of these major tasks are outlined here for your review:

1. You must continually and effectively supervise and evaluate secretarial-clerical personnel.
2. You must promote good human relations between yourself and secretarial-clerical personnel and between secretarial-clerical personnel and other school personnel.
3. You must convince secretarial-clerical personnel that their work is important toward accomplishing the school's objectives.
4. You must insure that secretarial-clerical personnel have physical facilities that (a) provide adequate space to get the work done; (b) are pleasant and provide privacy when needed; and (c) do not interfere with the traffic flow in and out of the office.
5. You must provide secretarial-clerical personnel with the necessary equipment to get the job done.
6. You must create a filing system that is efficient and up-to-date.
7. You must require the use of standardized forms that save time and energy.
8. You should encourage the use of electronic data processing and help secretarial-clerical personnel acquire the skills to operate these machines.[1]
9. You must provide each secretarial-clerical staff member an office manual that includes a job description, policies, procedures, and specific instructions.

This last task is particularly important and can lead to a better understanding by secretaries and clerical staff of their jobs, responsibilities, and how, when, and why they will be supervised and evaluated. Job descriptions for a principal's secretary should include, among other things, a description or listing of the tasks under (1) qualifications, (2) salary and working conditions, (3) receptionist, (4) office procedures, (5) records, (6) reports, and (7) other duties peculiar to a particular school.

Evaluating Office Services and Management

With these tasks in mind, there might be a need to find out from school personnel and others who use the services of the school office how they perceive or rate this service. The evaluation form shown in Figure 9-1 is designed to help you do this.

Directions: The purpose of this questionnaire is to obtain your rating of office services. This rating is designed to determine ways to improve services to all school personnel. Please answer each question carefully and as completely as time will allow. Your answers will be held in confidence.

Name: _____

For questions one and two, use this rating scale:
4 – Excellent; 3 – Good; 2 – Fair; 1 – Poor (circle one).
A.   How would you rate the service the school office provides:

1.   Administrators?   4 – 3 – 2 – 1
2.   Teachers?   4 – 3 – 2 – 1
3.   Staff (custodian, etc.)?   4 – 3 – 2 – 1
4.   Students?   4 – 3 – 2 – 1
5.   Parents?   4 – 3 – 2 – 1
6.   Others? (specify)   4 – 3 – 2 – 1

B.   How would you rate the service the school provides:

1.   The instructional program?   4 – 3 – 2 – 1
2.   The guidance program?   4 – 3 – 2 – 1
3.   Health services?   4 – 3 – 2 – 1
4.   Food services?   4 – 3 – 2 – 1
5.   Transportation services?   4 – 3 – 2 – 1
6.   Library/media services?   4 – 3 – 2 – 1
7.   The athletic program?   4 – 3 – 2 – 1
8.   Student activities   4 – 3 – 2 – 1
     programs?

C.   Are you aware of any major problems and/or complaint about the school office services?
_____ Yes _____ No   If so, please specify:
_____
_____

D.   What office services are you not receiving that should be considered?
_____
_____

FIGURE 9-1
Evaluating Office Services

Results from this kind of questionnaire may provide you with several ideas that you may wish to consider in order to help make the school office the communication and production center it is intended to be. After an evaluation of what is, you could generate ideas for what ought to be. Obviously, not all the ideas will be implemented, because of district restrictions, budget, and/or certain school factors that make the implementation of the idea impractical or impossible. But you should list the ideas now and evaluate the chances of implementation later. Today's idea may be tomorrow's practice. Here are a few ideas:

- Add additional secretarial-clerical help, if needed; even part-time assistance will help.
- Use student clerks; particularly at the high school level a program may be worked out with the business department to provide actual work experience for youngsters.
- Take a course or design your own independent study guide for learning effective office management techniques.
- Create a small committee of people to develop an office procedures manual.
- Find parents in the community who are managers of large business offices and ask them to do a study of the effectiveness and efficiency of the school office.
- Post a master calendar that identifies important due dates, activities, reporting dates, etc.
- Consider the use of additional part-time secretarial-clerical help during peak-load periods such as the opening and closing of school.
- Try a POW squad (a group of parent-office workers who would be willing to volunteer their services when called upon to do so).
- Plan a year's program of inservice activities-training for your office staff. Don't forget to include the office staff in the planning.
- Have your office staff do an analysis of their job by logging the tasks and activities over a week or two; tabulate and summarize by the day or week, and/or type of task. You can use the results to help the staff plan for a more efficient operation of the office, if needed.
- Design a daily task analysis chart for the office staff to complete. Use the results as the focal point for a conference with each one and obtain their opinion of how time may be better utilized.

SCHOOL OFFICE MANAGEMENT

In this section, three areas of school office services will be discussed. We begin with student records and reports, then, a self-evaluation procedure, and we conclude with a recommendation for evaluating office personnel.

Evaluating Use of Records and Reports

It should be the intent of all school principals, faculty, pupil personnel staff, and other school employees who have responsibilities regarding student records and reports, to know and carry out school district policies regarding student records. The established practices in an individual school regarding the collection, maintenance, and dissemination of information about students should assure a balance between a student's right to privacy and the need to use information for designed educational purposes.

The management of school records and reports is time-consuming but necessary. There are many more records and reports to be monitored at the secondary level than at the elementary level. Most of the records maintained in individual schools are those about students, thus the principal must asure that necessary skills are developed to manage not only students personnel records, but also the plethora of other records and reports.

The "paper chase" is a burden faced by all administrators. A rule-of-thumb principle should be that each record, each report, each form used in school should be justified by its function. The use of machines, computerizing as much as possible, helps reduce the workload.

There are, however, several questions that you, teachers, and pupil personnel staff should ask about school records and reports as a means for self-evaluation:

1. How efficiently and effectively do we organize and administer the use of records and reports in this school?
2. Do we try to eliminate multiple and duplicate records, reports, forms, etc., wherever possible?
3. How much time do teachers use in completing school forms, slips, records, and reports?
4. Have we tried to computerize records when and where possible?
5. What is our policy relative to the confidentiality of student/faculty records and reports?
6. How have we helped each other learn to interpret material that appears in our school's records and reports?
7. What guidelines have we prepared for teachers and staff relative to the collection, maintenance, and use of information in student reports?
8. Have we evaluted our management of records and reports including existing policies and practices?
9. What information should be collected about each student in our school?
10. How should this information be categorized? For example, will we have separate files on each student such as a cumulative record file, behavior file, teacher professional file, with each file containing different kinds of information?
11. Who has access to student records and reports? Are there policies and procedures for identifying who examined a student's file? Are policies available regarding access by students and parents, by authorized school personnel, by third parties?
12. How is confidentiality assured?
13. When should some records be destroyed?
14. How may student records be amended?
15. What strategies are necessary to carry out the functions implied in these questions?

These questions and others focus on the issues of confidentiality, invasion of privacy, and the right to know. The principal has a responsibility to obtain information that will be of value for the interpretation of and planning for the educational progress of each student. It is also the responsibility of the principal to have this information used discreetly and professionally. If the axiom "what you don't know can hurt you," is applicable to anything dealing with school, it is in this area that it takes on validity. Because of social circumstances, legal uses, and specific laws, it is imperative that each school and school district have a specific set of policies and procedures, in writing, that should be required reading by all school personnel handling student records and reports. To help focus on this problem, the following questions should be considered:

1. Does your school district have written policies regarding pupil personnel records?
2. If your school district does have a policy, do you and your faculty/staff know what it says? (Suggestion: Is it time for a review?)
3. If your district does not have a policy, do you feel that you and the faculty/staff could work out a procedure that would include the following:
   a. Identify the minimum pupil data necessary for meeting the needs of the school district?
   b. Establish behavioral records helpful toward meeting the educational needs of each child?
   c. Create temporary teacher files with information helpful to teachers for instructing that child?
   d. Develop procedures under which each of the above are to be retained, for how long, and where they are to be filed?
   e. Develop a list of procedures that insure the confidentiality of information released?
4. Are you and your faculty/staff aware of the various forms used by the district regarding the requests and release of pupil personnel records? (Suggestion: If you currently do not have such forms, consider using forms modeled from other schools who have had success with them. Ask your administrative colleagues for suggestions.)
5. How would you and the faculty/staff rate knowledge about the issues, state statutes, and laws governing pupil personnel records and reports?

Each state has laws regulating student records. Each state requires the local school board to adopt policies and procedures to carry out these regulations. Each school, under the direction of the principal, must establish procedures and practices that implement school board policies. To carry out the functions implied and described previously, the principal, faculty, pupil personnel staff, and clerks must know these policies, and the practices required for each function. In summary, a school principal should have forms available for a student or parent who requests to inspect the records; for informing graduating students (and those leaving school) about the destruction of records; for notifying students and parents of the destruction of material in a student's temporary file; for obtaining consent for the release of a student's record to a third party; for notification that a student's record has been provided to a third party who does not need student consent; for releasing certain information to a student's new school; for the possible publication of certain student information during the school year; and for maintaining a log of persons who have obtained access to a student's records.

The second major school-office-responsibility faced by building principals relates to establishing and administering the school budget.

Self-Evaluating Office Management

The self-evaluation checklist shown in Figure 9-2 is based upon eighteen recommendations in the literature regarding the effective and efficient management of the school office.

With modifications in the wording of this checklist, it may be used by teachers, students, school office staff, and others to asses their perceptions of how well the school office is managed and how well it functions. The purpose is to find out what you have to do to improve the services provided or to maintain the quality of such services.

Evaluating Office Personnel

Needless to say, school office personnel should be evaluated on the basis of their performance and their relationship with others in the school. Most school districts, through contract negotiations with local unions, have specific regulations and assessment instruments for performance review of classified personnel.

The school site administrator should assume certain responsibilities for new classified personnel assigned to the school. In a conference with the new person, he/she should discuss the importance of the job as it relates to the school objectives and its culture and climate, review the evaluation procedures to be used and the criteria for evaluation, and give the new employee a copy of the evaluation form to be used. Either you or your delegate should provide a tour of the facilities and introductions to other school personnel. If you have written office policies and procedures, this person should have a copy and be given some time to review and ask questions about its content. During the first two or three weeks, arrange for a mentor to whom this person can go to to get questions answered. If this is not possible, do it yourself. You should also informally check the new

1. How would you rate the organization and administration of the school office?
   ____Excellent   ____Good   ____Fair   ____Poor
2. Does the office run efficiently in the principal's absence?
   ____Definitely   ____Somewhat   ____Not at all
3. Do the office functions seem to be properly delegated to appropriate office personnel?
   ____Yes   ____No   ____For some, but not all
4. Is there a procedural manual for each member of the office staff?
   ____Yes   ____No   ____We don't need one
5. Is the office organized in such a way that it provides a direct service to the school's educational program?
   ____Definitely   ____Somewhat   ____Not at all
6. Are in-service training opportunities provided members of the office staff?
   ____Regularly   ____Sometimes   ____Never/Seldom
7. Is the filing system effective and efficient?
   ____Yes   ____No
8. Does each member of the office staff know the daily tasks they are expected to perform?
   ____Yes   ____No
9. Is there a job description for each member of the office staff?
   ____Yes   ____No
10. Are appropriate time-saving machines and equipment available to the office staff?
    ____Yes   ____No   ____A few are, but we need more
11. Is there an office schedule (routine but flexible) for each member of the office staff?
    ____Yes   ____No   ____We really don't need one
12. Is there a procedure for faculty and staff to follow should they wish to use school office services?
    ____Yes   ____No
13. Is there a cooperative system for the supervising and evaluating of office staff?
    ____Yes   ____No
14. Does the layout of the office (color, work space, ventilation, light, etc.) contribute to efficiency and favorable working conditions?
    ____Definitely   ____Somewhat   ____Not at all
15. Is there an office work-climate that is friendly, cooperative, and one of high morale?
    ____Definitely   ____Somewhat   ____Not at all
16. Is the procedure for obtaining school supplies and equipment efficient enough so that it requires a minimum amount of time and effort?
    ____Yes   ____No
17. Does the office staff respond politely and courteously to the inquiries and/or visitations by faculty, students, parents, and others?
    ____Most do   ____Some do, some don't   ____Few do
18. Is the office staff encouraged to share their ideas and suggestions for more effective management with the principal or his or her representative?
    ____Yes   ____No   ____Yes, but few do

FIGURE 9-2
Office Management Self-Evaluation Checklist

person's progress during the first two or three weeks by observing his/her performance and by informal conversations with the new employee.

All new and experienced classified personnel should be evaluated. The form shown in Figure 9-3 is used by the San Diego Unified School District (California). While it is not the intent here to review the detailed instructions that this district provides in its booklet, *Performance Evaluation Guide for Classified Employees,* some explanation of the content of the form would be helpful. A summary of instructions for using the form follows:

General

- After marking very lightly with pencil each factor in Section A, the rater shall review the report with his/her principal or department head, if any. Markings and comments shall then be typed or inked in. Either the rater or reviewer (or both) shall then review the rating with the employee in a private interview. All signatures shall be in ink. Changes and corrections shall be initialed by the employee.
- If space for comments is inadequate, attachments (either typewritten or in ink) may be included, but each must be signed and bear the same date as the Performance Evaluation Report Form.
- Unscheduled reports may be filed at any time to record progress achieved or specific work performance deficiencies.

Section A

Check (✓) one column for each factor. N/A may be used when a factor is considered "not applicable" to a particular job. Each check mark in *Unsatisfactory* or *Requires Improvement* must have a specific explanation in Section B.

Section B

Desribe outstanding qualities and superior performance. Give specific reasons for check marks in *Unsatisfactory* or *Requires Improvement* columns. Record here any other specific reasons why the employee should not be recommended for permanent status, or—if the employee is already permanent—any specific reasons for required improvement. Attachments, if included, should be indicated in space provided.

Section C

Enter the dates employee was counseled on noted deficiencies. SUMMARY EVALUATION: Check the appropriate box to indicate overall performance here, taking into account all factors and total performance for the full period of service being evaluated.

Unsatisfactory: Performance is clearly inadequate in one or more critical factors as explained or documented in Section B. Employee has

PERFORMANCE EVALUATION REPORT
Classified Personnel - except
Supervisory and paraprofessional
San Diego City Schools

| Use ink or typewriter for final markings |

Reference: Proc. No. 4530

EMPLOYEE NAME		SOCIAL SECURITY NO.	COST CENTER NAME		COST CTR NO
POSITION TITLE		EMPLOYEE STATUS	IF UNSCHEDULED REPORT CHECK HERE ☐	DUE DATE:	

SECTION A

Unsatisfactory / Requires Improvement / Meets Standards

Immediate supervisor must check each category in appropriate column.

FACTOR CHECK LIST

1. **Observance of Work Hours:** Dependable and punctual attendance.

2. **Productivity/Quality of Work:** Completes an acceptable level of quality work.

3. **Job Skill Level:** Demonstrates required skills.

4. **Communication Skills:** Communicates well orally and in writing; effectively carries out verbal and written instructions.

5. **Working Relationships:** Works with and relates to others effectively.

6. **Adaptability/Flexibility:** Accepts change; works effectively under stress; responds to varying needs.

7. **Observance of Safety/Health Standards:** Demonstrates knowledge of district safety/health/sanitary procedures.

SECTION B
Superior performance in any category should be described in detail. Check marks in "Unsatisfactory" or "Requires Improvement" must be supported with documentation.

ATTACHMENTS ADDED   YES ☐   NO ☐

SECTION C
Employee was counseled on noted deficiencies: (Dates) _____   _____   _____

SUMMARY EVALUATION: Unsatisfactory ☐   Requires Improvement ☐   Meets Standards ☐
(Check one)

SECTION D
Goals and Objectives:

RATER: _____   REVIEWER: _____

Signature   Date   Signature   Date

My supervisor has discussed this report with me and given me a copy of this evaluation report. I understand my signature does not necessarily indicate agreement.
Comments:

ATTACHMENTS ADDED   YES ☐   NO ☐   _____
Signature   Date

DS 1085   —SEE INSTRUCTIONS ON REVERSE —   **PERSONNEL DEPT. COPY**

FIGURE 9-3
Courtesy of the San Diego City School District.

demonstrated an inability or unwillingness to improve or to meet standards. Performance is not acceptable for position held. (Note: Such summary evaluation bars the employee from promotional examinations for one year.)

Requires Improvement: Total performance periodically or regularly falls short of normal standards. Specific deficiencies should be noted in Section B. This evaluation indicates the supervisor's belief that the employee can and will make the necessary improvements.

Meets Standards: Indicates consistently competent performance meeting or exceeding standards in all critical factors for the position. Most employees will fall into this category. If margin is narrow and standards are barely met, explain in Section B.

IF PROBATIONARY: Make recommendation regarding permanent status.

Section D

Record progress or improvements in performance resulting from employee's efforts to reach previously set goals. Record agreed upon or prescribed performance goals for the next evaluation period.

Signatures

Both the rater and the employee shall date and sign the report. The employee's signature indicates that the conference has been held and that he/she has had an opportunity to read the report. If he/she refuses to sign for any reason, explain that his/her signature does not necessarily imply or indicate agreement with the report and that space is provided to record any disagreement. Further refusal to sign shall be recorded on the report. Attachments, if included, should be indicated in the space provided.

Appeal

Evaluation reports express the judgment and opinions of supervisory authority and as such are not subject to appeal under rules of the merit system unles there has been a resultant action taken to suspend, demote, or dismiss a permanent employee.

While the discussion in this section focuses mainly on office personnel, district evaluation procedures center on all classified personnel. Near the end of this chapter assessment of food service and transportation service personnel will be described. But a few thoughts about the evaluating and supervising of classified personnel is in order.

In most school districts, there is a five-step process regarding the employment of staff personnel. The details of this process are usually negotiated in advance with union representatives. Three of the five steps—recruitment, selection, and training—are usually done at the district level.

The school principal, while having some input into these three tasks, is required to attend to the remaining two steps—supervision and evaluation.

The recruitment process in any school district should involve personnel from individual schools as well as from the district office. A representative committee of administrators, teachers, staff, parents, union representatives, and, in some cases, students should be involved in some manner. All applicants should be required to file a written application with references, and any other information necessary to help the selection process.

The selection of personnel should be based on the evidence at hand and on the regulations required by the equal employment opportunity mandates. The selection should be made only after the finalists in the recruitment process have completed required tests—written, oral, or performance—and after they have been interviewed by the committee at the school level.

The training of personnel should coincide with a probationary period during which time the new employees are carefully supervised and trained to accomplish the tasks required for the job. Orientation programs, procedure books, handbooks, and in-service programs should be made available to all new employees.

Procedures for supervising employees should be detailed, in advance, so that the supervisor and the employees know the criteria for supervision, i.e., based on job description, use of an observation instrument, a required conference, etc. Supervisory practices should be viewed as a positive process focusing on ways to help employees improve skills, attitudes, and performance.

The evaluation process, in conjunction with the supervision tasks, is a major responsibility of the school principal. The school principal is, and should be, responsible for providing periodic supervisory and evaluation reports. The evaluation should be based on the job description, the employee's performance, and the purpose of the evaluation (whether it be for retention/dismissal or promotion/compensation).

The second major school-office-responsibility faced by building principals relates to establishing and administering the school budget.

BUDGET AND ACCOUNTING PROCEDURES

There are four basic steps for establishing a school budget: preparing the budget, presenting it to the board of education and eventually to the public, administering the approved budget, and evaluating the plan to determine how the money appropriated was used and for what purpose.

There are a multitude of management systems designed to facilitate (and in some cases complicate) the process of budget planning. General practice has the school principal active in each phase, particularly in the preparation, administration, and evaluation of the school budget. It seems apparent, then, that a school principal must be able to demonstrate knowledge and skill in:

- Understanding budget-making procedures
- Developing a school budget that results from consultation with faculty and staff
- Preparing a school budget that supports the school's educational program
- Keeping accurate financial records of receipts and expenditures
- Preparing and delivering sound financial reports to the superintendent (or the superintendent's designated school business manager), the board, and the school's public
- Effectively managing and evaluating budget allocations made to the school.

No pretense is made here to provide a short course on school budget and finance. Experienced principals have probably had a course called school business management and have learned from on-the-job-training. Aspiring principals will probably have to take a school business management course that may or may not answer all of their questions. What is presented here is an overview designed to help you evaluate how to go about the task of budgeting, and if you are a practicing administrator, how skillfully you administer and account for budget allocations. Information, then, will be presented (for your self-evaluation) relative to three primary responsibilities: the preparation of the school budget, the administration of that budget, and the managing and accounting procedures you use in your school.

Preparing the Budget

The first step to budget preparation is to know about the classification system used in the school district. Principals should ask themselves these questions:

1. Do I know the basic budget categories used by my school district?
2. Do I use these categories in the preparation of my school budget?
3. Do I know how the total school budget is put together?
4. Is the school district's classification system of value to me as I prepare and evaluate my school budget?

Recommended procedures for preparing a school budget are identified in the evaluation scale in Figure 9-4. You might begin by determining which of the ten procedures you actually used last year.

Following your evaluation of the extent to which you use these procedures in preparing your school budget, it is important that you and your staff consider each school program and service. Use the following outline in evaluating and preparing a budget for these programs and services:

- Purpose of the program and/or service
- Specific activities and procedures required in providing this program and/or service
- Personnel needs and costs for each program and/or service
- Support personnel needed (example: part-time secretary for speech pathologist) and cost
- Supplies and equipment needed for each program and/or service
- Building space needs for each program and/or service

Evaluate the extent to which your budget preparation procedures:

	Great	*Moderate*	*Little*
1. Assess the educational needs of:			
a. students.	——	——	——
b. teachers.	——	——	——
c. staff.	——	——	——
d. professional service personnel.	——	——	——
2. Involve careful thought on your part.	——	——	——
3. Reflect the objectives of the instructional program.	——	——	——
4. Reflect the objectives of student activities and services.	——	——	——
5. Reflect the priorities established by you and others.	——	——	——
6. Reflect cost-estimates.	——	——	——
7. Include alternatives should budget not be approved or be reduced.	——	——	——
8. Reflect evaluation of monies spent during the past year.	——	——	——
9. Require teachers and others to provide rationales for requests.	——	——	——
10. Reflect your consultation with superintendent and/or central office staff.	——	——	——

FIGURE 9-4
Evaluation of Budget Preparation Procedures

- Last year's evaluation of program and service activities, costs, benefits, and personnel.

This review procedure requires that you and your faculty/staff give some serious thought to the programs and services provided to the young people in attendance. Not only does it provide an overall view of programs and services, but it encourages a yearly examination of program success and failures, personnel performance, and use of funds.

In review, the principal, with the cooperation of the personnel in the school, prepares the budget after examining school programs and services in relation to the:

- Purpose (objectives) of each
- Activities and procedures
- Personnel needed
- Support personnel needed
- Supplies and equipment needed
- Building space needed
- Evaluation results from previous and current year
- Projected cost estimates for next two or three years.

Administering the Budget

My experience as a school board member convinces me that school principals can be a valuable asset in the preparation and administration of the school budget. Public response to school budget meetings is not impressive, yet there is widespread concern about the budget—the cost of educating young people. Minimal attendance at annual budget meetings places a greater burden on board members and school administrators to get the budget message to the people. The usual school district activities of holding public hearings, publishing budget information in newspapers, bulletins, and newsletters, and meeting with community groups can be supplemented by a school principal who is probably closer to the school's public than is the central office staff, the superintendent, and/or any particular board of education member. In preparing and administering the budget, the principal can use a variety of methods for informing the school's clientele about it. Some ideas are presented in the chapter on school-community relationships. The point here is that the principal should not underestimate his or her influence in this area.

Once the school budget has been approved, the monies are to be put to use for the purposes intended. Most school districts employ automated accounting procedures that save time and effort. Most systems now have procedures that centralize purchasing; require competitive bids for supplies, equipment, and repairs; include methods for the requisitioning of supplies and equipment; and provide guidelines to school principals for the management of individual school accounts.

The tasks of the school principal in this area will vary according to the size and level of the school. Junior-senior high school principals will have many more accounting tasks to perform than will middle-elementary school principals. Some of the tasks may be common to both, in kind, but certainly vary in degree. For example, an elementary principal may have responsibility for book fees, as will the high school principal, but the high school principal's tasks are increased because of the number of students, the variety of programs, and the procedures used. Nevertheless, each and every principal has a responsibility for accounting for the revenue and expenditures for their individual school.

Evaluating Accounting Procedures

Almost every textbook on school administration has a chapter on school financial accounting. Few provide a method that principals can use to evaluate current practices. Adequate, effective financial procedures are essential. The major question is how can school principals evaluate the effectiveness of their current accounting practices? To answer this question an evaluation form was designed and is recommended for use by principals (Figure 9-5).

It should be noted that each "procedure" item is based upon recommendations from the literature and/or actual administrative practices. A principal who rates a particular item "sometimes" or "seldom" should take the time to examine the reasons for the rating, his or her current procedures, and ways these procedures can be changed.

Evaluating Budget Management

If a school principal has prepared the individual school budget carefully and with proper justifications, the use of monies should be evaluated with the same care and concern. No doubt the school district will have some specific method for evaluating the school budget. As suggested earlier, most school districts are required to submit to an annual audit. For a school principal, the evaluation of the budget centers on how the monies were spent, what accounting procedures were used, how the supplies and equipment were purchased and used, and how the principal managed school funds. The form provided in Figure 9-6 illustrates an idea for evaluating how effectively and efficiently the principal manages the budget.

As the figure shows, the principal can obtain a rating from his or her superiors (the superintendent, business manager) and from faculty and staff. Comparisons may be made. Additional items may be added to assess varying school policies and procedures.

Write the appropriate number in the box using the following scale: 1—Definitely; 2—Sometimes; 3—Seldom or Never; 4—Not Applicable	Bookstore	Student sales	Athletic funds	Luncheon sales	Petty cash	School fees	Tickets for school events	Special programs	School supplies	School equipment	Book rentals	Comments
My Procedure: is efficient												
requires receipts												
requires vouchers												
is subject to audit												
requires monthly reports												
requires an annual report												
requires all persons handling money to be bonded												
includes the use of forms that are clear and accurate												
includes banking all money received												
includes a method for authorizing expenditures												
requires that expenditures be paid only by check												
in general, provides an effective accounting system												

FIGURE 9-5
Evaluating Procedures for School Fund Accounting

Directions: This form is designed to help me determine how effectively and efficiently I manage the school budget. Please circle the number that best reflects your perception of that item. Thank you for your time and cooperation.

Respondent: ____Administrator   ____Teacher   ____Staff

Item	*Excellent*		*Good*		*Poor*
1. Preparation of the school budget	1	2	3	4	5
2. Management of school funds	1	2	3	4	5
3. Management of school supplies and equipment	1	2	3	4	5
4. Involves faculty and staff in budget preparation	1	2	3	4	5
5. Involves faculty and staff in budget evaluation	1	2	3	4	5
6. Keeps school personnel informed about budget throughout the school year	1	2	3	4	5
7. Demonstrates leadership in attaining program and service objectives within budget limitations	1	2	3	4	5
8. Demonstrates leadership in identifying needs and resources to meet these needs	1	2	3	4	5
9. Other	1	2	3	4	5

FIGURE 9-6
Form for Evaluating School Principal's Management of School Budget

In review, this discussion has focused on several major administrative responsibilities regarding office services including the evaluation of office service and management, the evaluation of school records and reports, and the evaluation of budget and accounting procedures.

There are two additional services worthy of discussion and evaluation—food and transportation. The remainder of this chapter will examine ways to evaluate these services and the personnel who provide them.

EVALUATING FOOD SERVICES

Here is a scenario regarding the food service program in the typical elementary or secondary school. Let's assume it is your school. There is a lunch program operating daily, serving a "Type A" lunch supplemented by other food options (sandwiches, snacks, etc.). Many students bring a sack lunch and purchase only milk and dessert. The food is either prepared in your school building or it is delivered to the school from a centralized food preparation area in the school district. You have limited or no responsibilities regarding the selection, preparation, or portioning of the daily lunches (and breakfast in some school districts). You administer the lunch program following policies established by the school board and rules and regulations established by the district's food director.

You notice and can expect over the next decade an increase in student participation in the school's food service programs. You have come to realize that there are various reasons for this current or expected increase in the number of students remaining at school for lunch. One reason may be that the school board has established a "closed" lunch period (students are not allowed to leave school grounds during the lunch period). Other reasons, all obvious to you, include the fact that more of the students in your school are coming from single-parent homes; there is a significant increase in families in which both parents work; there are many more students qualifying for a governmentally-subsidized lunch (and breakfast); and for many of your students the breakfast and/or lunch they receive at school may be their most nutritious meal of the day.

With this scene in mind, an examination of ways you can evaluate and improve the food services in your school may be worthwhile. An outline of a principal's specific responsibilities will help set the stage for the recommended evaluation techniques.

Principal's Responsibilities

This section includes an outline of specific responsibilities each school principal should follow in order to operate an effective and efficient food service program. You might use these responsibilities as a guide for self-evaluation and/or as a means for improving what you currently do regarding this school service. Therefore, to insure a sound and productive food service program, you should:

1. Use school board policies as guidelines for developing program rules and regulations.
2. Insure that teachers, students, and food service personnel understand and implement ways that the food service program contributes to and is incorporated into the school's educational program.
3. Create a representative committee to establish food service program goals and objectives, if these are not currently available.
4. Clearly establish "line" responsibilities regarding the evaluation and supervision of food service programs and personnel.

5. Create an environment in the lunchroom/cafeteria that contributes to healthy eating habits, manners, behavior, and decorum.
6. Provide adequate and attractive space and facilities for food service personnel and participants.
7. Continually assess administrative methods of operating the food service programs; i.e., scheduling, food selection, preparation, delivery, distribution, traffic flow, etc.
8. Inspect and evaluate the equipment and supplies and the need for repair and/or replacement.
9. Establish simple, reliable accounting procedures for budgeting and handling cash receipts.
10. Encourage and promote cooperation and communication between food service personnel and the faculty and staff.
11. Periodically solicit participants' attitudes and opinions regarding the school's food service program.
12. Work with the food service director (dietician) in providing in-service training opportunities for food service personnel.
13. Find out and then disseminate to others the different and interesting things other school districts are doing regarding food service programs.

Food Service Evaluation Plan

Since there is no uniform food service program operating in all school districts and since each school food service operation is conditioned by a variety of on-site factors (availability of a lunch room, conversion of gym to lunch facility, preparation of food in or out of the school, etc.), school principals should develop their own plans and procedures to insure effective and efficient operating of the food service program. As suggested in Chapter 1, establishing a school committee may be the best approach in assessing the food service program, its procedures, and its personnel. The following items may be worthy of evaluation. Reasons for evaluating the particular items are described with some suggestions for how and when the item should be assessed.

Philosophy

Why? Increasingly, school teachers are examining and using the food service program as part of the educational outcomes of the curriculum. "However, the primary role of the food services operation is that of providing tasty, tempting, balanced meals of reasonable costs to the students."[2]

How? Have teachers discuss, illustrate, and assess how the food service program could be incorpoated into such courses as chemistry, biology, health, consumer economics, and sociology. Teachers may also be encouraged to show how they use the food service program to provide student opportunities for learning:

- To select the right foods (nutrition)
- To maintain a proper diet
- Career education possibilities in the service occupations
- Socialization skills, manners, decorum, and proper behavior
- About cleaniness, waste, and sanitation
- About foods of various cultures and nationalities.

When? If the curriculum possibilities of the food service program have not been examined in your school, it may be a good idea to ask the teachers to consider this opportunity at the next curriculum meeting. If your school does incorporate some of these ideas, an evaluation of the worth and progress to date may be warranted.

Problems/Issues

Why? Principals should be aware of national and state issues because knowledge and understanding of these may be helpful in decision making at the local level. For example, there has been much debate and discussion of such topics as open and closed lunch periods, waste of food in school lunch programs, junk foods from school vending machines, use of student help in the cafeteria, the need for schools to serve breakfast, mass feeding psychology, student behavior, and alternate ways of providing food services to students.

How? A great deal of information can be obtained by reading appropriate educational journals, using the resources at the end of this chapter, and by attending educational conferences with programs on these topics.

When? Spend fifteen to twenty minutes each day reading about these topics. Seek out conferences and, if you have time, start educating yourself now.

Personnel

Why? Like other school personnel, food service personnel need to be supervised and evaluated so that strengths and limitations of each member and the entire group are identified and defined.

How? In cooperation with the district's food service director, the union representative (if your food service employees belong to a union) and the school principal should establish a supervisory and evaluation plan. There must be agreement on who is going to do what; that is, in the supervision and evaluation of food service personnel what will be the responsibilities of the food service director vis-à-vis the school principal? In most school districts, the school principal? In most school districts, the school principal assumes supervisory responsibilities of personnel working in that school. (An example of the type of rating scales that can be used for evaluating food service is shown in Figure 9-7.)

When? Food service personnel should be evaluated yearly, as should all faculty and staff in your school, with the purposes, criteria, and procedures understood and accepted by those involved.

Accounting

Why? Since the principal is primarily responsible for the security of cash, checks, and the accounting procedures used in the school, an evaluation of the procedures used in carrying out this responsibility is paramount.

How? A school principal could benefit from observing how lunch monies are collected and transported either to the school office or the bank each day. Careful observation may suggest that better ways of collecting and transporting these monies are necessary. Recall the discussion regarding ways to evaluate accounting procedures (Figure 9-8). In addition, the checklist in Figure 9-8 may provide ideas and serve as a check on what you are currently doing in your school regarding school lunch accounts.

When? A few minutes to observe your procedures over the next two or three days may save you hours of explanations later on. After completing the observation and the checklist, take a few more minutes to decide if there is, indeed, a better, safer, more responsible way of accounting for school food service monies.

Operation

Why? The school principal carries the primary responsibility for the management of the school's food service operation. This responsibility includes, among other things, the preparation and delivery of food; the quality and quantity of food served per lunch; the number of students and others participating in the lunch program; the scheduling and supervising of students; the traffic flow to and from the cafeteria; the equipment and supplies in the kitchen and cafeteria; the physical facilities and atmosphere in the cafeteria; the collection and handling of monies; an adherence to the school district's policies and procedures; the school's compliance with state and local health and sanitation laws; the attitude of students and others toward the food service program and its personnel; and the working relationship among food service personnel, district office staff, and the school's faculty and staff.

Date of Evaluation _____

Period Covered _____ to _____

Social Security #

Name _____

Present Position _____

School and/or Department _____

INTERPRETATION OF RATING SCALE

UNSATISFACTORY	Performance is unacceptable. Two or more markings in this category or four or more markings in the marginal area in any one reporting period will be cause for appropriate action to be initiated.
MARGINAL	One to three markings in this category indicates barely acceptable performance. Requires a high degree of supervision, needs improvement.
SATISFACTORY	Performance is mostly acceptable and may require supervision in other than routine matters. Performance is considered average.
GOOD	Performance is usually acceptable. Requires little or no supervision.
VERY GOOD	Performance is usually highly acceptable. Performs most duties in an exemplary manner.

AREAS MARKED UNSATISFACTORY AND/OR MARGINAL MUST BE EXPLAINED IN WRITING. A PROGRAM FOR IMPROVEMENT IN UNSATISFACTORY OR MARGINAL AREAS MUST ACCOMPANY THIS APPRAISAL.

JOB FACTORS	8 VERY GOOD	6 GOOD	4 SATISFACTORY	2 MARGINAL-NEEDS IMPROVEMENT	0 UNSATISFACTORY	RATER COMMENTS
(1) Quality of Work						
(a) Accuracy						
(b) Neatness						
(c) Thoroughness						
(2) Quantity of Work						
(a) Completion of Work as Scheduled						
(b) Amount of Work Performed Consistently						
(c) Ability to Organize Work						
(3) Job Knowledge						
(a) Knowledge of Materials & Equipment						
(b) Knowledge of Methods						
(c) Care and Use of Equipment						
(4) Judgment, Dependability & Initiative						
(a) Ability to Follow Directions						
(b) Ability to Perform Tasks with Little or No Supervision						
(c) Observance of Regulations, Procedures, & Policies						
(d) Adaptability to New & Unusual Situations						
(5) Interpersonal Relationships						
(a) Ability to Work Harmoniously with Other Employees						
(b) Ability to Work with/for Those Who Supervise						
(c) Ability to Meet & Relate with the Public						
(d) Attention to Personal Hygiene						
(e) Attention to Personal Appearance						
(6) Attendance						
(a) Regularity in Attendance						
(b) Punctuality in Attendance						
(7) Observance of Safety Precautions						
(a) To Prevent Injury to Self						
(b) To Prevent Injury to Others						
CRITERIA FOR EVALUATION OF ASSISTANTS I & II & MANAGERS						
(a) Organizing & Assigning Work						
(b) Delegation of Authority & Responsibility						
(c) Analysis and Resolution of Problems						
(d) Training & Development of Employees						
(e) Maintaining Employee Morale						

OVERALL RATING: _____

(cont.)

FIGURE 9-7
Denver Public Schools
Department of Food and Nutrition Services
Performance Evaluation
Courtesy of the Denver Public Schools.

Recommendations, Time Lines, and Plans for Improving Performance _____

_____

_____

Employee Comments: _____

_____

Appraisal Prepared by _____   _____
              (Rater)   (Date)   (Reviewer)   (Date)

Signature of Employee _____ Date _____

(Employee's signature does not indicate approval, only that he/she has seen and discussed it with the appraiser.)

White - Personnel Services   Canary - Department   Pink - Employee

FIGURE 9-7 (*cont.*)

	We Do This Now	Good Idea; We Should Do This	No Need To Do This In Our School
1. A cash register, with printed tape recording each cash transaction, is used for lunch payments.	_____	_____	_____
2. Each teacher collects monies for snacks and lunches, then files a daily accounting report with the school secretary.	_____	_____	_____
3. Students/others buy food tickets daily or weekly from the homeroom teacher or the school office (store).	_____	_____	_____
4. A ledger is used for keeping lunch records of expenditures and receipts.	_____	_____	_____
5. Money is placed in a safe area, preferably in the school safe.	_____	_____	_____
6. Daily cash vouchers are transported to the district's business office or bank in locked moneybags each day.	_____	_____	_____
7. All persons handling school food service monies are bonded.	_____	_____	_____
8. Receipts are obtained for all monies deposited each day/week.	_____	_____	_____
9. A monthly financial accounting statement should be filed with the business manager.	_____	_____	_____

FIGURE 9-8
Lunch Fees Accounting Checklist

How? There are a number of ways principals can assess the extent to which they are successfully managing each of the responsibilities listed above. A few examples will illustrate this point:

1. *Rating scales* can be effective in soliciting lunch participants' attitudes about the program.
2. *Observing and recording* aspects of the daily operation such as student behavior, length of time it takes to get lunch and pay for it, handling of trays and cash registers, food waste, and quantity of food per lunch can provide useful information to solve potential or current problems.
3. *Opinionnaires* can be used to find out about users' opinions for improving the school lunch program.
4. *Interviews* with students, teachers, and food service personnel may provide helpful information for better management of this program.
5. *Conferences* with groups of students, teachers, and food service personnel may reveal concerns, problems, issues, strengths, and weaknesses in the way the program is operating and managed.

When? Principals should use at least one method of assessing the food service operation in their school each school year.

Student Participation and Behavior

Why? It is well known, at least among students, that participation in the lunch programs is directly related to a variety of factors, some of which are the behavior of students, the attractiveness and decor of the cafeteria, the quality and variety of foods, the time it takes to get and eat lunch, and so on.

In some schools, the cafeteria, like the restrooms, is the last place most students wish to visit. In other schools, students can hardly wait for the lunch period so that they can rest, relax, and enjoy a delicious lunch while socializing with their friends.

Student participation is essential if the school food service program is to be an educational and financial success. It is estimated that at least one-third to one-half of the student body must participate. For this reason, principals should rely on student judgment regarding participation, quantity and quality of foods served, the atmosphere of the cafeteria, and other factors that will influence their willingness to participate. Many times the perceptions and judgments of the principal and teachers regarding the school's lunch program will differ from those of the student body. Principals and teachers may want a quiet, restful, atmosphere and shorter lunch

Directions: We want your opinion and your rating of this school's lunch program. The information you provide will help us improve and do a better job. "Grade" each of the items below by circling the letter that best describes your rating of that item.

Item	*Excellent*	*Good*	*Fair*	*Poor*
1. Time for lunch	A	B	C	D
2. Lunchroom atmosphere	A	B	C	D
3. Quality of lunch	A	B	C	D
4. Quantity of lunch	A	B	C	D
5. Behavior of students	A	B	C	D
6. Variety of lunches	A	B	C	D
7. Cost of lunch	A	B	C	D
8. Cafeteria workers	A	B	C	D
9. Student workers	A	B	C	D
10. Length of lunch times	A	B	C	D
11. Condition of trays and utensils	A	B	C	D
12. Attractiveness of lunchroom	A	B	C	D
13. Traffic flow to and from lunch	A	B	C	D
14. Waste disposal procedures	A	B	C	D
15. Teacher/aide supervision	A	B	C	D

16. What *improvements* do you suggest regarding:
    a. physical facilities?

    b. food offerings?

    c. student conduct?

    d. lunch period (time)?

    e. other (specify)?

17. If you were in charge of this school's lunch program, what would you change and/or improve?

18. Name two or three major things that "bug" you about this school's lunch program.
    a. _____
    b. _____
    c. _____

FIGURE 9-9
Student Rating Scale for Lunch Program

period while students prefer a longer time for eating lunch in an atmosphere of noise, talk, and opportunity for socializing. It is important to underscore the point that student participation is dependent upon their attitudes and desires to eat in the school cafeteria.[3]

There are several factors that tend to increase student participation in the school lunch program. Some of the major factors include teachers and students eating together, an increase in the number of students bussed to school, a history of cafeteria service in the school, sufficient seating capacity, publishing the menu in advance, a variety of food choices, food quality and quantity, shorter lines and an adequate eating time, closed lunch periods, and a lack of nearby restaurants.

How? The evaluation techniques recommended under the discussion of the "Operation" of the food service program would be appropriate here. In addition, it may be helpful to have an example of a student rating scale that you can use or adapt to evaluate the lunch program in your school. Figure 9-9 is an example of such a student rating scale.

When? One is tempted to suggest that this evaluation be done yearly, but time and other tasks suggest that a principal should assess student opinions when participation decreases, when there are more lunchroom problems than usual, and when and if an assessment has not been done for two or three years.

EVALUATING TRANSPORTATION SERVICES

What was once a rural phenomenon has become an important service for over 40 percent of the school children in this country. From the concept of transportation to get children to their local schools and for transportation to school-sponsored events, school districts now provide transportation services for handicapped and other special students, for students attending special "magnet" schools, and for helping the community racially balance the schools.

The managerial responsibilities of the school principal are carried out within the parameters of the school board's transportation service policies. In reality, the principal has administrative and supervisory responsibilities for services provided only to the students at the school level. However, these responsibilities must be discharged with knowledge and understanding of federal, state, and local laws and regulations and the school district's policies and procedures.

There are concerns regarding pupil transportation issues. Farmer[4] lists and desribes five such issues: demands from community pressure groups, reductions in proposed budgets, driver militancy and turnover, reduced purchasing power of the tax dollar, and increased on-board disciplinary problems.

Your reponsibility for administering and supervising transportation services are based upon decisions others have made regarding:

- Who will receive transportation services
- What other transportation services will be provided students in the school district; i.e., athletics, field trips, etc.
- How federal, state, and local regulations offset the district's transportation plans
- How students qualify for these services
- What rules and regulations guide student behavior, pick-up and delivery, safety measures, etc.
- What the district can and cannot afford
- The best way to provide transportation services, i.e., contract for the service or have a district-owned service
- The best routing and scheduling methods to serve all qualified students in all schools
- The standards, specifications, inspection, and maintenance of transportation vehicles
- The methods for recruiting, selecting, and training of transportation personnel
- The plans and procedures for evaluating transportation services and personnel.

Most school districts have procedures for evaluating transportation personnel. For example, school bus drivers should be evaluated in three ways: written evaluation, behind-the-wheel observations, and on-the-road observations. These three categories would include such factors as: observation of the driver's pre-trip safety inspection of the bus, safe driving practices, adherence to routes and schedules, unauthorized use of the school bus, bus driving habits and skills, attendance at training sessions, handling of children riding the bus and the like.

Evaluating Administration Responsibilities

It may be best to provide you with a list of responsibilities you, as principal, should be doing about transportation services for the students in your school. As you read each item on this list, decide whether (1) this item is something you are currently doing; (2) if so, how well are you doing it?; and (3) if not, why aren't you doing it? This procedure offers a means for self-evaluation. So, as principal you should:

- Know and implement school board policies
- Know and implement the transportation and director's rules and regulations
- Keep school personnel informed of policies, rules, and regulations

- Inform parents, students, and teachers about local school rules, regulations, and procedures
- Provide for the supervision of students while loading and unloading buses
- Solve problems relating to bus services as quickly as possible
- Attend to the needs of special students (see next section)
- Maintain adequate accident records and reports
- Maintain adequate misbehavior records and reports
- Establish simple, easy-to-use forms for teachers, coaches, and others requesting special transportation services
- Publish bus routes and schedules periodically throughout the school year
- Evaluate bus services for your school annually
- Develop notification procedures for students who ride the buses should they become ill during the school day
- Develop procedures that will provide for children who miss the school bus
- Develop an after-school bus schedule and procedure if your school has after-school activities programs
- Encourage teachers to incorporate safety program content into their curriculum
- Establish standards of bus conduct that students must follow
- Develop procedures for handling cases of misconduct
- Encourage teachers and others to develop transportation (bus/bike) safety programs
- Check on the district procedures for vehicle maintenance and repairs
- Ride the buses at least once a year
- Follow a school bus in your car to check on driving and student behavior
- Report concerns and compliments to the district's transportation director
- Establish and publish emergency procedures should the school close for some reason
- Respond immediately to parent concerns and requests
- Work with teachers to develop constructive activities students can do on the bus while riding to and from school.

In addition to these responsibilities, building principals must attend to the transportation needs of special students. Although each school district is responsible for providing safe, reliable transportation for handicapped students, it is the building principal's tasks to:

- Identify students in the school who need special transportation
- Arrange with the district's transportation director the kind of transportation needed; i.e., taxicab, private automobile, minibuses, buses with wheelchair lifts, regular school bus

- Notify the parents and teachers of the kind of transportation that will be provided
- Insure that adequate procedures are implemented for vehicle loading and unloading at the school and the home or shop
- Promote pre-service and in-service training opportunities for drivers servicing handicapped students
- Periodically supervise and evaluate transportation services for handicapped students in the school.

A FINAL COMMENT

The principal's major responsibility is the instructional program. Instructional leadership has become the watchword for school administrators. And well it should be, because instruction is or should be the major focus of what goes on in school. Everything else is tangential to it. Now, for you, the leader-manager, this is easier said than done as you well know. Your success as instructional leader is somewhat related to your skill in managing the services the school provides the students. Effective management of school offices and services might best be summarized in these ten administrative skills:

1. Arrange your personal schedule so that you spend at least two hours each week in a classroom.
2. Assess the time and tasks you spend in doing office work.
3. Organize the school office and services so that they are an example of efficiency and effectiveness.
4. Seek additional help if you really feel you need it.
5. Keep the office open to communication from all sources.
6. Periodically assess office, food, and transportation services.
7. Assess accounting and budgeting procedures that hold people who handle money responsible for what they do with it.
8. Involve faculty and staff in the preparation and evaluation of the school budget and the evaluation of school services.
9. Keep yourself, the faculty, and the staff up-to-date on current issues and trends in school funding and accounting procedures, as well as food and transportation services.
10. Automate records, files, budget, and accounting procedures as much as possible.

NOTES

1. See Chase W. Crawford, "Administrative Uses of Microcomputers Part I: Needs Evaluation," *Bulletin of the National Association of Secondary School Principals* (March 1985): 70–72; and "Administrative Uses of Microcomputers, Part II: Specific Tasks," (April 1985): 53–60.

2. I. Carl Candoli et al., *School Business Administration: A Planning Approach* (Boston: Allyn and Bacon, 1978), p. 228.

3. Emergy Stoops; Max Rafferty; and Russell E. Johnson, *Handbook of Educational Administration: A Guide for the Practitioners* (Boston: Allyn and Bacon, 1975), pp. 463–464.

4. Ernest Farmer, "Current Issues in Pupil Transportation," *School Business Affairs* 50 (April 1984): 20–21.

REFERENCES

Comeau, Lee F. *How to Make a Critical Analysis of Your Transportation System* (New Orleans: Paper presented at the Annual Meeting of the Association of School Business Officials, 1980).

Hensarling, Paul R. *Instruments for the Evaluation of School Special Services: Organization and Administration* (Bryan, TX: Demand Publishing Company, 1983).

Seitz, Charles A., et al. *Report on the Division of Transportation Management, Operations, Review, and Evaluation* (Rockville, MD: Department of Educational Accountability, Montgomery County Public Schools, 1983).

CHAPTER 10

Evaluating the Effectiveness of Managing School Plant and Facilities

The virtue of a man ought to be measured, not by his extraordinary exertions, but by his everyday conduct.

Blaine Pascal

The physical aspects of the school plant and maintenance of its facilities contributes to or detracts from a school environment—its culture and its climate (see chapter three). The school principal has the responsibility to supervise, manage, evaluate, and improve, with assistance from other personnel, the school's physical plant and its facilities. The purpose of this chapter is to help you carry out this charge. Evaluative data should focus on five major factors: the efficient and effective use of the building itself, the operation and care of the building and grounds, the proper management of school supplies and equipment, the safety and security of the people that work in the school as well as the safety and security of the plant and facilities, and the evaluation of personnel responsible for its care and upkeep. Attention to these five factors, coupled with the recommendations in other chapters, should help you manage the school plant more effectively, more efficiently, and even more creatively.

PRINCIPLES AND PRACTICES

Recognizing the changes that take place educationally and socially, the school principal should reflect upon the following principles and practices before evaluation plans are implemented:

1. Theoretically, the school plant and its facilities should be influenced by the education programs and school services. In practice,

281

and in many instances this is not the case, the school plant sometimes influences the school programs. The principal and others
should be aware of the extent to which this exists.

2. Plans should be developed to use all of the space within the school.
   Space should not be wasted.
3. The school plant and its facilities should be modified to meet the
   needs and changes required by the educational program and/or
   school services (including special education students).
4. Safety, security, comfort, and adaptability should be essential factors in plant and facilities management.
5. The proper care of school plant and facilities requires the involvement of faculty, staff, and students.
6. Plans should be developed for the proper supervision and management of the plant and its facilities, supplies, and equipment.
7. Wherever possible, the principal should delegate responsibility for
   plant management to an assistant principal and/or custodian.
8. The principal should continuously evaluate educational needs and
   services and determine the extent to which the physical facilities,
   supplies, and equipment are meeting these needs.
9. School grounds and its equipment should reflect educational, recreational, and community needs.
10. Purchasing of school supplies and equipment should, wherever
    possible, be centralized and result from bids.

HOW TO EVALUATE UTILIZATION
OF SCHOOL SPACE

Evaluating and planning for the efficient use of the school building requires the cooperation of teachers and staff. They are in a central position
to inform the principal about the use of space in the building regarding
the educational program. In planning for evaluation, you, as principal,
should consider two factors: one is the efficient use of the school plant
during the day, when the usual educational program is in session, and the
other is the use of school plant and facilities when school is not in session.

Determining Building Use

One method for determining the use of the school building is the utilization of a building-use chart. The purpose of such a chart is to determine
how, when, and why specific space is used in the school building. The
information gleaned from a chart of this kind may help principals, teachers, and staff plan for a more creative use of school space for programs
and services provided. Figure 10-1 shows a daily building-use chart that
may be useful in determining room utilization except for classrooms. The

Day:_____ Date:_____	Room Capacity	8:00	9:00	10:00	11:00	12:00	1:00	2:00	3:00	4:00	5:00	Utilization Percent Average
Library	50	10 20%	15 30%	40 80%	25 50%	20 40%	45 90%	40 80%	30 60%	10 20%	5 10%	48%
Band room												
Auditorium												
Multipurpose room												
Science laboratory												
Cafeteria												
Art room												
Business Education room												
Home Economics room												
Industrial Arts room												
Gymnasium												
Special Education room												
Guidance Center												
Health Care Services												
Speech Service area												
Bookstore												
Study Hall												
Other												
Building Utilization Summary												

FIGURE 10-1
Daily Building-Use Chart

chart provides a way to examine specific room use for each hour. However, you may find it more effective to include the school's time schedule rather than an hourly schedule.

When using this chart, you should write in the room capacity for each room in the building and the number of students using the room during each time frame. This could also be accomplished by asking each person in charge of a particular room to indicate the room capacity and the number of students in the room each hour (or each scheduled period), each day for one week. For example, you might ask the librarian to provide you with the preceding information. You could duplicate the chart and, using the above procedure, have the band director, music teacher(s), art teacher(s), and others gather the needed information. It should be noted that the chart provides two spaces per time frame. The space at the top is used to record student use. The space at the bottom of the block is the utilization percentage averaged for the day. An example is shown under the Library section. Note that the room capacity is fifty people and that on this particular day ten used the library room at 8:00 A.M., fifteen at 9:00 A.M., and so on. Also, note the percentage of utilization for each hour. This figure is obtained by dividing the number of students using the room by the room capacity. The utilization percent average is computed by adding the percentages and dividing by the number of scores. Thus, on a particular day this library is used every hour, with certain low and peak periods, and an average utilization rate (in relation to room capacity) of a little less than 50 percent.

The principal can obtain some idea of building use by examining the percentages found in the Building Utilization Summary column. Again, this figure is derived by adding the percentages for the time frame and dividing by the number of rooms on the chart.

Teacher: John Jones   Room Capacity: <u>30</u>
Room Number: <u>101</u>   Date:_____

Period	M	T	W	Th	F	Room Available	Used Less Than 70 Percent of Capacity
Before School	0	0	0	0	0	M–F	M–F
Home Room	26	26	26	26	26	0	None
1	28	24	29	18	22	0	Th
2	19	0	22	28	30	I	M
3							
4							
5							
6							
7							
8							
After School							

FIGURE 10-2
Classroom Utilization Chart

Determining Class Use

Figure 10-2 is an example of a classroom-use chart. The chart can be duplicated and given to classroom teachers and others if the principal decides to use this form to collect classroom-use data as well as use of other rooms in the building.

The example shown allows the teacher to identify room use for each day of the week. It also provides a quick summary of non-room use that may be of value when a room is needed for a special reason. The variation in the figures shown is due to different class sizes resulting from grouping and/or the scheduling of sections in each subject matter area. The last two columns of the chart enable the principal to determine quickly when the room is available (unless used for other purposes not charted) and when the room is being used at less than 70 percent capacity (an arbitrary figure).

The point to this analysis of school and classroom usage is the need to have the facility in operation for a significant period of time so that it won't be a waste of taxpayer's money. For example, in Montgomery County, Maryland, surplus school space is leased to qualified users under joint occupancy agreements, thus creating income on otherwise surplus school space![1] That's one way. Another would be to offer the facility to community groups.

EVALUATING COMMUNITY USE
OF SCHOOL FACILITIES

Many communities now offer a variety of programs in school buildings after school hours. Adult education programs, special programs for the youth of the community, and recreational and cultural programs are all scheduled on existing school facilities. In many instances, the school plant is open twelve to fourteen hours a day. For example, a middle school in Colorado serves as a branch of the local library, a recreation center, a preschool, and a meeting place for scouts, churchgoers, and home-owners associations.[2] Community use of the school has many advantages and some problems. There are six particular problems to consider before opening schools to community groups: cost, conditions for use, insurance, school personnel for supervisory work, scheduling, and security.[3] Let's examine these factors in more detail.

Problems with Community Use

Extensive use of school plant and facilities does create several problems for school principals that require attention. Among the major concerns are the following:

1. There is a need for supervision of groups using the facilities.
2. There is also a need for supervision and care of the plant and its

facilities during and after school hours. This requires additional cus-todial staff or paying extra fees to the existing custodial staff.
3. School use costs money for heating, lighting, ventilating, cleaning, and supplies and equipment.
4. A schedule must be made by the principal and/or the principal's designee. This may cause problems when a number of groups want to use the facilities at the same time.
5. Scheduling groups for use of school facilities requires that priority be provided in this fashion: school-concerned activities, extra-curricular activities, local groups, and then other self-supported agencies, organizations, and associations. This procedure some-times causes problems for the school principal.

Regardless of these disadvantages, it is important to remember that the school is a community facility and the advantages certainly outweigh the disadvantages. The disadvantages can be lessened somewhat by spe-cific board of education policies on community use of school facilities.

Checklist for Developing Policies

In general, community use of school buildings is guided by policies and procedures of the board of education. The principal's job is to carry out the school board's policies, clarify these policies to community groups when necessary, and record and report the extent of community use and its effect on the school plant, facilities, supplies, and equipment. To assist principals with this task the following checklist is provided.

_____ 1. Does your school board of education have a policy regarding com-munity use of the school plant and its facilities?
_____ 2. Do you know what the policies are or at least where to find them if needed?
_____ 3. Does your school policy provide classifications of uses?
_____ 4. Does the policy provide a rental fee for use of school facilities?
_____ 5. Does the policy state what procedures should be followed by groups requesting the use of school facilities?
_____ 6. Does the policy state the arrangements necessary for custodial ser-vices?
_____ 7. Does the policy provide guidelines for safety and security during those times community groups are using school facilities?
_____ 8. Does the policy provide guidelines for each school administrator?
_____ 9. Do you file a report of community use of school facilities that in-cludes:
  a. Calendar of events scheduled?
  b. Groups using facilities?
  c. Building condition after each event?

      d. Special concerns?

      e. Fees collected?

___ 10. Does the policy require the filing of an application? (Example: The application should require specific information, including a guarantee regarding damage and/or injuries.)

HOW TO EVALUATE MAINTENANCE
OF PLANT AND FACILITIES

The principal is responsible for the proper maintenance of the school plant, its facilities, and its grounds. The primary goal should be to keep the building in good operating condition, including safety and security, for daily use. The resource for these tasks is the school's custodial staff.

Self-Evaluation Questions

A principal should have specific plans and procedures for the care and maintenance of the school plant and facilities. To insure this, you should consider each of the following questions:

1. Do you have a monthly or biannual plan for supervising/inspecting the school plant, its site, and its facilities?
2. Do you involve custodians and others in planning for the care and maintenance of the school and facilities?
3. Do you have procedures that require teachers and staff to determine the extent to which existing facilities meet the needs of the instructional program, extracurricular programs, and school services?
4. Do you have procedures that identify major alterations, expansion, or remodeling that should be made to better serve the school's programs and services?
5. Do you regularly evaluate any plans and procedures you implement to asssess care and maintenance of the school and facilities?

The evaluation checklists that follow enable a principal, custodian, or both to rate the condition of each item. They provide a means for determining what action should be taken and when. The schedule column enables the principal to engage in short- and long-range planning. The forms provide an excellent way to plan courses of action and a schedule for budgeting for the actions to be taken. The items are by no means a complete listing but they are as comprehensive as will be found in the literature. The principal should add items that reflect factors peculiar to his or her own particular school and grounds.

Checklist for the Inspection of a School's Interior

The checklist shown in Figure 10-3 may be used monthly or biannually by the principal and/or custodian. The data from this checklist can be used for establishing priorities for alterations, remodeling, or additions to the interior of the school.

Checklist for the Inspection of Classrooms

Figure 10-4 illustrates a list of points that should be considered when inspecting classrooms. Periodic inspection of classrooms should be planned by the principal and custodian. However, the key to classroom conditions is the teacher. Each teacher should be required to complete the checklist at least once each year. This procedure, coupled with an inspection by the principal and the custodian, will contribute to safe and functional classrooms.

Checklist for the Inspection of a School's Exterior

One's first impression of a school is obtained by observing the exterior of the school plant. Old schools can be made just as attractive as new schools. Inspection of exterior items is essential because failure to repair items such as roofing, gutters, etc., can often lead to greater expense later on. Therefore, it is essential that the principal and custodians regularly inspect the exterior of the school building. Some of the major items that deserve special attention are identified in Figure 10-5.

Checklist for the Inspection of School Grounds

The school's grounds and its equipment cannot be supervised all the time. Community use of these facilities takes place after school hours. In most cases the use is recreational; sometimes it is destructive. These factors call for the school principal and custodians to insure that regular inspection takes place. It is best to document the inspection in case of liability suits regarding safety of grounds and equipment. Monthly inspections using the checklist in Figure 10-6 is recommended.

Checklist for Asbestos Abatement

Dr. William Nicholson estimates that asbestos in a typical school having 1,000 students could lead to five potential deaths over the lifetime of the school.[4] While the responsibility for an asbestos abatement program is a school district one, there are certain tasks you can do as a school principal

School:_____ Date:_____
Inspected by:_____

Items	Condition			Action					Schedule			Comments/ Notations
	Good	Fair	Poor	Repair	Replace	Remodel	Paint	Clean	This Year	Next Year	Year After	
Plumbing												
Drinking fountains	—	—	—	—	—	—	—	—	—	—	—	———
Toilets	—	—	—	—	—	—	—	—	—	—	—	———
Sinks	—	—	—	—	—	—	—	—	—	—	—	———
Dryers	—	—	—	—	—	—	—	—	—	—	—	———
Showers	—	—	—	—	—	—	—	—	—	—	—	———
Water pipes	—	—	—	—	—	—	—	—	—	—	—	———
Drainage pipes	—	—	—	—	—	—	—	—	—	—	—	———
Electrical												
Fixtures	—	—	—	—	—	—	—	—	—	—	—	———
Lights	—	—	—	—	—	—	—	—	—	—	—	———
Bulletin boards	—	—	—	—	—	—	—	—	—	—	—	———
Ceilings	—	—	—	—	—	—	—	—	—	—	—	———
Wood/Metal trim	—	—	—	—	—	—	—	—	—	—	—	———
Hardware	—	—	—	—	—	—	—	—	—	—	—	———
Floors	—	—	—	—	—	—	—	—	—	—	—	———
Carpets	—	—	—	—	—	—	—	—	—	—	—	———
Safety Devices												
Firehose cabinet	—	—	—	—	—	—	—	—	—	—	—	———
Fire extinguishers	—	—	—	—	—	—	—	—	—	—	—	———
Water shutoff valve	—	—	—	—	—	—	—	—	—	—	—	———
Gas shutoff valve	—	—	—	—	—	—	—	—	—	—	—	———
Electrical master switches	—	—	—	—	—	—	—	—	—	—	—	———
Plates	—	—	—	—	—	—	—	—	—	—	—	———
Switches	—	—	—	—	—	—	—	—	—	—	—	———
Lights	—	—	—	—	—	—	—	—	—	—	—	———
Wiring	—	—	—	—	—	—	—	—	—	—	—	———
Heating/ Ventilation												
Boilers	—	—	—	—	—	—	—	—	—	—	—	———
Pumps	—	—	—	—	—	—	—	—	—	—	—	———
Radiators	—	—	—	—	—	—	—	—	—	—	—	———
Ducts	—	—	—	—	—	—	—	—	—	—	—	———
Corridors/ Halls												
Walls	—	—	—	—	—	—	—	—	—	—	—	———
Stairways	—	—	—	—	—	—	—	—	—	—	—	———
Railings	—	—	—	—	—	—	—	—	—	—	—	———
Door panic bolts	—	—	—	—	—	—	—	—	—	—	—	———

FIGURE 10-3
Checklist for Regular Inspection of Individual School—Interior
(Excluding Classrooms)

School:_____ Date:_____

Inspected by:_____

Items	Condition			Action					Schedule			Comments/ Notations
	Good	Fair	Poor	Repair	Replace	Remodel	Paint	Clean	This Year	Next Year	Year After	
Ceiling	—	—	—	—	—	—	—	—	—	—	—	_____
Walls	—	—	—	—	—	—	—	—	—	—	—	_____
Floor	—	—	—	—	—	—	—	—	—	—	—	_____
Trim	—	—	—	—	—	—	—	—	—	—	—	_____
Hardware	—	—	—	—	—	—	—	—	—	—	—	_____
Cabinets	—	—	—	—	—	—	—	—	—	—	—	_____
Bulletin boards	—	—	—	—	—	—	—	—	—	—	—	_____
Chalk boards	—	—	—	—	—	—	—	—	—	—	—	_____
Furniture	—	—	—	—	—	—	—	—	—	—	—	_____
Electrical fixtures	—	—	—	—	—	—	—	—	—	—	—	_____
Heating ducts	—	—	—	—	—	—	—	—	—	—	—	_____
Ventilation unit	—	—	—	—	—	—	—	—	—	—	—	_____
Shades/blinds	—	—	—	—	—	—	—	—	—	—	—	_____
Intercom system	—	—	—	—	—	—	—	—	—	—	—	_____
Plumbing	—	—	—	—	—	—	—	—	—	—	—	_____
Plumbing fixtures	—	—	—	—	—	—	—	—	—	—	—	_____
Bookcases	—	—	—	—	—	—	—	—	—	—	—	_____
Clock	—	—	—	—	—	—	—	—	—	—	—	_____
Lockers	—	—	—	—	—	—	—	—	—	—	—	_____

FIGURE 10-4

Checklist for Regular Inspection of Classrooms

to insure that your school isn't a health hazard to its occupants. Here is a checklist:

____ 1. Find out about the district's asbestos abatement program.

____ 2. Find out if the program is in compliance with the Environmental Protection Agency's interpretation and notification rules.

____ 3. Get the information about the Federal government's Asbestos School Hazard Act.

____ 4. Be sure that your school is periodically checked for asbestos hazards, particularly in walls, ceilings, around pipes and boilers, through heating and cooling systems.

____ 5. Inform school personnel and parents about the steps you and the district have or have not taken regarding asbestos abatement in your school and school district.

____ 6. Recommend to school district personnel that when they hire an asbestos contractor they:

a) Check references

b) Hire a consultant or an independent air monitoring firm

c) Ask contractor for prequalifications

School:_____ Date:_____
Inspected by:_____

Items	Condition			Action					Schedule			Comments/ Notations
	Good	Fair	Poor	Repair	Replace	Remodel	Paint	Clean	This Year	Next Year	Year After	
Roofing	—	—	—	—	—	—	—	—	—	—	—	_____
Skylights	—	—	—	—	—	—	—	—	—	—	—	_____
Roof vents	—	—	—	—	—	—	—	—	—	—	—	_____
Chimneys	—	—	—	—	—	—	—	—	—	—	—	_____
Walls	—	—	—	—	—	—	—	—	—	—	—	_____
Columns	—	—	—	—	—	—	—	—	—	—	—	_____
Windows	—	—	—	—	—	—	—	—	—	—	—	_____
Sashes	—	—	—	—	—	—	—	—	—	—	—	_____
Facia	—	—	—	—	—	—	—	—	—	—	—	_____
Soffits	—	—	—	—	—	—	—	—	—	—	—	_____
Doors	—	—	—	—	—	—	—	—	—	—	—	_____
Entrance/ Exit stairs	—	—	—	—	—	—	—	—	—	—	—	_____
Downspouts	—	—	—	—	—	—	—	—	—	—	—	_____
Gutters	—	—	—	—	—	—	—	—	—	—	—	_____
Louvers	—	—	—	—	—	—	—	—	—	—	—	_____
Screens	—	—	—	—	—	—	—	—	—	—	—	_____
Fire escapes	—	—	—	—	—	—	—	—	—	—	—	_____
Footing/ Foundation	—	—	—	—	—	—	—	—	—	—	—	_____
Masonry	—	—	—	—	—	—	—	—	—	—	—	_____

FIGURE 10-5
Checklist for Regular Inspection of Individual School—Exterior

d) Beware of the lowest bid
e) Check insurance
f) Document everything
g) Check certification for handling and dumping.[5]

Energy Management Checklist

Like the asbestos abatement program it should be the responsibility of the school board and the district administration to initiate an energy conservation program and to manage this program effectively and efficiently.[6]

The school principal can take the lead in organizing and managing an energy conservation program both at the district level and on his/her own school site. To carry out this responsibility, several questions have to be answered. A checklist of questions will help you get started.

1. ____ Do you currently have an energy conservation program?
2. ____ Do you plan to start a program within the next school year?
3. ____ Is energy conservation an established priority by the school board or superintendent?

School:_____ Date:_____
Inspected by:_____

Items	Condition			Action					Schedule			Comments/ Notations
	Good	Fair	Poor	Repair	Replace	Remodel	Paint	Clean	This Year	Next Year	Year After	
Curbs and gutters	—	—	—	—	—	—	—	—	—	—	—	_____
Driveways	—	—	—	—	—	—	—	—	—	—	—	_____
Sidewalks	—	—	—	—	—	—	—	—	—	—	—	_____
Parking lot	—	—	—	—	—	—	—	—	—	—	—	_____
Water meter	—	—	—	—	—	—	—	—	—	—	—	_____
Gas meter	—	—	—	—	—	—	—	—	—	—	—	_____
Electrical meter	—	—	—	—	—	—	—	—	—	—	—	_____
Fences	—	—	—	—	—	—	—	—	—	—	—	_____
Gates	—	—	—	—	—	—	—	—	—	—	—	_____
Bicycle racks	—	—	—	—	—	—	—	—	—	—	—	_____
Flag pole	—	—	—	—	—	—	—	—	—	—	—	_____
Turf	—	—	—	—	—	—	—	—	—	—	—	_____
Lawns	—	—	—	—	—	—	—	—	—	—	—	_____
Trees	—	—	—	—	—	—	—	—	—	—	—	_____
Shrubs	—	—	—	—	—	—	—	—	—	—	—	_____
Sprinkling system	—	—	—	—	—	—	—	—	—	—	—	_____
Fertilizer/ sand	—	—	—	—	—	—	—	—	—	—	—	_____
Top soil	—	—	—	—	—	—	—	—	—	—	—	_____
Benches/ bleachers	—	—	—	—	—	—	—	—	—	—	—	_____
Drainage	—	—	—	—	—	—	—	—	—	—	—	_____
Playground equipment	—	—	—	—	—	—	—	—	—	—	—	_____

FIGURE 10-6
Checklist for Regular Inspection of School Grounds

4. ____ Does the program involve teachers, staff, and community experts?

5. ____ Do you provide school personnel, parents, and your public with information about energy conservation programs at the local, state, and national level?

6. ____ Do teachers implement units or discuss energy conservation topics with students in their classes?

7. ____ Have teachers and students explored ways to save energy at home and at school?

8. ____ Have you devoted at least one faculty meeting to the topic of energy conservation?

9. ____ Have you created a committee to help you implement an energy conservation program?

10. ____ Have you, with the committee, conducted energy surveys and audits of the school building?

11. ____ Has the committee helped you determine the opportunities present in your school for conserving energy?

12. ____ Has the committee estimated the cost of implementing energy conservation practices?

13. ____ Has the committee estimated the potential benefits (savings) if some or all of the energy conservation recommendations are implemented?

14. ____ Has the committee established a list of priorities for implementing recommended energy conservation practices?

15. ____ Have the energy conservation recommendations been implemented?

16. ____ Have you established, with the committee, ways to monitor the energy conservation measures?

17. ____ Have you and the committee constructed or purchased appropriate forms and checklists for recording the data to be collected?

18. ____ Have you and the committee documented the energy conservation results in a manner that is readable and understandable to the public?

19. ____ Have you considered ways you will share the results of the "audit" and program with the school personnel and the public?

In summary, the principal is responsible for managing others in the efficient and effective use of the school plant and its facilities. The previous sections of this chapter have described ways to evaluate school-space utilization, community use of the building, maintenance of plant and facilities, asbestos abatement, and energy conservation programs.

The building principal also has responsibilities regarding the management of supplies and equipment, safety and security measures, and the evaluation of custodial personnel and services. These are discussed in the following sections of this chapter.

MANAGING SCHOOL SUPPLIES
AND EQUIPMENT

There are seven functions that principals must implement to effectively manage the school's supplies and equipment:

- Requisitioning—What procedures do you use to find out supply and equipment needs of teachers, custodians, secretaries, librarians, and other school personnel?
- Purchasing—What procedures do you use to purchase needed supplies and equipment?

- Receiving—What procedures do you employ for receiving supplies and equipment?
- Storing—What procedures do you use to store school supplies and equipment?
- Distributing—What procedures are used in your school for distributing supplies and equipment?
- Inventorying—What procedures do you use to keep records and reports on school supplies and equipment?
- Evaluating—What evaluating methods do you use to determine how effectively and efficiently you manage school supplies and equipment?

Principles and Practices

When one considers the cost of school supplies and equipment and the contribution they make to the instructional program, the importance of proper management takes on added significance. For this reason, a school principal should consider these principles and practices.

1. The selection of school supplies and equipment should result from a team approach; that is, the principal should involve teachers, custodians, secretary, and others in the selection process.
2. Standardized procedures for requisitioning and purchasing supplies and equipment should be implemented.
3. Standardized supply and equipment lists should be utilized.
4. School personnel should consider cooperative (sharing) use of some supplies and equipment, particularly those that are very expensive.
5. The principal, teachers, and staff should decide whether to use an open or closed stockroom approach. Open stockroom means that personnel are allowed to take supplies as needed. Closed stockroom means that personnel requisition needed supplies and, if approved by the principal, the material is delivered to the classroom by the custodian.
6. The principal or the principal's designee should employ a method for receiving, storing, and inventorying all school supplies and equipment.
7. A team approach should be employed for evaluating the extent to which supplies and equipment ordered and received contributes to the purposes for which it was purchased.

Selecting and Requisitioning

To answer the questions asked in the introduction to this section, examine your current procedures for selecting and requisitioning supplies and equipment with the suggestions that follow:

1. A school team or committee is appointed to obtain supply and equipment needs of all school personnel.
2. The committee uses standardized catalogs for the selection of supplies and equipment.
3. The committee recommendations go to the principal with priority ratings for each item.
4. The committee is given opportunities and responsibilities for the evaluation of supplies and equipment to be purchased (quality, economy) as well as matching supply and equipment requests with the needs of the school program and personnel.
5. The principal prepares a suggested supply and equipment budget establishing his or her own priority ratings.
6. All forms used should meet certain criteria: completed in triplicate, ordering date, priority rating, name of person ordering, school or department, vendor, item, price, etc.
7. Whenever possible use an electronic data processing system to simplify ordering procedures.

Purchasing

The major question here is whether or not purchasing is done by the individual school principal or the school district. Centralizing the purchasing procedures has been found to be of benefit to school districts because buying material in bulk and obtaining bids saves money. The principal's main task is to be sure the purchase orders are ready (usually late spring or early summer) so that the materials are received when the school year opens. The procedure in most school districts requires the principal to submit purchase lists by a certain date, and then let the central office coordinate all requests, prepare orders and appropriate requisition and order forms for carrying out these procedures.

Receiving, Storing, and Distributing

Consider the following guidelines in your receiving, storing, and distributing procedures:

1. Check the item against the invoice.
2. Check the item against the requisition.
3. Check the item for damage.
4. Store supplies and equipment in safe, convenient places.
5. Require that storage facilities be neat, orderly, and uniform.
6. Allow some supplies and equipment to be stored in classrooms, media center, etc., on shelves, in closets, and the like for easier access for teachers and others.
7. Determine whether the open or closed stockroom approach will be used.

Inventories

The major purposes of maintaining inventories of supplies and equipment are:

1. It helps you determine what you have and what you'll need; therefore, it is a good method for budget preparation.
2. It helps you to know what you had in case of fire, theft, or loss through some other reason.
3. It helps school personnel appreciate what they have, and it enables them to plan what they need.

Inventories can be taken annually or continuously throughout the school year. It may be best to inventory equipment on an annual basis and supplies on a continuing basis. That is, teachers and staff should list supplies they have used three or four times throughout the school year rather than wait until the end of the year. When these are filed with the principal at the end of each school year, it serves as an overview of what is and is not available. The principal can use these inventories to prioritize the requisitions received from individuals or a committee.

A useful inventory form for annually itemizing school equipment is shown in Figure 10-7. One of the advantages of a form such as this is that it helps whoever does the inventorying to evaluate the condition of the equipment. This helps the principal establish priorities for repair or replacement and thus contributes to equipment budget preparation.

Figure 10-8 illustrates a form that may be used by the teachers, secretaries, and others for implementing a procedure that continuously records the use of school supplies. Teachers can select certain students to help them complete the inventory in each of the three months. If a central, closed storeroom is used for the distribution of supplies, the secretary or custodian can use the inventory form as well. One of the advantages of this kind of form is that it informs the teachers and principal when crucial supplies are getting low.

Instructional Material Inventory

Inventories of instructional material such as textbooks, workbooks, reference books, and supplementary texts should be of special concern to principals and teachers for these reasons:

1. These materials are subject to theft, fire, and misplacement.
2. They are expensive items to repair or replace.
3. They usually last four to five years.
4. New textbook adoptions cost money and should be carefully budgeted in advance.
5. They are essential to the instructional program.

Name:_____Date:_____

School:_____

Equipment Item	*Date of Purchase*	*Number*	*Condition* E—Excellent G—Good F—Fair P—Poor	*Repair*	*Replace*	*Repair Priority*	*Replace Priority*	*Estimated Cost*	*Comment*

FIGURE 10-7
Equipment Inventory Form

So, the inventorying of instructional materials will tell you what you have and what you'll need—two essential factors for instructional and budget planning.

Inventories of instruction materials should be an annual activity. Depending on the individual school situation, it can be done during the final days of school or, if the principal wishes to use the information for budget preparation, it can be completed during the spring recess. Some students are more than willing to help teachers with tasks such as this. In fact, I believe that students should be given a much more active role in the housekeeping activities necessary in keeping the school lively, bright, and clean. It not only develops responsibility but it provides opportunities for teachers and students to interact in settings other than the classroom.

Name:_____Grade/Dept.:_____
School:_____

Items	No. at Start of Year	Number Left In			Amount to Replace	Est. Cost
		November	February	June		

FIGURE 10-8
Continuous Supply Inventory Form

The inventorying of instructional materials should be complete. That is, it should include textbooks, supplementary texts, reference books, workbooks, trade books, programmed texts, special master packages, periodicals, games and puzzles, and all of the audio-visual material in the classroom or in the department resource center. There are numerous forms that can be used for keeping an inventory. One example is shown in Figure 10-9.

As you will note, this inventory has several features not found in traditional textbook inventory forms. It enables the teacher to determine how many texts have been lost, misplaced, or stolen within the year. It helps identify how many years the texts have been in use. It asks the teacher to judge the condition of the texts and to make recommendations. This information enables the principal and/or committee to plan accordingly. The same kind of form can be used for other instructional materials, i.e., workbooks, reference books, etc.

Name:_____Grade/Dept:_____
School:_____

Title	C	No. B	No. E	YP	YU	Condition U Rb Rp	Recommendations

Code:
C   = Copyright Date
No. B = Number of book at start of this school year
No. E = Number of book at end of this school year (or at spring recess)
YP   = Year Purchased
YU   = Years in Use
U   = Usable for Another Year
Rb   = Needs Rebinding
Rp   = Needs Replacing

FIGURE 10-9
Textbook Inventory Form

Evaluating Management of School Supplies and Equipment

Now that you have been introduced to several ideas, some old and some new, hopefully you are ready to grasp the opportunity to evaluate your current procedures for managing school supplies and equipment. Figure 10-10 provides a scale to help you do this.

Directions: Circle one number in your column that best describes how you rate the procedure. Scale: 1—Every Time; 2—Most of the Time; 3—Some of the Time; 4—Little of the Time; 5—Never.

Procedures	*Principal*	*Faculty/Staff*	*Central Office/Supt.*
1. Selection is based on needs of program and personnel.	1 2 3 4 5	1 2 3 4 5	1 2 3 4 5
2. Selection procedures involve faculty and staff.	1 2 3 4 5	1 2 3 4 5	1 2 3 4 5
3. Standard catalogs are used for ordering.	1 2 3 4 5	1 2 3 4 5	1 2 3 4 5
4. Orders are placed promptly and accurately.	1 2 3 4 5	1 2 3 4 5	1 2 3 4 5
5. Faculty and staff are informed when requisitions are not approved.	1 2 3 4 5	1 2 3 4 5	1 2 3 4 5
6. Procedures for receiving items include invoice and order check, damage check, etc.	1 2 3 4 5	1 2 3 4 5	1 2 3 4 5
7. Storage facilities are adequate.	1 2 3 4 5	1 2 3 4 5	1 2 3 4 5
8. Distribution to faculty and staff is adequate.	1 2 3 4 5	1 2 3 4 5	1 2 3 4 5
9. Requisitioning classroom supplies and equipment is efficient and not time-consuming.	1 2 3 4 5	1 2 3 4 5	1 2 3 4 5
10. Annual inventory checklists and directions are required and provided.	1 2 3 4 5	1 2 3 4 5	1 2 3 4 5
11. Equipment is replaced and/or repaired promptly.	1 2 3 4 5	1 2 3 4 5	1 2 3 4 5
12. Instructions are provided for using equipment.	1 2 3 4 5	1 2 3 4 5	1 2 3 4 5
13. Conservation and nonwaste of supplies is promoted.	1 2 3 4 5	1 2 3 4 5	1 2 3 4 5
14. Care and protection of equipment is promoted.	1 2 3 4 5	1 2 3 4 5	1 2 3 4 5
15. Yearly evaluation of the value of certain supplies and equipment to the instructional program is encouraged.	1 2 3 4 5	1 2 3 4 5	1 2 3 4 5

FIGURE 10-10
Evaluation Scale for Managing School Supplies and Equipment

Although all of the items may not be appropriate because of the nature of your situation, they may be changed to meet specific needs. This evaluation scale allows you to evaluate yourself while obtaining evaluative information from your faculty-staff and from the central office/superintendent. As suggested in other sections of this book, discussion and decisions relative to discrepancies in the ratings are worth your time and effort.

EVALUATING AND IMPROVING
SCHOOL SAFETY

This section focuses on a discussion of evaluation and improving school building safety related to fire and accident prevention.

A safe school results when the principal performs the following:

1. Establish a safety-conscious tone.
2. Implement a safety education program.
3. Provide in-service training for faculty and staff.
4. Promote special safety programs and assemblies.
5. Establish a school safety patrol.
6. Participate in safety campaigns.
7. Utilize community resource personnel.
8. Actively demonstrate concern about the safety of all people in the school.

Self-Evaluation Checklist

As a school principal you may wish to check yourself on the items in Figure 10-11. The checklist enables you to assess what you did during the past year and, if you think the item has merit, plan when you will implement the suggestion.

Fire Inspections

The importance of regular building inspections for potential fire hazards cannot be understated. Besides requesting that fire officials inspect the building regularly (usually once each year), the principal would benefit from a self-inspection plan that includes the involvement of the school custodian as well as other school personnel. A useful self-inspection checklist is available to schools from the American Fire Insurance Association (Figure 10-12).

Fire Drills and Evacuations

The principal has the responsibility to become acquainted with state laws and local ordinances regarding fire and accident regulations for school

During the Past School Year:	Yes	No	Good Idea! I'll Do This Next Year*
1. I invited fire officials to inspect the school.	____	____	____
2. I regularly inspected the school building for fire hazards.	____	____	____
3. I regularly checked fire fighting equipment.	____	____	____
4. I prepared a checklist of things to be inspected regularly by the custodian.	____	____	____
5. I provided written safety procedures for school personnel.	____	____	____
6. I prepared a list of safety activities that teachers and students can use in the classroom.	____	____	____
7. I promoted the inclusion of topics on safety and accident prevention for in-service and faculty meetings.	____	____	____
8. I honestly tried to create a safety-conscious atmosphere.	____	____	____
9. I held regular fire drills and building evacuation activities.	____	____	____
10. I encouraged the use of safety topics in our curriculum.	____	____	____

*Write below the date, week, or month you plan to do something about this item.

FIGURE 10-11
Principal's Self-Evaluation Safety Checklist

buildings. Most states require a monthly fire drill. Evacuation procedures have taken on greater importance because coupled with the potential for fire has been the phenomenon of bomb threats. Managing procedures for the efficient and safe evacuation of the school building should not be taken lightly. To assist you in this task, the following questions deserve your attention:

1. Do all school personnel know what to do when an evacuation signal is given no matter where they are in the school building?
2. Do all school personnel know the evacuation signals? Exits? Returns?
3. Are you convinced that teachers have instructed students, at the beginning and middle of each school year, regarding procedures for evacuating the school building?
4. Do teachers and students know what to do while evacuating a room? (Example: Close all outside windows; close door after all

Prepared by
AMERICAN INSURANCE ASSOCIATION
Engineering and Safety Service
85 John Street. New York. N Y 10038

INSTRUCTIONS

Inspection to be made each month by the custodian and a member of the faculty at which inspection only Items 1 to 23 need be reported. At the quarterly inspection, a member of the fire department should accompany the above inspectors, and the complete blank should be filled out The report of each inspection (monthly and quarterly) is to be filed with the Board of Education or School Commissioners.

Questions are so worded that a negative answer will indicate an unsatisfactory condition.

Date . . . .

Name of School   Address . . . .

Class. Elementary   Junior High   .Senior High . . . .

Capacity of School   Number now enrolled . . . .

1 Are all exterior exit doors equipped with approved panic hardware when serving 100 or more persons? . . . .
   Is the hardware tested each week?   Is it readily operable? . . . .

2 Are all outside fire escapes free from obstructions and in good working order? . . . . Are they used for fire drills?
   . . . .

3 Are all doors in smoke control partitions in operable condition? . . . . .Free from obstruction?. . . . .

4 Is all heating equipment. including flues. pipes. ducts and steam lines:-
   (a) in good servicable condition and well maintained?
   (b) properly insulated and separated from all combustible material by a safe distance? . . . .

5 Is the coal pile inspected periodically for evidence of heating? . . . .

6 Are ashes placed in metal containers used for that purpose only? . . . .

7 Is remote control provided whereby oil supply line may be shut off in emergency and is it readily accessible? . . . . . .

8 Is an outside shut-off valve on the gas supply line provided?   Is it readily accessible and marked? . . . .

9 Has automatic heating and air-conditioning equipment been serviced by a qualified service man within the past year?
   . . . .

10 Are the following locations free of accumulations of waste paper, rubbish, old furniture. stage scenery, etc?
    attic?   basement?   furnace room?   stage?. . . . . .dressing rooms in connection with
    stage?   other locations?   (explain No ' answers under Remarks.)

11 Are spaces beneath stairs free from accumulation or storage of any materials? . . . .

12 If hazardous material or preparation is used for cleaning or polishing floors: Is the quantity limited as much as practicable?   Is it safely stored?   . . . .

13 Are approved metal cans. with self-closing covers or lids. used for the storage of all oily waste, polishing cloths, etc?

14 Are approved safety cans with vapor-tight covers used for all kerosene, gasoline, etc., on the premises and are they stored away from sources of heat or ignition?   . . . .
    Is it essential that such materials be kept on the premises? . . . .

15 Are premises free from electrical wiring or equipment which is defective? . . . .
    (If answer is No. explain under Remarks)

16 Are only labeled extension or portable cords used?   . . . . •

17 Is the correct size fuse being used in each electrical circuit?   . .   . .

18 Are electric pressing irons equipped with automatic heat control or signal and provided with metal stand? . . . .
    . . . .

19 Are sufficient proper type fire extinguishers provided on each floor so that not over 75 feet travel is required to reach the nearest unit?   . . . .
    In manual training shops and on stage. 30 feet or 50 feet depending on extinguisher rating? . . .   .

20 Is date of inspection or recharge shown on tag attached to extinguisher?   . . .   .
    Have fire extinguishers been inspected or recharged within a year?   . . . .

21 Is the building equipped with standpipe and hose with nozzle attached?   . .   . .,
    Is the hose in good serviceable condition?   . . .

22 Where sprinklers are installed Are all sprinklers clean and unobstructed?   . . . .
    Are all sprinkler valves open?   Has the system been thoroughly inspected within the past year?   . . . . .

23 Are large woolen blankets readily available in kitchens and science laboratories for use in case clothing is ignited?
    . . . .

Remarks (Note any changes since last inspection)
The following items to be included in each quarterly inspection -

24 Are there at least two means of egress from each story of the building?   . . . .
    Are these so located that the distance to any single exit measured along the line of travel, does not exceed:-
    From any point in any classroom. 150 feet?   . . . .
    From any point in an auditorium. assembly hall or gymnasium. 150 feet?   . . . . . .

FIGURE 10-12   *(cont.)*
Inspection Blank for Schools

25 Are all windows free from heavy screens or bars? . ...
26 Do all exit doors open in direction of exit travel? . ...
27 Are all interior stairways enclosed? . ...
    Are doors to these enclosures of automatic or self-closing type? ... Are they unobstructed......... and in operable condition? ....
    If automatic closing type, are they closed as routine part of fire exit drill? ....
28 Are windows within 10 feet above, 35 feet below and 15 feet horizontally of fire escapes glazed with wire glass? ....
29 Are manual training, domestic science, other laboratories and the cafeteria so located that a fire in one will not make the means of egress from other nearby rooms or spaces unusable? ....
30 Are heating plant and fuel supply rooms separated from other parts of the building by fire-resistant walls or partitions, and fire doors? ....
31 Do all ventilating ducts terminate outside of the building? ... .
32 State type of construction of any temporary buildings in the school yard ... .
    .. . .
33 Is nearest temporary building at least 50 feet from the main building? ... .
34 State frequency of fire drills   State average time of exit .. . .
35 Are provisions made for sounding alarm of fire from any floor of building? .. ..
    Is sounding device accessible?   Plainly marked? . ...
36 Signs giving location of nearest city fire alarm box posted? ....
    Give distance from the premises to box ....
             Inspector ... . Title ....
             Inspector ... . Title ....
             Fire Chief and/or Building Inspector . .. .

FIGURE 10-12 *(cont.)*

have left the room; students line up in orderly manner; if exit is blocked, follow teacher; and routes to follow for each room).

5. Do the evacuation instructions emphasize orderliness, seriousness, and respect for potential danger?
6. Are copies of evacuation procedures given to each teacher and staff?
7. Are evacuation orders posted in each room?
8. Do you plan monthly evacuation drills at different times, under various circumstances, each month?
9. Do you keep a record of each evacuation drill? Does it include the date, time of day, evacuation time, and effectiveness?
10. Are all school exits clearly marked?
11. Is special attention given for the evacuation of special places like the school gym, auditorium, etc.?
12. Do you have special procedures for assisting handicapped students, teachers, or staff?
13. Do teachers and others know what to do if their specified exits are blocked when the order to evacuate is given?
14. Are procedures for returning to the school building provided to each teacher and staff member?

Accident Prevention

Part of the management responsibilities of a school principal is to assure the safety for school personnel. Accidents happen; some because of negligence, others because of happenstance. The best that a principal can do

(check one)

(check one)	**RECOMMENDED**	(check one)
☐ School Jurisdictional	**STANDARD STUDENT ACCIDENT REPORT**	Recordable ☐
☐ Non-School Jurisdictional		Reportable Only ☐

School District:
City, State:

General	1. Name	2. Address
	3. School	4. Sex — Male ☐ Female ☐ — 5. Age — 6. Grade/Special Program
	7. Time Accident Occurred — Date: — Day of Week: — Exact Time: — AM ☐ PM ☐	
Injury	8. Nature of Injury	
	9. Part of Body Injured	
	10. Degree of Injury (check one) — Death ☐ — Permanent ☐ — Temporary (lost time) ☐ — Non-Disabling (no lost time) ☐	
	11. Days Lost — From School: — From Activities Other Than School: — Total:	
	12. Cause of Injury	
Accident	13. Accident Jurisdiction (check one) — School: Grounds ☐ Building ☐ — To and From ☐ — Other Activities Not on School Property ☐ — Non-School: Home ☐ Other ☐	
	14. Location of Accident (be specific)	15. Activity of Person (be specific)
	16. Status of Activity	17. Supervision (if yes, give title & name of supervisor) — Yes ☐ No ☐
	18. Agency Involved	19. Unsafe Act
	20. Unsafe Mechanical/Physical Condition	21. Unsafe Personal Factor
	22. Corrective Action Taken or Recommended	
	23. Property Damage — School $ — Non-School $ — Total $	
	24. Description (Give a word picture of the accident, explaining who, what, when, why and how)	
Signature	25. Date of Report	26. Report Prepared by (signature & title)
	27. Principal's Signature	

Student Accident Reporting Guidebook (Chicago: National Safety Council, 1966).

FIGURE 10-13
Student Accident Report Form

is try to instill in the faculty, staff, and students concepts of accident prevention. Be prepared! Be safety-minded! Don't be negligent! Think before you act! This is not an easy thing to do as you watch some students "burn rubber" getting out of the parking lots, or when you view children chasing each other around the playground swings as others are swinging. But try you must. Those in charge must be constantly on the check for conditions or activities that may contribute to accidents. Special attention should be given to areas such as showers, gyms, lavatories, halls, stairways, boiler room, swimming pool, parking lots, playground, and so on. Teachers of specific subjects such as industrial arts, physics, and chemistry should be aware of the dangers of power tools, chemical elements such as acids, electrical units, and the like.

A recommended form for securing data about student accidents appears in Figure 10-13. The information from forms such as this one can be used to plan safety and accident prevention programs.

HOW TO ORGANIZE AND MANAGE CUSTODIAL SERVICES

While the direct responsibility for the maintenance of plant and facilities belongs to the principal, it is carried out by the custodial staff. The importance of custodial personnel to the daily operation of the plant and to the educational program within the school cannot and should not be minimized. Therefore, both the principal and the custodial staff have specific responsibilities that are special to plant and facilities management.

Principal's Responsibilities

The principal's major responsibilities are threefold: to supervise, to administer, and to evaluate. As supervisor, the principal should define the custodian's job if the school district does not provide a job description. A division of labor should also be developed if there is more than one custodian. And, most important, the principal should seek to have others respect and dignify the position of custodian. As the administrator of custodial services, the principal should comply with the following duties:

1. Cooperate with custodians; come to appreciate them for the services they provide.
2. Assist custodians by developing reasonable work schedules.
3. Communicate with custodians by being open to their suggestions, listening to their problems and concerns, and sharing with them information about plant and facilities management.
4. Develop and demonstrate pride in the importance of each custodian's position and work efforts.

5. Mediate potential conflicts between custodians and teachers by using "work requests" and keeping teachers aware of each custodian's duties and problems.
6. Provide custodians with an office and workroom for maintaining records and reports and storing tools and equipment.

The principal's additional task is to evaluate the quality of work and the effectiveness of performance.

Custodians' Responsibilities

Like the principal, the custodians also have specific responsibilities.

1. They must work cooperatively with the principal, teachers, and school personnel.
2. They should demonstrate pride in their position and in their work.
3. They must show concern for the health and safety of all school personnel.
4. They must maintain high housekeeping standards.
5. They must be particularly helpful in times of emergencies, problems, and special school activities.
6. They must properly clean, repair, replace, and maintain the school plant and its facilities.
7. They must periodically inspect the building and equipment.
8. They must keep an up-to-date inventory of supplies and equipment.
9. They must anticipate and prevent many maintenance problems.
10. They should evaluate themselves and encourage others to evaluate their work.

Evaluating Principal-Custodial Relations

In order to help you and the custodians in your school determine the extent to which you cooperatively carry out some of the responsibilities previously identified, a rating scale has been constructed (Figure 10-14).

The purpose of such a scale is to help you and the custodian(s) evaluate some crucial factors important in a positive, pleasant working environment. It will also produce information that you and the custodian can discuss during follow-up conferences. For example, the scale may reveal that a custodian feels that you don't keep the faculty informed about some "clean up" problems, but it doesn't reveal why the custodian feels this way; that is the purpose of the conference.

Rate the extent to which you:	Principal		Custodian
1. Communicate	⎯⎯	Great	⎯⎯
	⎯⎯	Some	⎯⎯
	⎯⎯	Little	⎯⎯
	⎯⎯	No	⎯⎯
2. Establish maintenance plans	⎯⎯	Great	⎯⎯
	⎯⎯	Some	⎯⎯
	⎯⎯	Little	⎯⎯
	⎯⎯	No	⎯⎯
3. Schedule workload	⎯⎯	Great	⎯⎯
	⎯⎯	Some	⎯⎯
	⎯⎯	Little	⎯⎯
	⎯⎯	No	⎯⎯
4. Define job requirements and limitations	⎯⎯	Great	⎯⎯
	⎯⎯	Some	⎯⎯
	⎯⎯	Little	⎯⎯
	⎯⎯	No	⎯⎯
5. Work cooperatively to solve plant/facilities problems	⎯⎯	Great	⎯⎯
	⎯⎯	Some	⎯⎯
	⎯⎯	Little	⎯⎯
	⎯⎯	No	⎯⎯
6. Prepare budget for custodial needs	⎯⎯	Great	⎯⎯
	⎯⎯	Some	⎯⎯
	⎯⎯	Little	⎯⎯
	⎯⎯	No	⎯⎯
7. Prepare building and grounds repairs/ replacements	⎯⎯	Great	⎯⎯
	⎯⎯	Some	⎯⎯
	⎯⎯	Little	⎯⎯
	⎯⎯	No	⎯⎯
8. Keep faculty/staff informed about custodial problems/duties/needs	⎯⎯	Great	⎯⎯
	⎯⎯	Some	⎯⎯
	⎯⎯	Little	⎯⎯
	⎯⎯	No	⎯⎯

FIGURE 10-14
Principal-Custodian Rating Scale

Evaluating Custodial Performance

Evaluating the performance of custodians, like that of other school personnel, must result from an accurate and comprehensive job description, continual and regular supervision, and the use of a written evaluation. Whether the evaluation is done by a principal or the head custodian, the evaluation instrument used should have resulted from input by the administration and the custodial staff.

Figure 10-15 shows a school district's evaluation scale that is based upon a comprehension job description. It should be noted that in this district's schools, where a head custodian does the evaluations, each custodian meets with the head custodian to discuss the evaluation—the quality of work performance and services. The intent is to show and help the custodians to find out how they are doing and what is expected of them. Hopefully, the result of the meetings is a cooperative approach toward obtaining higher quality performance which will lead to high quality school maintenance standards and services in each building. Each custodian, however, has the option to discuss any aspect of the job evaluation with the school principal. This procedure, which insures open communication and high morale, is worth your consideration.

Self-Evaluation/Teacher Evaluation

Self-evaluation is as valuable for a custodian as it is for the principal. Few administrators recommend self-evaluation procedures for classified personnel, yet the results can be informative and contribute to a more positive annual performance rating. The example shown in Figure 10-16 is easy to use and does not require a great deal of time to complete. The principal and custodian can add items to fit particular job requirements. The scale may be used twice a year with a follow-up conference between the principal or head custodian and the custodian. The results may head off potential problems and will provide additional information that can be discussed during the conferences.

The self-evaluation process can take on added significance when the results are compared to an evaluation by those who are the recipients of custodial services and performance. To help you collect information from teachers and others about the custodial staff, a sample form appears in Figure 10-17.

In summary, a principal can bring three sets of data to the custodial evaluation conference: self-evaluation, teacher evaluation, and administrator evaluation. The information gleaned from these three sources should be extremely useful for obtaining or maintaining high quality performance and service.

ELMBROOK SCHOOLS

Merit evaluation of custodial/maintenance Personnel

In appraising the several aspects of job performance, consider the following:

1. TECHNICAL COMPETENCE
   - (a) extent to which the employee possesses the knowledge and skills necessary to his position;
   - (b) his effectiveness in applying skills and acceptable techniques;
   - (c) comprehension of instructions and successful completion of assigned tasks;
   - (d) systematic approach to the duties of the position and thoroughness of accomplishment;
   - (e) recognition of problem situations and resourcefulness in developing ways and means of meeting them; and
   - (f) soundness of judgment.

2. RELATIONSHIPS
   - (a) employee's personal appearance and impression he generally makes on others;
   - (b) nature of response to guidance and extent to which he makes constructive use of criticism offered by superiors;
   - (c) the degree to which he cooperates and works with fellow employees;
   - (d) the tact and courtesy he exercises in dealing with the public;
   - (e) degree to which he understands his fellow workers and inspires their confidence and respect.

3. RELIABILITY
   - (a) degree of confidence and trust which may be placed in employees to carry out assignments without undue checking;
   - (b) sense of responsibility to the job and conscientiousness in performance;
   - (c) readiness to adjust to changing character of assignments and conditions of employment;
   - (d) temperament and emotional stability as they affect performance;
   - (e) regular attendance and punctuality; and
   - (f) loyalty to the standards and ideals of the School System.

4. QUANTITY OF WORK
   - (a) degree to which employee organizes his work effectively;
   - (b) accuracy of results with a minimum of waste, spoilage and loss of time;
   - (c) rate or production in relation to other employees in this category of position;
   - (d) ability to turn out a satisfactory amount of acceptable work under pressure; and
   - (e) degree to which he devotes himself steadily to the job.

5. WORK INTEREST
   - (a) his demonstration of originality in meeting new problems and developing ways to improve existing procedures;
   - (b) his recognition and utilization of opportunities to improve himself so as to perform his duties more efficiently;
   - (c) willingness to be personally inconvenienced when responsibilities of the job place unusual demands on his time or energy;
   - (d) his practice of keeping himself physically and mentally fit for the proper discharge of his duties;
   - (e) his readiness to accept special assignments beyond daily routine.

MERIT RATING FORM

Name: _____ Work Location _____

Title _____ Period: From _____ to _____

Instructions: Read carefully the descriptive statements on the lower section of this page and on the other page. For each job element select and encircle the numerical value most nearly representing the degree of the employee's accomplishment. Do not rate the element "Supervisory Effectiveness" unless a significant portion of the employee's responsibility is in the supervision of other employees. After encircling the appropriate figure for each element, place corresponding figures in the right hand column and total.

		UNSATISFACTORY	AVERAGE		MAXIMUM	RATINGS
1.	Technical Competence	1	2	3 4	5	_____
2.	Relationships	1	2	3 4	5	_____
3.	Reliability	1	2	3 4	5	_____
4.	Quantity	1	2	3 4	5	_____
5.	Work Interest	1	2	3 4	5	_____
6.	Supervisory Effectiveness	1	2	3 4	5	_____

Total Rating _____

Signature: Rater _____ Reviewing Officer _____

To obtain rating, you are to divide the total rating by the number of classifications the employee was rated on. In most cases there will be five, but where the employee has supervisory responsibility, the employee will be rated for six classifications.

6. SUPERVISORY EFFECTIVENESS
(a) his effectiveness as a leader, manifested by his ability to inspire confidence, provide guidance, set appropriate standards and to follow through on performance.
(b) his interest and effectiveness in training subordinates for satisfactory quantitative and qualitative performance;
(c) adequacy of his over-all planning, his willingness to make appropriate delegation of responsibilities and to give the necessary authority for their proper discharge;
(d) soundness of judgment and validity of decisions;
(e) willingness to make decisions;
(f) extent to which his handling of subordinates develops and sustains a satisfactory level of employee morale.

The following table is to be used in converting numerical ratings:

4.67-5.00	Excellent
4.00-4.66	Very Good
3.00-3.99	Good
2.00-2.99	Fair
0.00-1.99	Unsatisfactory

FIGURE 10-15
Custodial Evaluation Form

Courtesy of the Elmbrook School District, Elmbrook, Wisconsin.

Directions: The purpose of this scale is to help you evaluate yourself in your day-to-day custodial duties in this school. Check the appropriate space following each item.

Items	*Outstanding*	*Adequate*	*Needs Improving*	*Inadequate*
1. Performance of duties	___	___	___	___
2. Speed of operation	___	___	___	___
3. Quality of work done	___	___	___	___
4. Ability to get along with others:				
a. Students	___	___	___	___
b. Teachers	___	___	___	___
c. Administrators	___	___	___	___
d. Other school personnel	___	___	___	___
5. Accept criticisms and suggestions	___	___	___	___
6. Physically healthy	___	___	___	___
7. Pride in your position	___	___	___	___
8. Positive attitude toward your work	___	___	___	___
9. Appearance	___	___	___	___
10. Attendance	___	___	___	___
11. List other items				

FIGURE 10-16
Custodian Self-Evaluation Scale

A FINAL COMMENT

The effectiveness of a school plant and its facilities can be viewed in what people say about the building, what they do when using the facility, and whether they perceive it as a facility that contributes to or detracts from carrying out the day-to-day business of education.

Your challenge, the challenge of all school-site administrations, is to insure that the school plant and its facilities are useful, attractive, safe and secure. With the emphaiss on instructional leadership, student achievement, teacher performance, school culture and climate, it would be rather easy for a principal to worry less about managing the school plant and facilities, turn the task over to others, and get on with the educational aspects of the job. However, since these factors are interrelated, the challenge is to attend to all the tasks, give some priority, delegate what you can, but keep an eye on the physical facilities in which the educational activities take place.

Performance Rating for:_____(Name and/or Position)

Directions: The rating sheet is designed to assist the principal in determining the efficiency and effectiveness of the custodian(s) in this school. Please indicate your rating by circling the appropriate number.

Items	Excellent	Good	Fair	Poor	Cannot Evaluate
1. Service to teachers	4	3	2	1	0
2. Understands duties	4	3	2	1	0
3. Carries out duties	4	3	2	1	0
4. Is efficient	4	3	2	1	0
5. Is cooperative	4	3	2	1	0
6. Is productive	4	3	2	1	0
7. Is courteous	4	3	2	1	0
8. Quality of work	4	3	2	1	0
9. Is punctual	4	3	2	1	0
10. Self-motivated	4	3	2	1	0
11. List other items					
_____	4	3	2	1	0
_____	4	3	2	1	0

Comments:

FIGURE 10-17
Teachers/Others: Rating Scale of the Custodian

This chapter was designed to provide you with ideas and suggestions for evaluating a variety of factors that are an integral part of managing the school plant and its facilities. Regardless of the kind of building you manage—old, new, flexible, inflexible, single or multiple-story construction—you have the responsibility to supervise, manage, evaluate, and improve the school plant and its facilities.

NOTES

1. Robert Posilkin, "Turn Unused Classrooms into Big Bucks by Following These Guidelines," *American School Board Journal* 52 (February, 1981): 25–26; also see C. William Brubaker, "What to Do with Surplus School Space," *American Schools and Universities* 52 (February, 1980): 37–41.
2. Joan B. Grady, "Expanding the Use of the School Building to Improve Community Support," *Bulletin of the National Association of Secondary School Principals* 69 (February, 1985): 89–92.
3. Robert L. Monks, "Six Things You Must Consider Before Opening Schools to Community Groups," *American School Board Journal* 51 (July, 1980): 34.

4. Kathleen McCormick, "Progress and New Problems Mark Your Battle Against School Asbestos," *American School Board Journal* 72 (March, 1985): 25–29.
5. *Ibid.*, p. 27.
6. See Larry W. Bickle and John Emry, "These Eight Steps Will Lead You To a Systematic Energy Management Program," *American School Board Journal* 66 (August, 1979): 37–38.

REFERENCES

Blauvelt, Peter D. *Effective Strategies for School Security.* Reston, VA: National Association of Secondary School Principals, 1981.

Energy Management in Education Facilities. Washington, D.C.: Electrification Council, 1984.

Stone, Ronald R. "Managing Employees Through Progressive Discipline." *Educational Leadership* 38 (February 1981): 407–408.

Rubel, Robert J. "Enter the Security Audit." *American Schools and Universities* 57 (June 1985): 47–48.

Total School Energy Management Program. Washington, D.C.: U.S. Government Accounting Office, No. 061-000-00396-7, 1980.

School Facilities Evaluation Instrument. Trenton, NJ: Department of Education, Division of Field Services, 1977.

School Facilities Maintenance and Operations. Park Ridge, IL: Association of School Business Officials, GA 231024, Report Number ISBN-0-919179-25-8, 1982.

Index